Tacit Knowledge and
Spoken Discourse

Also Available From Bloomsbury

Continuum Companion to Discourse Analysis, Edited by Ken Hyland and Brian Paltridge
Available in paperback as *Bloomsbury Companion to Discourse Analysis*
Discourse of Twitter and Social Media, Michele Zappavigna

Tacit Knowledge and Spoken Discourse

Michele Zappavigna

B L O O M S B U R Y
LONDON · NEW DELHI · NEW YORK · SYDNEY

Bloomsbury Academic

An imprint of Bloomsbury Publishing Plc

50 Bedford Square
London
WC1B 3DP
UK

175 Fifth Avenue
New York
NY 10010
USA

www.bloomsbury.com

First published 2013

British Library Cataloguing-in-Publication Data
A catalogue record for this book is available from the British Library.

ISBN: HB: 978-1-4411-2840-9

Library of Congress Cataloging-in-Publication Data
Zappavigna, Michele.
Tacit knowledge and spoken discourse / Michele Zappavigna.
p. cm.
Includes bibliographical references.
ISBN 978-1-4411-2840-9 (hardcover) – ISBN 978-1-4411-2383-1 (ebook) –
ISBN 978-1-4411-6102-4 (pdf) 1. Discourse analysis. 2. Silence. 3. Knowledge, Theory of.
4. Conversation analysis. 5. Speech acts (Linguistics) I. Title.
P302.Z36 2013
401'.41–dc23
2012035233

Typeset by Newgen Imaging Systems Pvt Ltd, Chennai, India
Printed and bound in Great Britain

This book is dedicated to three fine men: my grandfather

Allan Roy Horton and

my sons Orlando and Joseph

Contents

Acknowledgements

I would like to acknowledge and thank my PhD supervisor, Professor Jon Patrick, whose generous help and guidance allowed me to complete the thesis upon which this book is based.

1

Tacit Knowledge and Technology

Introduction

Most of us have been in the situation where we have been frustrated by technical discourses, perhaps through an encounter with an Information Technology (IT) helpdesk or when trying to understand the resident technical 'guru'. The language of technologists[1] can be opaque to outsiders. One of the reasons for the impenetrability of 'tech talk' is that technologists hold extensive tacit knowledge about working with technology. This book seeks to uncover this kind of tacit knowledge by probing the grammatical patterns of technologists working in corporate organizations.

Using the discourse of technologists working in three corporate organizations as a case study, the fundamental argument that will be made is that tacit knowledge cannot be divorced from language. Instead, the process of knowing is a process of transforming experience into meaning with language. This perspective arises out of a systemic functional orientation to language and knowledge:

> Instead of experience being construed by the mind, in the form of knowledge, we can say that experience is construed by the grammar; to 'know' something is to have transformed some portion of experience into meaning. (Halliday and Matthiessen 1999: 603)

In order to make this claim I will begin by critically reviewing Polanyi's (1966b: 4) famous assumption that 'we know more than we can tell', which he used to justify the notion that tacit knowledge is ineffable. I will argue that Polanyi's axiom does not account for a sufficiently nuanced view of linguistic communication and that analysing latent grammatical patterns in spoken texts can in fact illuminate tacit knowledge. Linguistics as a discipline is very much concerned with making visible patterns in language (and thus in experience and knowledge) that are not readily visible to the untrained eye.

This chapter begins by considering Polanyi's Theory of Tacit Knowing (TTK), focusing in detail on his principle that tacit knowledge is ineffable. I will then review how various domains, from philosophy of science, linguistics, psychology to organizational science, have theorized concepts akin to tacit knowledge, employing different kinds of technicality.

The tacit turn away from language

Much of human experience is below-view, unattended to as we operate in the world, but integral to our performance as social creatures. We hold the experiential agility to be at once creative and efficient, to assimilate the novel and the familiar: in essence, to develop expertise. Over human history we have mythologized experts, such as the artisan, the witchdoctor and the physician by culturally locating their knowledge as hidden and unspeakable, in other words, as 'tacit'. Thus it is not surprising that the dominant contemporary research perspective on what has been termed *tacit knowledge* maintains that it cannot be understood in terms of how people communicate with language (Polanyi 1969). This book, however, seeks to demonstrate that analysing latent linguistic patterns in spoken discourse, the kinds of patterns that linguists regularly explore, reveals tacit knowledge.

As a folk term, tacit knowledge has come to be associated with prosodies of meaning relating to silence and the unspoken. *Tacit* originates in the Latin, *tacitus*, meaning silent. Its synonyms refer to ineffability (e.g. *unsaid, unspoken, unuttered, wordless, silent, undeclared, unexpressed* and *unvoiced*) and to indirectness (e.g. *implicit, implied, inferred* and *understood*). Antonyms of tacit include *explicit* and *expressed*. These folk meanings about linguistic inexpressibility have directed research away from investigating how tacit knowledge might be manifest in language patterns. We should, however, consider whether silence is an attribute of tacit knowledge or an artefact of our lens.

The researcher attributed with coining tacit knowledge as a technical term is Michael Polanyi, though the general concept of practical knowledge can be traced at least as far as Aristotle's notion of *phronesis*. While Polanyi may have introduced tacit knowledge into scholarly discourse, *tacit knowing* was his preferred term for the act of 'tacit integration' that his theory developed to explain the experience of knowing something. This conceptual position, casting knowing as a process rather than an object, (knowledge) is in accord with the movement in disciplines such as semiotics and linguistics away from a constituency-based view of meaning, towards a view of meaning as 'in the making' as we construe our experience of the world.

Polanyi's TTK introduced a post-critical perspective on what it means to know, arguing that personal judgement characterizes knowledge claims even in disciplines such as the sciences that assert their objectivity. Despite his claim that 'all knowledge is either tacit or rooted in tacit knowledge' (Polanyi 1969: 144), most studies drawing on TTK presuppose a dichotomy of tacit and 'explicit' knowledge. Indeed, the impetus to classify human knowledge as either tacit and intuitive, or conscious and experiential, has ancient pedigree. For example, Basque, the oldest language of Europe, originating some 7,000 years ago, distinguishes between knowing intrinsically (*ezagutu*) and knowing by learning (*jakin*).

Before exploring TTK, I will deal with Polanyi's most famous axiom regarding the ineffability of tacit knowing since it is the principle that this book seeks to reconsider. The intent is not to invalidate TTK but to show how employing linguistic theory in conjunction with Polanyi's work can extend our insight into tacit knowledge. As we will see in the chapters that follow, consideration of the complexities of human meaning-making, using a functional, stratified model of language can extend Polanyi's theory and show that there are patterns in what we say that can give us further clues about tacit knowing.

The ineffability principle: What does it mean 'to know more than we can tell'?

One of the central tenants of Polanyi's TTK is that tacit knowledge cannot be articulated. Instead it is a form of ineffable knowledge which is not expressed through language but rather lived through experience:

> I shall reconsider human knowledge by starting from the fact that we can know more than we can tell. This fact seems obvious enough; but it is not easy to say exactly what it means. Take an example. We know a person's face, and can recognize it among a thousand, indeed among a million. Yet we usually cannot tell how we recognize a face we know. So most of this knowledge cannot be put into words. (Polanyi 1966b: 4)

The claim that 'we can know more than we can tell' is an argument that tacit knowledge is not carried in language. It positions ineffability as a criteria for asserting the epistemological significance of knowledge of which we are not intentionally aware. According to the principle of ineffability, an identifying attribute of this knowledge is its a-linguistic instrumentality since while 'the expert diagnostician, taxonomist and cotton-classer can indicate their clues and formulate their maxims, they know more than they can tell, knowing them only in practice, as instrumental particulars, and not explicitly, as objects' (Polanyi 1958: 88).

However, it important to carefully consider what it means *to tell* in theorizing how we might know more than can be told. If *telling* means directly 'transferring' information to the mind of the listener, then this it is not a possible means for exposing tacit knowledge. This impoverished view of communication has been characterized by Reddy (1979) as employing a conduit metaphor whereby words are boxes with meanings inside that we send to other people. As Reddy (1979: 287) has noted with the following examples of lexical metaphor, the metalingual resources of English privilege this kind of view:

> Whenever you have a good idea practice capturing it in words.

> You have to put each concept into words very carefully.

If, however, we allow that *telling* involves negotiating meanings that are latent in the often implicit patterns of spoken discourse (and in turn subject to the interpretation of the listener), linguistic communication is reinstated as relevant to understanding tacit knowledge. Our account of telling should also allow for language to be considered as a social practice, being used as it is to enact the various genres that constitute social life.

The view of language characterized by the conduit metaphor is not a view that Polanyi would have condoned. Despite his claims about ineffability, Polanyi had a lot to say about language and, as I will cover later, developed a theory of 'sense-making and sense-giving' (Polanyi 1967). Given that Polanyi's thesis about 'personal knowledge' was aimed at undermining the notion that science deals in objectivity, it is unlikely that TTK intended to adopt this kind of mathematical model of communication. Indeed TTK acknowledges that language use is itself tacit to the knower rather than an object ready to be transferred to someone else's head:

> While language expands human intelligence immensely beyond the purely tacit domain, the logic of language itself – the way language is used – remains tacit. (Polany 1966a: 7)

However, and importantly, Polanyi's model neglects the very significant point that the field of linguistics has developed many tools for describing the complex patterns that can be uncovered in discourse and that these tools can make these tacit patterns visible. While Polanyi's theory involves contemplating meaning, it does not acknowledge the role that linguistics and semiotics can play in exploring tacit language patterns. In theorizing tacit knowledge as unable to be communicated in language, Polanyi has factored out the power of linguistics to describe and explain what Polanyi terms 'the tacit coefficients of language' (Polanyi 1958).

Nevertheless, Polanyi's concept of knowing more than one can express in language has been taken up by theorists in a variety of disciplines with vigour. The enthusiasm has meant that the opportunity that linguistic analysis affords in giving us greater insight into the nature of tacit knowledge has been obscured. The strong standpoint on ineffability is a superficial reading of Polanyi's theory. Rather than arguing that one cannot speak at all about tacit coefficients, Polanyi focuses on the 'adequacy' of representation:

> To assert that I have knowledge which is ineffable is not to deny that I can speak of it, but only that I can speak of it adequately, the assertion itself being an appraisal of this inadequacy. (Polanyi 1958: 91)

Explicit maxims that attempt to encapsulate or explain the craftsman's practice are limited in their utility as 'these never disclose fully the subsidiary known particulars of the art', that is, they do not adequately represent the object of subsidiary awareness (Polanyi 1958: 90).

Polanyi's arguments about knowing and telling separate knowledge and language. A functional approach to language, however, suggests that it does not make sense to distinguish between knowledge and language in the same way that it does not make sense to distinguish between language and thought (Butt 1985). Relevant to this perspective, is Douglas's account of the misleading nature of the verb 'to express':

> That word establishes a distinction between the expression and that which is expressed. The object of our study discloses no such cleavage. Knowledge is a continuous process of realization involving both the implicit and the explicit. (Douglas 1975: 8)

This 'continuous process of realization' can be modelled by looking how meanings are realized in language. We may articulate what we know tacitly through patterns and features of language to which we do not directly attend. This is an argument that articulation is not the equivalent of codification. It is the work of the discourse analyst to uncover the implicit meanings that are made in spoken texts, affording the potential for these implicit patterns to be celebrated or, where they may be impeding some social process, offer suggestions on how they might be changed (see for example the extensive tradition in Systemic Functional Linguistics (SFL) of making explicit the language patterns of pedagogic discourse so that classroom teaching might be improved; summarized in Rose 2012).

Part 1: Introducing Polanyi's TTK

TTK draws upon the perspective on human perception afforded by Gestalt psychology. In particular, it references the Gestalt idea of perceiving the whole while not being aware of the particulars. Two levels of awareness are presented as central to tacit knowing: focal awareness and subsidiary awareness. These are mutually exclusive states distinguished by the nature and degree of attention deployed: focal awareness is conscious, while subsidiary awareness is below-view. Polanyi (1969: 212) illustrates how these two systems of awareness operate with the example of stereovision. A person looking at a stereoscopic image is focally aware of the integrated stereoscopic image but has only subsidiary awareness of the two slightly different images that each eye sees. The knower integrates the differences in the two stereo images to form a joint visualization that has spatial depth. Such a process of integration is the fundamental configuration of tacit knowing and termed, *tacit integration*.

Tacit integration is the basis of our capacity to perform skilful action. For example, when hammering a nail 'I have subsidiary awareness of the feeling in the palm of my hand which is merged into my focal awareness of my driving the nail' (Polanyi 1958: 55). The structure of such integration is likened to the proximal–distal relation in anatomy figured as the unusual construction of attending *from* something *to* something else:

> Such is the functional relation between the two terms of tacit knowing: we know the first term only by relying on our awareness of it attending to the second. (Polanyi 1966b: 10)

In this way, the functional structure of tacit knowing, that is, the act of integrating subsidiary clues and a focal object, is directional since in 'subordinating the subsidiary to the focal, tacit knowing is directed from the first to the second' (Polanyi 1969: 141). It is.

Subsidiary awareness is further specified by TTK as incorporating two kinds of clues: *subliminal* or *marginal* (Table 1.1). On the one hand there are things that a knower cannot directly perceive. These subliminal clues include any of the

Table 1.1 Types of awareness in Theory of Tacit Knowing

Type of awareness	Nature
Subsidiary	
Subliminal	Knower cannot directly perceive object
Marginal	Knower could perceive object if it were the focus of their attention
Focal	Knower can perceive object directly

neurophysiological bases of perception such as eye muscle contraction. On the other hand there are things which the knower could perceive if they were the focus of attention. These are marginal clues such as objects in the periphery of a knower's field of vision.

While subsidiary awareness appears to loosely correspond to the popular conception of the unconscious,[2] TTK is careful to distance it from this common-sense view, reiterating that, as a form of awareness, it must be considered in terms of the to–from structure at the heart of tacit knowing:

> If this analysis convinces us of the presence of two very different kinds of awareness in tacit knowing, it should also prevent us from identifying them with conscious and unconscious awareness. Focal awareness is, of course, always fully conscious, but subsidiary awareness, or from-awareness, can exist at any level of consciousness, ranging from the subliminal to the fully conscious. (Polanyi and Prosch 1977: 39)

In this way, the model of awareness does not equate with models of the subconscious, preconscious, 'or with the fringe of consciousness described by William James'. Instead, TTK casts the functional structure of tacit knowing as a form of logic similar to drawing inferences from a premise, the difference being that the inferences drawn by tacit knowing are not explicit.

Indwelling and interiorization

TTK posits knowing as an act of 'personal participation' involving the body (Polanyi and Prosch 1977: 73). The term *indwelling* is used to describe the active participation of the knower and their body in the process of tacit integration. For example, subliminal subsidiary awareness in the form of neurophysiological reaction to stimulus is a form of indwelling experienced by a knower but not attended to at the level of focal awareness. Both sensory perceptual experience and internal bodily functioning that is not part of our direct experience are encompassed by subsidiary awareness. Knowing is cast as an *interiorization* with meaning being made by dwelling in something rather than merely looking at it. We experience via subsidiary awareness something not as solely itself, but as its relation to a more comprehensive entity. For example, indwelling is central to performing and learning a skill:

> Two kinds of indwelling meet here. The performer co-ordinates his moves by dwelling in them as parts of his body, while the watcher tries to correlate these moves by seeking to dwell in them from the outside. He dwells in these moves by interiorizing them. By such exploratory indwelling the pupil gets the feel of a master's skill and may learn to rival him. (Polanyi 1966b: 30)

This is a view of knowledge as embodied whether the skill is physiological or semiotic. Indwelling is at the centre of both everyday perception and complex scientific theorizing: a dancer dwells in a dance just as a chemist dwells in an experiment.

The tacit coefficients of language: The structure of meaning in tacit knowing

Polanyi developed an account of 'sense-giving and sense-reading' where he set out to outline 'the total structure of language, comprising both its formal patterns successfully established by modern linguistics and its informal semantic structure, studied so far mainly by philosophy' (Polanyi 1969: 181). Nevertheless his work on language has largely been ignored by theoretical and applied linguists (Tóth 2008). As I flagged earlier, there are many references to 'meaning' in TTK that a functional linguist might find promising, particularly in their appeal to the experiential rather than to logical formalism. Polanyi specifies tacit knowing as a process of making meaning without which consciousness is not possible:

> All human thought comes into existence by grasping the meaning and mastering the use of language. Little of our mind lives in our natural body; a truly human intellect dwells in us only when our lips shape words and our eyes read print. (Polanyi 1969: 160)

Making meaning is an active process involving the two forms of awareness (focal and subsidiary) introduced in the previous section. These forms of awareness are described by TTK in terms of how they function semiotically:

It is our subsidiary awareness of a thing that endows it with meaning: with a meaning that bears on an object of which we are focally aware. A meaningful relation of a subsidiary to a focal is formed by the action of a person who integrates one to the other, and the relation persists by the fact that the person keeps of this integration. (Polanyi 1969: 182)

In figuring tacit integration as producing relations in meaning, Polanyi is essentially suggesting that tacit knowledge is a semiotic act. It therefore seems entirely at odds with the TTK to argue that tacit knowledge is not carried in language when we speak, particularly as Polanyi goes on to specify three types of linguistic meaning that involve tacit integration: words functioning as indicators, as symbols and as metaphors. Perhaps this failure to fully account for the possibilities that understanding grammatical patterning might afford in understanding tacit knowledge results from the fact that this linguistic description is undertaken solely at the word level without factoring in the power of linguistic stratification. Another problem may be that Polanyi is employing a model of meaning as external to language, a kind of 'transcendent' model of semiosis that figure meanings as outside the linguistic system:

. . . as reference, meaning as idea or concept, meaning as image. These notions have in common that they are 'external' conceptions of meaning; instead of accounting for meaning in terms of a stratum within language, they interpret it in terms of some system outside language, either the 'real' world or another semiotic system such as that of imagery. (Halliday and Matthiessen 1999: 416)

By way of contrast the functional approach adopted in this book sees meaning as realized in language, that is, as 'something that is constructed in, and so is part of, language itself' (Halliday and Matthiessen 1999: 416).

According to TTK, linguistic reference utilizes the 'from–to' structure of tacit integration with words functioning as 'indicators, pointing in a subsidiary way to that focal integration upon which they bear' (Polanyi and Prosch 1977: 70). Other kinds of signs such as road signs and mathematical formulae may function like denotative words as subsidiary indicators of meaning:

. . . they have in common with these words that, when they are viewed in themselves (not as they appear to us when they are serving their function of bearing on something else), there is little interest to be found in them. (Polanyi and Prosch 1977: 70)

Polanyi employs the following notation to describe the to–from relation, where S is a subsidiary clue, F is the object of focal intent and the arrow represents the relationship of 'bearing upon':

$$S \rightarrow F$$

For example, S might be a particular word which, according to the way TTK theorizes meaning, is in itself is not of 'intrinsic interest' to the knower. The word is endowed with meaning once it serves its 'function of bearing upon something else' (Polanyi and Prosch 1977: 70). The general class of this type of relation is defined as the following, where +ii is 'our intrinsic interest' and –ii represents those clues that are not of intrinsic interest:

$$+ii \quad -ii$$
$$S \rightarrow F$$

Consider the example of a blind man operating a cane to navigate. The potentially dangerous objects that he encounters with the stick are the focal objects (F), while the feelings he experiences in his hand as the cane hits an object are subsidiary clues (S) that he integrates with the focal object to draw his conclusions about the safety of his path. Polanyi suggests that this is a 'self-centred integration' as it relies upon the indwelling of the self, attending 'from' subsidiary clues 'to' the focal object (Table 1.2 shows 12 examples of other self-centred integrations that he provides).

Table 1.2 Self-centred integrations involving clues lacking the intrinsic interest of the focal object

Kinds of self-centred integration
Sensory clues fused to perception
Two retinal images fused to three-dimensional sight
Two stereo pictures fused to three-dimensional sight
Deliberate motions fused to intended performance
Actions taken in causing something to happen
Establishment of part-whole relations
Structure of a complex entity, e.g. a physiology
Series of integrations forming a stratification
Use of clues to establish reality of a discovery
A simulation identified with a simulated object
Recognition of a member of a class
Use of a name to designate an object

The next class of words considered is where they function as symbols, rather than as indicators of other things. Instead of being outside our interest, 'it is the subsidiary clues that are of intrinsic interest to us, and they enter into meanings in such a way that we are carried away by these meanings' (Polanyi and Prosch 1977: 71). The focal object is of interest to us because of its symbolic relation to the subsidiary clues. Hence the + and − symbols used in the notation for symbolization are the inverse to indication. For example, in the case of a flag, the subsidiary object is the person's cultural experience of living in the particular country and 'we, as selves, are picked up into the meaning of the symbol' (Polanyi and Prosch 1977: 73). The looped, 'somersaulting' arrow used in the notation below represents the involvement of our embodied, personal experience (as people living in a country) in our understanding of the symbol. The notation is intended to capture the idea that it is 'a wholistic achievement imaginative achievement of meaning, not a serialized mechanical one':

$$\underset{S}{-ii}\; \overset{\curvearrowright}{\circlearrowright}\; \underset{F}{+ii}$$

On the other hand, an example where S and F are both of intrinsic interest to the meaning made is metaphor. This is the case where 'a symbol embodying a significant matter has significance of its own and this is akin to the matter that it embodies' (Polanyi and Prosch 1977: 78). In other words, the target of the metaphor and its vehicle are both significant:

> The tenor bears on the vehicle, but, as in the case of a symbol, the vehicle (the focal object) returns back to the tenor (the subsidiary element) and enhances its meaning, so that the tenor, in addition to bearing on, also becomes embodied in the vehicle. (Polanyi and Prosch 1977: 78)

The view of metaphor proposed may be seen as a misreading of Richards' (1936) conception that tenor and vehicle are integrated in metaphor to produce a new meaning rather than the vehicle being a focal object (Gulick 1993). This may be notated as follows, where t (tenor) and v (vehicle) are given as:

$$\underset{\underset{S}{+ii}}{\text{ourselves}}\; \overset{\curvearrowright}{\circlearrowright}\; \underset{\underset{F}{+ii}}{(t\; \overset{\curvearrowright}{}\; v)}\; +ii$$

It is because of the involvement of ourselves in the meaning of a metaphor that we experience the emotional response so integral to its use in poetry and other written art.

The account of meaning provided by Polanyi is very different to the Saussurean and Firthian-inspired model that developed into SFL, the account of language deployed in this book. Polanyi's focus on words factors out the other strata of language (context, discourse-semantics, phonology/graphology). In so doing it factors out the interpersonal, social dimension of meaning. Meaning is more than a relation between different kinds of attentive states, it is a way of getting things done in the social word, and is in this sense a social semiotic (Halliday 1978). There is, however, some alignment between a functional and Polanyian perspective with both descriptions figuring meaning as experience rather than as formal logic. Nevertheless, making meaning with language involves construing experience, interacting with others and organizing these two dimensions (Halliday (1978) theorizes these functions of language as metafunctions explained in Chapter 2). Polanyi's account of attention in relation to words does not adequately address these kinds of functions of language.

Tacit semiosis: Translating tacit integration into peircean semiotics

In *Knowing and Being*, a collection of essays, Polanyi (1969) translates TTK into the technicality of Peircean semiosis. Semiosis is a term used in semiotic theory to describe the making of meaning with signs. Peirce's semiosis posits a triadic relation between a sign, interpretant and object in an account that emphasizes the relational and perspectival nature of representation. A sign is 'grounded' by the interpretation of the entity that perceives it:

> A sign, or representament, is something which stands to somebody for something in some respect or capacity. It addresses somebody, that is, creates in the mind of that person an equivalent sign, or perhaps a more developed sign. That sign which it creates I call the interpretant of the first sign. (Peirce et al. 1931).

Peirce's claim that the meaning of a sign is mediated by further signs is a rejection of the notion of immediate access to 'understanding' and in this way is aligned with Polanyi's critique of scientific objectivity. Figure 1.1 depicts the mediating role of the interpretant in a triadic conception of signification (meaning-making).

Polanyi (1969) translated his ideas about tacit integration into the terms of Peircean semiotics, possibly to further specify the way he conceived tacit knowing to be an active process of making meaning. The triadic relation between

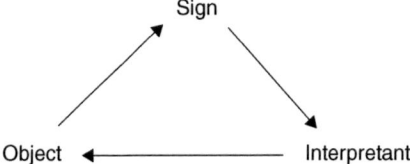

Figure 1.1 A triadic conception of semiosis.

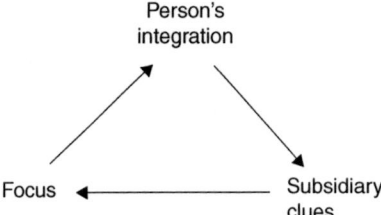

Figure 1.2 Tacit integration represented in terms of Pierce's triadic semiosis.

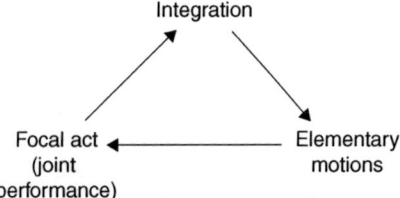

Figure 1.3 The tacit integration of a skill.

an object, an interpretant and a sign posited in Peircean semiosis is presented in Figure 1.1. Polanyi's concept of subsidiary awareness, when translated into the Peircean model, becomes the interpretant, that is, the socially situated consciousness of the 'knower' (see Figure 1.2). This representation accords with the idea that the social and cultural influences on our meaning-making are often below our attention.

For example, the tacit integration of a skill can be represented using the Peircean triad as in Figure 1.1. Polanyi (1969: 183) argues that 'the major skills of our body and mind are all based on a meaningful integration of our body and of sensations felt by our body'. The elementary motions that are integrated to perform the skilful action are subsidiary in the sense that the performer does not attend to them. Thus they are placed in the position occupied by the interpretant in Figure 1.1. These elementary motions are integrated with the focal act (Figure 1.3). In this way, Polanyi argues that an action with our bodies, such as riding a bike, is skilful because physical action involves the integration of subsidiary elements that are interiorized by the subject. External objects are made internal to the body in the process of tacit integration, here rewritten as 'tacit semiosis'.

Such subsidiary sensing figures meaning as internalization, that is, rendering meaning-making as the integration of subsidiary and focal elements (Polanyi 1969: 183). Things of which we are not directly aware, being subsidiary to our attention 'resemble our body closely by the fact that we rarely know them focally' (Polanyi 1969: 183). For example, consider Figure 1.4 which depicts tacit integration in navigating blindfolded with a stick. In this case, the impact that the stick makes on the hands and fingers of the knower is part of their subsidiary awareness and this is integrated with the position of the object where it is hit by the stick. The integration allows the knower to assess potential hazards in the environment and navigate the space.

Figure 1.5 depicts tacit integration in the speculative skill of deciding a chess move. Here the knower integrates the potential moves of chess-men, the entire scope of which he does not readily have conscious access to at once, with the chess-men that he is focusing on moving.

Polanyi suggests that the Peircean triad, with subsidiary perception added for the case of tacit knowing, is directly applicable to fields such as zoology and botany. In these fields understanding the characteristic appearance of biological phenomena is 'based on features that are hardly identifiable in themselves' (Polanyi 1969: 184). Figure 1.6 portrays the tacit integration of reading a physiognomy, an example of how integrating clues or features imbues meaning

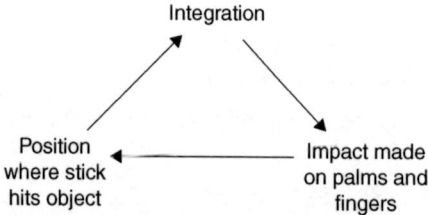

Figure 1.4 Tacit integration in navigating blindfolded using stick.

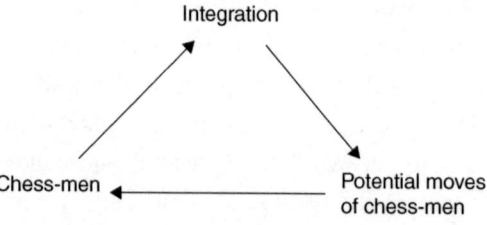

Figure 1.5 Tacit integration in a speculative skill: deciding a chess move.

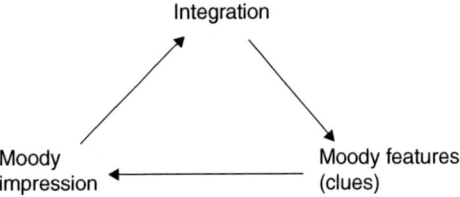

Figure 1.6 Tacit integration in reading a physiognomy.

through combination. The specific moody features are integrated by the knower with the moody impression of the face.

Polanyi developed this argument about subsidiary awareness to assert that this quality of tacit knowing is part of scientific discovery itself which is often 'guided by many unidentifiable clues' (Polanyi 1969: 184). In this way TTK is a critique of the possibility of objective scientific knowledge. The move to recasting TTK in this Peircean form opens the way for looking at tacit knowledge with semiotic tools.

We will now shift gear to consider how practical, implicit knowledge has been theorized across disciplines. While the term 'tacit knowledge' is currently in popular use, many disciplines employ related concepts using different technicality.

Part 2: An interdisciplinary archaeology of tacit knowledge

Philosophical perspectives on tacit knowing

While Polanyi's work in the 1950s is the dominant contemporary perspective on tacit knowledge, it is a concept that dates back to the Ancient Greeks. TTK has been used in an argument for tacit knowledge as ineffable, however this view is incommensurable with a research tradition beginning with the Aristotle. The psychoanalytical concept that we can learn about our tacit knowledge through our own talk originates in Plato and Aristotle's ideas about introspection and peripateticism. The peripatetic walks, as was Aristotle's habit, and talks, not knowing what they may say but nevertheless learning from that talk. Greek philosophical traditions are probably preceded by earlier interest in tacit knowledge but our knowledge of them is limited

Aristotle and practical wisdom

Aristotle is perhaps the first philosopher in the western tradition to develop a theory about tacit knowledge. He liked to walk as he discussed issues of philosophy with his students, a practice with gave the 'peripatetic' tradition he found its name (from the Greek 'peripatao' meaning 'walk around'). Peripatetics privileged perception over the intellect, as Kant usefully summarized:

> ... [Aristotle] rejected all a priori cognitions, and said that all cognitions were empirical, or that they were based on the first principle of experience. (Kant 2001: 309)

Later this idea would be interpreted by Thomas Aquinas as the peripatetic axiom, 'Nothing is in the intellect that was not first in the senses' (*Nihil est in intellectu quod non prius in sensu*). Such a position is the central idea in empiricism.

Aristotle was interested in how to explain the relationship of human ability and experience. In Nicomachean Ethics he defines practical wisdom (phronesis) as a virtue that governed how to use experience to determine how to best act in particular situations. Practical wisdom is developed with experience and, as such, is unlikely to be found in the young:

> The cause is that such wisdom is concerned not only with universals but with particulars, which become familiar with experience, but a young man has no experience, for it is length of time that gives experience; indeed one may ask this question too, why a boy may become a mathematician, but not a philosopher or a physicist. (Aristotle 1998: 148)

This perspective distinguishes between practical and philosophic wisdom, specifying that 'each is a virtue of a different part of the soul' (Aristotle 1998: 153):

> A young boy is capable of mathematical reason since it involves abstraction rather than lived experience. Philosophy or physics, on the other hand, require experience to exercise even their first principles. Indeed, experience may be considered a first principle of these domains. Thus, practical wisdom is different from scientific knowledge, 'for that which can be scientifically known can be demonstrated, and art and practical wisdom deal with things that are variable'. (Aristotle 1998: 144)

Aristotle further distinguishes practical wisdom from intuitive reason. The latter deals with premises, the logic behind which is not understood by the individual. On the other hand practical wisdom involves with 'the ultimate particular' afforded by the increased perception that experience engenders (Aristotle 1998: 148). However, even as Aristotle foregrounds the differences between the virtues, he suggests their convergence in their human realization:

> ... for when we speak of judgement and understanding and practical wisdom and intuitive reason we credit the same people with possessing judgement

and having reached years of reason and with having practical wisdom and understanding. (Aristotle 1998: 152)

A person who holds practical wisdom does not merely perform acts which are 'good', she understands how to act depending on the particularities of a given context because she has accustomed herself with different instances and contexts over time. To act virtuously in one context does not necessarily directly map to expectations in another context: practical wisdom allows a person to recognize the difference.

Ryle (1949) – knowing how/knowing that

Jumping forward considerably in time we see the Aristotelian distinction about forms of knowledge still in currency. Ryle (1949) is attributed with introducing a philosophical distinction between 'knowing how' and 'knowing that'. Ryle (1949) sought to renegotiate the relation of theory and practice in an argument against Cartesian mind–body separation. Tacit knowing is not, according to this framework, following internal matrices of rules that are translated into suitable behaviours. Instead 'there are many classes of performances in which intelligence is displayed, but the rules or criteria of which are unformulated', for example telling a joke (Ryle 1949: 30). Rules are inadequate because 'intelligent practice is not the step-child of theory' as theorizing is itself a practice (Ryle 1949: 26). It is the way the practice is carried out that makes it a skill rather than any 'special antecedents' to the act (Ryle 1949: 32). If antecedents to the skilful practice were formulated they would result in an infinite regress where no action would be logically possible:

> . . . if for any operation to be intelligently executed, a prior theoretical operation had to be performed and performed intelligently, it would be a logical impossibility for anyone ever to break into the circle. (Ryle 1949: 30)

This perspective that intelligent action is not preceded by intellectual formulation questions the intellectualist position that to perform intelligently 'is to do a bit of theory and then to do a bit of practice' (Ryle 1949: 29).

Ryle criticized Cartesian dualism, which situates theory as a private activity located in the mind, as a 'dogma of the ghost in the machine'. The ghost is the mind, locus of private experience, contained in the machine, the publicly knowable, physical body. Instead, intelligent action is not composed of two distinct processes but one practice. Polanyi (1969) presented his theory of tacit knowing as a way of getting around the problems Ryle identified with the

Cartesian framework. Tacit knowing, in TTK, is an interface through which the mind and body interact and 'it is this logic that disposes of the Cartesian dilemma by acknowledging two mutually exclusive ways of being aware of our body' (Polanyi 1969: 223).

Ryle's thesis sought to apply the principle of 'linguistic philosophy' (otherwise known as 'ordinary-language philosophy') that philosophical problems are problems generated by linguistic misunderstanding. The kind of misunderstanding he was concerned with was the category mistake: confusion in the attribution of logical types. He aimed 'to show why certain sorts of operations with the concepts of mental powers and processes are breaches of logical rules' (Ryle 1949: 8). He argued that the Cartesian perspective on intelligent action ascribes mental processes to an erroneous category and thus that the Cartesian mind–body division is a philosophical myth resulting from a category-mistake. According to Ryle this category-mistake may be attributed to Descartes' attempt to retain a religious conception of the mind while leveraging the explanatory power of Galileo's mechanics. The mistake is a distortion resulting from adopting an inappropriate grammar:

> Still unwittingly adhering to the grammar of mechanics, he tried to avert disaster by describing minds in what was merely an obverse vocabulary. The workings of minds had to be described by the mere negatives of the specific descriptions given to bodies; they are not in space, they are not motions, they are not modifications of matter, they are not accessible to public observation. Minds are not bits of clockwork, they are just bits of not-clockwork. (Ryle 1949: 20)

In keeping with the methodological position that philosophical problems can be solved by looking at the language in which they are raised, Ryle grounded his discussion of knowing how/knowing that in what appears akin to semantic analysis. He uses linguistic selection restrictions as evidence for philosophical arguments:

> We speak of learning how to play an instrument as well as learning that something is the case; of finding out how to prune trees as well as finding out that the Romans had a camp in a certain place... (Ryle 1949: 28)

While this kind of semantic inquiry appears useful in foregrounding the issues to be dissected, the question of whose semantics they reflect remains. Ryle predates the corpus-based linguistics arising in the 1960s that use large databases of speech and writing in what was to become a more quantitative approach to understanding linguistic usage. Ryle's approach is instead that of individual judgement about what is commonly said, generalized as statements of philosophical 'truth'.

Wittgenstein, rule-following and language-games

Wittgenstein's investigation of rule-following and language-games is a significant study in tacit knowledge. At its core is the question of whether a rule can be explicitly formulated as arising from human intention. Through examples of children learning concepts that are naturalized as adults he shows that action that seems intentional may be illusory. For example, children who have learnt how to play with trains are engaging in skilful activity. However, other children who have not been 'trained' in train playing are able to play the game using mimicry alone. The two groups of children appear to be doing the same thing despite having different intentions.

Wittgenstein also considered the case of making meaning in relation to rule-following. Making meaning with language is largely tacit despite the complexity of the 'tacit conventions' upon which language is based:

> Man possesses the ability to construct languages capable of expressing every sense, without having any idea how each word has meaning or what meaning is just as people speak without knowing how the individual sounds are produced. (Wittgenstein 1953/2001: 22)

To investigate this complexity he describes a series of thought experiments designed to foreground the role of culture and society in meaning-making. These thought experiments draw analogies between games and language. Consider for example the following language game from *Philosophical Investigations*:

> Now think of the following use of language: I send someone shopping. I give him a slip marked 'five red apples'. He takes the slip to the shop-keeper, who opens the drawer marked 'apples', then he looks up the word 'red' in a table and finds a colour sample opposite it; then he says the series of cardinal numbers – I assume that he knows them by heart – up to the word 'five' and for each number he takes an apple of the same colour as the sample out of the drawer. – I t is in this and similar ways that one operates with words – "But how does he know where and how he is to look up the word 'red' and what he is to do with the word 'five'?" Well, I assume that he 'acts' as I have described. Explanations come to an end somewhere. – But what is the meaning of the word 'five'? No such thing was in question here, only how the word 'five' is used. (Wittgenstein 1953/2001: 1)

In this language-game, the participants in the exchange did not possess internal mental representations of colours and numbers but they were nevertheless able to complete the transaction. Meaning here is how language is used and language has a function beyond naming objects. This account of 'language as use' connects meaning with what Wittgenstein terms 'forms of life'. In other words, meaning emerges from how we live. He argues that, for this reason, if a lion could speak we wouldn't understand what he was saying as we have no understanding of how lions construct their lives and hence no capacity to empathize with them.

Tacit knowledge in the sociology of science: Science, objectivity and tacit knowing

Revealing the tacit dimensions of scientific methods is an important concern within the history and philosophy of science within an area known as the sociology of knowledge that approaches science as a social practice. Polanyi's model of tacit knowledge was itself particularly directed at critiquing the scientific method and is cited by theorists within this discipline as providing a useful conceptual model for understanding scientific practice (Kuhn 1962; Ravetz 1971). TTK was aimed at providing 'a stable alternative', the seeming objectivity of science (Polanyi 1966b: 25). It is an example of deconstructing what Schuster (1984) refers to as the mythic construction of 'Method'. Method discourses in science typically try to generate the idea that they are systematic, explicit and objective (Ravetz 1971; Collins 2001a,b). As such, they present themselves as incommensurable with other practices such as astrology that they claim to be pseudoscience. Here we have an example of a technical discourse operating to efface the role of tacit knowing in the production of knowledge.

Ravetz and craft knowledge

Ravetz (1971) developed a view of scientific work as craft, acknowledging a debt to Polanyi's TTK. His claims about the craft-character of science were intended as a means for 'resolving the paradox of the radical difference between the subjective, intensely personal activity of creative science, and the objective, impersonal knowledge which results from it' (Ravetz 1971: 231). 'Craft' is popularly conceived as involving skill that is inherently unspecifiable, residing within the personal experience of the artist. Synonyms for craft skill include:

> adroitness, aptitude, artistry, craft, craftsmanship, creativity, dexterity, expertise, facility, imagination, ingenuity, inventiveness, knack, knowhow, knowledge, mastery, method, profession, trade, virtuosity. (Kipfer 2003)

These terms are closely associated with tacit knowledge. Ravetz suggests that the techniques of a craft-person are not reducible to explicit descriptions, invoking Polanyi's ideas about tacit knowing as resistant to articulation. The novice endeavouring to learn an art will need to gain a close familiarity with the objects used in the craft such that their use becomes tacit and automatized:

> Indeed, much of his technique may not even have the character of conscious knowledge; by experience, his hands and eyes have taught themselves. It is this subtle interaction of the craftsman with his material, producing slightly different copies of the same general model, which gives handicraft productions their special charm. (Ravetz 1971: 75–6)

Craft practice thus involves a below-view stratum that resists formalization of the kind typically associated with scientific knowledge. Tacit knowledge, or craftsman's knowledge, is required to undertake the work of producing and transforming materials use in science, be they artefacts or scientific theories. Scientists posses craft knowledge of both how to use the material in their laboratories and how to generate theory.

The scientist is a very particular kind of craftsman due to the mediated, artificial nature of the equipment he uses in practicing his craft. The interaction between the scientist and the scientific instrument is mediated by the understanding that the scientist holds about both the functioning of the instrument and higher-order assumptions. However, this understanding is not necessarily explicit, being the product of both the scientist's accumulated, idiosyncratic interaction with the instrument, and the practices that the scientist has assimilated during training. For example, in the case of systematic errors produced by a device (that are assumed not to be indicative of the nature of the phenomena upon which the device is operating), the scientist must rely on experience integrated into formal theories of how the apparatus operates:

> The scientist must know by experience what size of error is 'negligible'; he must be able to reduce the recognized errors to such a size; and he must be sensitive to clues announcing the presence of stable non-negligible errors from other sources. For this sort of work, the scientist must be a master of the operations of the apparatus. (Ravetz 1971: 75–6)

Here, Ravetz refers to the general problem in scientific practice, also identified by Kuhn and Bachelard, that interpretation plays a role in using experimental apparatuses and that 'instruments are nothing but theories materialised' (Bachelard 1984: 12–13). Scientific instruments are not divorced from the vagaries of theoretical constructs. Ravetz points to the circularity inherent in employing a theory-laden object to investigate a theory. An attendant implication is whether the instrument itself may be producing the phenomena it is being used to observe.

These ideas about craft knowledge of scientific equipment problematize the possibility of scientific objectivity. Bachelard (1984) suggests that scientific projects have a general bias towards finding phenomena by the very use of instruments themselves:

> ... the activity of scientific thought is to produce couplings of the abstract and the concrete via the installation of theoretically defined instruments and via setting up apparatuses according to programmes of rational realization. (Lecourt 1975: 77)

While scientific tools make scientific study possible, they also appear to make the discovery of phenomena inevitable. This tendency towards 'realization of the noumenon' complicates any claim of objectivity. It challenges the idea that scientific instruments merely translate existing phenomena into the discourse of measurement rather than altering or 'interpreting' such phenomena.

Ravetz's characterization of scientific knowledge as craft knowledge provides an alternative way of classifying knowledge to the widely deployed tacit/explicit dichotomy. A senior researcher brings to the socially accumulated knowledge in his particular field 'personal craft experience of his portion of it' (Ravetz 1971: 97). Tacit knowledge is considered in relation to this accumulated knowledge rather than solely to its relation to explicit, objectified knowledge.

A key component of the craft in scientist is the ability to avoid 'pitfalls'. Pitfalls prevent a research project from realizing its goals and can only be perceived in retrospect. They may result from a hidden systematic error by an apparatus, an error within a theory or a false deduction in reasoning:

> At every stage of our exploration of the unknown, we are at risk of being mistaken, and of remaining in ignorance of our mistakes until irretrievable damage has been done. (Ravetz 1971: 95)

Different pitfalls are associated with different types of instruments and the scientist must be apprenticed into recognizing the pitfalls that characterize their particular domain. Negotiating pitfalls ahead of time is a tacit process into which the scientist is apprenticed. We can attribute degrees of tacitness in terms of the extent to which a problem has been previously encountered within the practice of a field:

> ... we can distinguish between more or less solidly established knowledge, by the degree to which the ways around its common pitfalls are well charted,

and those encountered in the extensions of that knowledge can be sensed in advance. (Ravetz 1971)

This apprenticeship is embedded in the social processes of a given scientific field. Ravetz describes the process as being apprenticed into a 'tool' rather than a field due to the high level of specialized mastery of particular instruments that most scientific fields require. The tacit knowledge at the heart of this mastery precipitates certain social roles within the community:

> There is thus a natural division of labour between tool-experts and their clients; and the tool-experts are not merely individuals serving as auxiliaries to the clients in their work, but themselves can form a self-contained speciality, a tool-providing field. (Ravetz 1971: 90–1)

Depending on the goals of the different scientists, they will privilege distinct activities: for example acquiring existent 'reliable' data versus maximizing the reliability of an instrument. Competing goals may lead to conflict over what is essentially tacit knowledge:

> The two parties even perceive the situation differently, for their different interests correspond to different bodies of craft knowledge; and unless both parties enter the relation with considerable mutual comprehension and respect, only their respective incompetencies will be communicated, and conflict will ensue. (Ravetz 1971: 90–1)

The subject positions of the 'tool-expert' and their 'client' identified above are particularly relevant to the IT domain and hence the field studies explored in this book. In an organizational IT context we also have a division of labour among groups with different interests (IT professionals, project stakeholder, end users, etc). These groups are negotiating artefacts that are highly 'artificial' (in Ravetz's sense of mediated instruments). In a similar way to the client in Ravetz's description, the user in the IT domain wants systems that meet certain standards (typically referred to as the user requirements as we will see in Chapter 4). The tool-expert, or technologist, also possesses a preoccupation with the tools they are providing as entities in their own right.

Khun and the paradigm as tacitly enforced

Kuhn's (1962) seminal work *The Structure of Scientific Revolutions* introduced the concept of a 'paradigm' as the conceptual structure unifying communities of scientists. A paradigm is a form of tacit consensus among a scientific community about what counts as a solution to the research questions of a particular field.

As such, it constitutes the way in which general theoretical positions and their corresponding methodologies are deployed. Individual members of scientific research programmes assimilate the principles of the paradigm through their training. This involves carrying out standard experiments or working on problems which are deemed important to the discipline during their training. Students are apprenticed into a paradigm by working with a supervisor from whom they learns the standards of the field such as valid measurement and criteria for defining a problem. Because scientists working in different paradigms have been socialized into different ways of thinking about what counts as valid science, they will talk at cross-purposes when arguing with competing views from different paradigms: a property which Khun termed 'incommensurability'.

The paradigm is, however, not necessarily characterized by an explicit set of rules or foregrounded assumptions. It is on this point that Kuhn engages with Polanyi's TTK and Kuhn's reference to Polanyi in *The Structure of Scientific Revolutions* contributed to popularizing the notion of tacit knowledge. There is some controversy over the similiarity of Khun's notion of incommensurability and Polanyi's ideas about scientific controversy (Jacobs 2007). Both authors conceded that Polanyi's theory was a large influence on Khun's work.

The practice that goes on within a paradigm is termed 'normal science' and is essentially a process of 'mopping-up', that is, confirming and refining the principles of the paradigm rather than discovering novel phenomena. Deviation from the paradigm is seen as a failure to correctly apply method rather than a new discovery:

> Sometimes, as in wave-length measurement, everything but the most esoteric detail of the result is known in advance, and the typical latitude of expectation is only somewhat wider . . . the project whose outcomes do not fall in that narrower range is usually just a research failure, one which reflects not on nature but on the scientist. (Kuhn 1962: 35)

Kuhn goes on to describe the crisis state which ensues in the case of the discovery of a true anomaly as 'revolutionary' science. The revolutionary switch required to shift from one paradigm to another is a gestalt switch. Once the change has occurred the old paradigm seems obviously flawed.

The duplication of scientific skills

Tacit knowledge is a central problem in duplicating scientific skills across communities of that are geographically dispersed. Collins' (2001) study of attempts to replicate measurement of the quality factors (Qs) in sapphire in

Russia is an important case study in this area. He defines tacit knowledge as 'knowledge or abilities that can be passed between scientists by personal contact but cannot be, or have not been, set out or passed on in formulae, diagrams or verbal descriptions and instructions for action' (Collins 2001: 72). This is part of a ' "enculturational model" of skill transmission' suggesting that skills, such as how to perform an experiment, are shared through socialization rather than through codified prescriptions (Pinch et al. 1996: 164). The scientist is socialized into the practice of experimentation, assimilating its assumptions through interpersonal engagement with colleagues.

In Collins' example tacit knowledge is at stake in measuring the Q of a substance (the rate at which its resonance decays). Russian measurements of a high Q in sapphire had suggested that it would be the optimal material for mirrors in laser-interferometer gravitational wave detectors. Measuring Q required methods for suspending a crystal that avoided dissipating its energy of vibration. The suspension process required a high degree of expertise in the form of an intimate knowledge of the materials and instruments – craft knowledge in the sense established by Ravetz earlier in this chapter. Failed attempts were made to reproduce the Russian measurements by other universities in Europe, the United States and Australasia. The duplication process involved what one of Collins' subjects described as 'a great deal of "black magic"' (Collins 2001: 75).

Collins (2001) attributed the difficulties in replicating the Russian Q measurements to the absence of personal contact between the scientists. According to his model, five kinds of problems (relating to tacit knowledge) could have been overcome through such personal contact: concealed knowledge, mismatched salience, ostensive knowledge, unrecognized knowledge and uncognized/uncognizable knowledge (Table 1.3). Concealed knowledge is knowledge that is deliberately withheld or remains unnoticed due to circumstance. Ostensive knowledge refers to phenomena such as photographs or diagrams that can be

Table 1.3 Allocation of experimental practices in Collins' (2001a) tiered model of tacit knowledge

Knowledge	Type of tacitness
Degree of vacuum and length of suspension	Hidden knowledge/mismatched salience
Selection of material for suspension fibres	Hidden knowledge/mismatched salience/ostensive knowledge
Adjustments to clamp	Ostensive knowledge
Methods for greasing a fine silk thread	Ostensive knowledge

explained by some form of demonstration. Consider, for example, the example that Collins provides of a scientist describing a process important to getting a correct measurement:

> Ericson: It's very difficult to be precise about the amount of grease you apply because you're just applying grease to the thread. If you apply too much the Q tends to fall off because it's too loose and it will wobble and you will get an erratic ringdown. But if you have too little grease then the thread may stick and slip rather than sit smoothly on the mass. In this case I think there probably wasn't quite enough grease, which is why it [the Q] is slightly lower than what I thought it might be. But if you get it spot on you can usually get a very high result ... I think there's not quite enough.
>
> Collins: And that's just from your looking at it.
>
> Ericson: Yeh that's just empirical from my experience of doing this before, I can sort of tell. When you take off the greased thread and you see this band of grease, there's a feel for what's enough and what's too much. And that looked less but not too far off. (Collins 2001: 81)

On the other hand mismatched salience is about differences in determining which questions are addressed given a large number of possible variables. In addition, unrecognized knowledge is about habits (in experimental technique) only understood to be important once a field has developed. The last form of knowledge, uncognized/uncognizable knowledge, is the closest to Polanyi's tacit knowing. It refers to automatized practices transferred through apprenticeship and unconscious imitation. Collins suggests two schools of thought on this final class of knowledge: the reductionist position that claims that the physics and chemistry of the body may in future be able to explain this kind of knowledge, and enculturational model which argues that acquiring such knowledge is an irreducible social process.

Pinch et al. (2001) sought to complement this enculturational model of skill by investigating the 'second-order' coefficients of skill:

> In other words, we need to understand the role of information within knowledge. If virtually everything is culture, what is information? What can you know about being a member of a culture and without rediscovering it for yourself? In trying to answer this question it is important not to give up the enculturational model or compromise it with judicious admixtures of old ideas ... One might say that we are looking for the second order aspects of skill that a 'rediscoverer' might find useful. (Pinch et al. 1996: 166)

The study used participant observation, unstructured interviews and audio and video recording to analyse two elements of second-order knowledge about skill:

- Feasibility: whether the skilful action is 'doable'.
- 'Hardness': the degree of difficulty in learning and performing the skill.

Appending second-order information such as the difficulties encountered at different stages of an experiment to technical documents might aid the transfer of scientific knowledge between groups. Such information is typically effaced by published scientific works which typically adopt a passive voice that factors out the human actors performing experiments.

Callon (1994: 402) casts Collins' work as a 'thesis of the intrinsic inutility of statements', that is, the thesis that without personal experience descriptions or practical guidelines are largely useless:

> What he successfully demonstrated contrary to what he sometimes affirms was not so much the thesis of experimenters' regress as the impossibility of endowing a statement with any meaning if the work of the duplication of skills and instruments has not been done. In other words, it is impossible to mobilize the different elements independently of each other. (Callon 1994: 403)

According to this view, theoretical statements are not 'portable' in the way that is popularly conceived. Instead, they are embedded in the situational, experimental context in which they were engendered. Thus, the individual needs to be socialized into the personal and contextual particularities of a skill to understand the meaning of a theoretical statement. Later in his career Collins returned to the issue of tacit knowledge, proposing a three-phase model of weak, medium and strong tacit knowledge which covered 'respectively, . . . the contingencies of social life (relational tacit knowledge), the nature of the human body (somatic tacit knowledge), and the nature of human society (collective tacit knowledge)' (Collins 2010: x). Learning, he argues involves all three phases, however, it is largely the last form of tacit knowledge that 'requires a solution to the socialization problem' in order to be shared (Collins 2010: x).

The perspective of the social sciences

Many researchers in the social sciences have dealt with the notion that our social experience is constructed through implicit processes. Although some, such as Turner (1994), argue that theories of below-view action move theorists to unneccessary contortions. Work has considered the role implicit, 'backgrounded' (Douglas 1975) knowledge plays in solidifying power structures in society:

> If there is any one idea on which the present currents of thought are agreed it is that at any given moment of time the state of received knowledge is backgrounded by a clutter of suppressed information. It is also agreed that the information is not suppressed by reason of its inherent worthlessness, nor by any passive process of forgetting: it is actively thrust out of the way because of difficulties in making it fit whatever happens to be in hand ...
>
> By a less extreme process of relegation, some information is treated as self-evident. The logical steps by which other knowledge has to be justified are not required. This kind of information, never being made explicit, furnishes the stable background on which more coherent meanings are based... Through these implicit channels of meaning, human society itself is achieved, clarity, and speed of clue-reading ensured. In the elusive exchange between explicit and implicit meanings a perceived-to-be-regular universe establishes itself precariously, shifts, topples, and set itself up again. (Douglas 1975: 3–4)

Douglas and backgrounding

Douglas (1975) adopted an anthropological perspective on backgrounded meaning, adopting a version of the ineffability principle by suggesting that implicit meaning is external to language:

> What is actually said in words is only the tip of the iceberg. The unspoken understandings are essential. How do we reach the implicit? By studying the classifications by which people decide if action has been done well or badly, whether it is right or wrong. (Douglas 1975: vii)

Consdering 'how submerged ideas determine action' she argues beliefs underlying social structures have, to use Polanyi's term, 'tacit coefficients' that are backgrounded. For example the pervasive notion that 'dirt' is dangerous forms the largely implicit basis of deeply held ideas about forbidden behaviour (taboo) or moral failings causing affliction. Impurity becomes a moral symbol that affords order to a particular society. Douglas studied the Lele culture of Zaire. Within this culture there had developed a particular classifications system about what was considered to be polluted (e.g. blood and milk). Other cultures define particular animals or other phenomena as unclean. The classification forms a symbolic system rather than a literal catalogue of hygiene. We have tacit knowledge about this symbolic system by virtue of residing inside a culture. We may engage in symbolic activity such as religious rituals of purification that in turn affirm the implicit order. While explicit meaning can be directly contested and 'destroyed by being labelled untrue', such implicit meanings are beyond the reach of discursive deconstruction because they are 'regarded as too true to warrant discussion' (Douglas 1975: 3).

Bourdieu and habitus

Bourdieu (1990) suggested that individuals unconsciously internalize the cultural 'habitus' in which they reside that causes them to form dispositions to behave and construe their experience in certain ways:

> The habitus is the universalizing mediation which causes an individual agent's practices, without either explicit reason or signifying intent, to be none the less "sensible" and "reasonable". That part of practices which remains obscure in the eyes of their own producers is the aspect by which they are objectively adjusted to other practices and to the structures of which the principle of their production is itself the product. (Bourdieu 1977: 79)

An individual's model of the world is subject to 'structural constraints', manifested in the habitus, acquired by a process of acculturation into specific socially established groups or classes (Bourdieu 1990: 130). In this way people 'to some extent fall into the practice that is theirs rather than freely choosing it or being impelled into it by mechanical constraints' (Bourdieu 1990: 90). Bourdieu's position differs from the structuralist position that argues that we follow unconscious rules in enacting our practice. Instead, the habitus is socially constructed and will shift with changes in context.

In a similar way to Douglas, Bourdieu situates some kinds of implicit meaning as outside the realm of discourse. He terms this 'doxa': meanings that are beyond question for a social group in the sense that they have no means by which to articulate them. Doxa is defined through its compliment, 'the field of opinion', that is, the field of what can actively be contested. As 'the universe of the undiscussed', doxa lies outside 'opinion' with its competing discourses of 'orthodoxy' (hegemony) and 'heterodoxy' (heresy). Bourdieu further defines it as a form of practical knowledge:

> . . . doxa implies a knowledge, a practical knowledge. Workers know a lot: more than any intellectual, more than any sociologist. But in a sense they don't know it, they lack the instrument to grasp it, to speak about it. (Bourdieu and Eagleton 1994: 273)

This practical knowledge manifests 'theses tacitly posited on the hither side of all inquiry' and is only visible in retrospect (Bourdieu and Eagleton 1994: 168).

The tacit knowledge formed by doxa is even more powerful than more explicit forms of social control and can function to limit the possibilities that individuals in a society have to move out of certain roles. Bourdieu argued that the line that is drawn between opinion and doxa 'is itself a fundamental objective at stake in that form of class struggle for the imposition of the dominant systems of classification' (Bourdieu 1977: 169). The dominant class seeks to maintain doxa, while the dominated class aims to redefine its limits and win for themselves greater freedom. The struggle is below-view in the sense that these participants would be unable to explain exactly what is being contested as there are no words in the field of opinion to use.

Tacit knowledge as a psychometric

While tacit knowledge is typically described as resisting measurement, psychology is the main area claiming to have operationalized and measured a version of tacit knowledge. In this discipline tacit knowledge is closely aligned to the concept of automatized action. Bargh (1999) specifies two major strains of psychological research into automatic processes in the last century. The first of these is work on skill acquisition that investigates intentional, goal-directed processes. These processes are automatized through accumulated experience such that they can be practiced without conscious direction and are, in this sense, 'effortless' mental skills. The second area of research deals with 'preattentive' or 'preconscious' processes below the awareness of an individual.

Implicit learning

Learning is a key area of research in psychology. The role of implicit processes in learning is a contentious region in this work. The classic experiment is a finite state grammar test where subjects are presented with sets of letters ordered by a particular grammar. After this exposure, they are presented with randomized cases. Subjects are able to identify which cases conform to the grammar, even though they cannot say why these cases are 'grammatical'. Reber (1967) referred to this grammatical knowledge as 'implicit learning', claiming that his empirical studies on artificial-grammar and probability are the 'earliest studies touching directly on the acquisition of complex information without awareness'

(Reber 1993: 10). These studies conducted in the 1960s involved subjects who memorized sequences of letters generated by an artificial Markovian grammar who were tested to see if they could make decisions about well-formedness of novel cases.

There are many different models of implicit learning. For example Bargh (1999) suggested that conscious processes, being constrained by the amount they can process at a given time, are complemented by unconscious, automatic processes. These hidden processes constitute the major aspect of our mental operations, acting as ' "mental butlers" who know our tendencies and preferences so well that they anticipate and take care of them for us, without having to be asked' (Bargh 1999: 476). Three forms of automatic self-regulation do not involve the perceptual burden of conscious choice:

- Automatic effects of perception on action.
- Automatic goal pursuit.
- Continual automatic evaluation of one's experience.

The automaticity of perception is manifest in the way that our unconscious perceptive mechanisms activate internalized representations of experience:

> ... because perceptual activity is largely automatic and not under conscious or intentional control (the orange on the desk cannot be perceived as purple through an act of will), perception is the route by which the environment directly causes mental activity specifically the activation of internal representations of the outside world. (Bargh 1999: 465)

Many theories factor-in implicit, non-attentive processes into their model of mental processing. For example Bargh claimed that there were both 'intentiontal and unintentional routes to the automatization of a psychological process' (Bargh 1999: 469). The intentional path is the aim to learn a particular skill. For example, practising the violin every day is an intentional act that may lead to automatized, and hopefully proficient, musical skill. Conversely, an unintentional path is followed when 'mental processes recede from consciousness over time with repeated use' (Bargh 1999: 469). For example, we may learn to feel a certain way under a set of conditions that we habitually encounter.

Sternberg's theory of practical intelligence

Another example that figures implicit learning as central to skill acquisition is Stenberg's theory of practical intelligence (PI) which proposed three types of intelligence: analytical, creative and PI (Stenrberg 1985). Tacit knowledge forms the central aspect of PI, the type of intelligence that governs the skills required to meet the goals of everyday life. Sternberg claimed that PI is a measure that accounts for facets of experience not adequately assessed by intelligence metrics such as Spearman's (1927) general intelligence factor, g. In fact, he argues that tacit knowledge, as a subset of PI, is related to performance 'independently of IQ, personality variables, and job satisfaction' in the domain of management (Wagner and Sternberg 1991: 28). According to the theory of PI, tacit knowledge has the following characteristics:

- Not typically acquired by formal training.
- Less subject to awareness than other more formal types of knowledge.
- Procedural in nature and determined by complex, multifaceted rules rather than sets of rules.
- Has 'practical value' to the knower.

Because it is difficult to articulate, PI must be assessed through individual responses to descriptions of practical problems (Sternberg and Grigorenko 2001).

Various domain-specific tests were designed to measure an individual's tacit knowledge in different practical contexts. For example, Wagner and Sternberg (2000) developed a method for measuring tacit knowledge in academic psychology and business management. The method adopted a triadic view of tacit knowledge as manifest in the areas of managing self, managing tasks and managing others. According to this perspective 'managing self' is about the introspective knowledge 'an individual has about his or her individual motives and goals that might be useful in maximising productive accomplishment', while 'managing others' is about the interpersonal, social relationship a person has with work peers (Wagner and Sternberg 2000: 55). An example of this framework in use is the 'Tacit Knowledge in Management' (TKIM) inventory which sought to 'identify individuals whose "street smarts" indicate the potential for excellent performance in managerial and executive careers' (Wagner and Sternberg 1991: 1). The inventory has been shown to be a significant predictor of success in management (Wagner 1987).

Tacit knowledge in linguistics

Knowledge of language is a special case of tacit knowledge. It is both a practical skill and a fundamental medium for human expression. Most schools of linguistics agree that our ability to make meaning with language is an automatized process and scholars in linguistics have been analysing how we use language for centuries. The native speaker of a language has a complex practical understanding of the grammar, semantics and phonology of their language, however, they are unlikely to be able to articulate the nature of this competence. This is because they possess knowledge of language, as they use it, at a level below direct awareness. The grammars described in text books and used in teaching a language are examples where such tacit knowledge has been made explicit (Klein 1986: 40).

The approach of generative linguistics

One aim of the generative theory of linguistics is to provide an explicit representation of the tacit knowledge a native speaker has of their language. This theory asserts that such knowledge is dependent upon innate structures in the brain. Chomsky (1986: 1) adopts Leibniz's notion that 'languages are the best mirror of the human mind', defining tacit knowledge of language as follows:

> Linguistic competence is understood as concerned with the tacit knowledge of language structure, that is, knowledge that is commonly not conscious or available for spontaneous report, but necessarily implicit in what the (ideal) speaker-listener can say ... It is in terms of such knowledge that one can produce and understand an infinite set of sentences, and that language can be spoke[n] of as 'creative', as energeia. (Chomsky 1965: 19)

While Chomsky (1986) refers to linguistic 'competence' this is distinct from performance, the focus of functional approaches to language. Chomsky introduces the term 'cognizing' to describe 'knowing' a language. Cognizing has 'the properties of knowledge in the ordinary sense of the term, apart, perhaps, from accessibility to consciousness' (Chomsky 1986: 269). The focus is on investigating language as a mental state involving 'systems of mental representation and computation' (Chomsky 1986: 51). Language, according to this perspective, is the product of how the human brain is configured, and specifically, the result of the 'language faculty', a '"module" of the mind' (Chomsky 1986: 12). Chomsky's preoccupation with structure rather than function is seen in how he defines the effect of this module:

> The system of knowledge that has somehow developed in our minds has certain consequences, not others, it relates sound and meaning and assigns structural properties to physical events in certain ways, not others. (Chomsky 1986: 12)

These consequences, Chomsky argues, are seen in language acquisition. For example, he asks us to consider the following sentences:

John is too stubborn to talk to Bill.

John is too stubborn to talk to.

We cannot induce the meaning of (2) on the analogy of (1), however, once a child has passed through a certain developmental stage they no longer make errors confusing (1) and (2). A set of principles and parameters define the initial state of the language faculty and allow the child to acquire additional language as more linguistic data becomes available to them through experience. The 'universal grammar' exists as a meta-recipe for constructing any language-specific grammar.

Chomsky defines the way linguistics, as a science, should proceed in terms of this 'logical problem of language acquisition'. The role of linguistic explanation is to explain our tacit knowledge of language. The essential question this explanation needs to address is how a child with very little linguistic data to work with, is able to master the complex grammar of his language in a relatively short amount of time. In this way, the project of generative linguistics may be thought of as an exercise in tacit knowledge elicitation, where the aim is to understand the innate system that allows a speaker to construct grammar. As we will see as we now turn to consider a systemic functional approach to language, attempting to understand linguistic competence without understanding how language operates as a social practice within real-world contexts is an unusual undertaking.

The functional approach: SFL

A challenge to the generative perspective and its emphasis on structure is SFL, the theory of language used in developing the model of under-representation used in this book. SFL will be introduced in detail in Chapter 2. Rather than providing an overview of SFL, this section discusses specifically how SFL conceives of linguistic competence, in the sense of the tacit knowledge a speaker has about how to use their native language. Rather than an innate competence arising from a universal grammar, SFL figures a language user's ability to produce meaningful discourse as a socially constructed capacity oriented towards performing social tasks. In other words, language is a resource for making meanings in social contexts. Halliday (1973) argues that learning a language involves socialization into its different contexts of use:

> Learning one's mother tongue is learning the use of language, and the meanings, or rather the meaning potential, associated with them. The structures, the words, the sounds are the realisation of this meaning potential. Learning language is learning how to mean. (Halliday 1973: 24)

In this way, the tacit knowledge a speaker has of language is a functional: we learn 'how to mean' in context, rather than by learning sets of syntactic rules. For example, if we consider again a child attempting to learn their native tongue, the child's experience of language will be as part of trying to do something (e.g. demand someone to give them something), while the tacit coefficients of language production remain unconscious:

> The child looks through language and sees the social function of the interaction. It is for this reason that children become users, indeed proficient users of language, without achieving what has come to be called linguistic awareness, i.e. an understanding of what language is, rather than an understanding of how it is used. (Hall 1994: 23)

As adults we may make complex use of grammar even with minimal knowledge of grammatical structures. It is only when we choose to 'foreground' grammatical choice, for example, when studying how a poem is written, that we are directly aware of how grammar is used. Foregrouding is the opposite of automatization as it brings more meaning into conscious consideration. Poets make use of foregrounded language to draw attention to the texture of a poem by violating the linguistic patterns that might be expected: 'automatization schematizes an event; foregrounding means the violation of the scheme' (Mukarovský 1964: 19). In this way it is 'prominence that is motivated' (Halliday 1973: 112).

According to the SFL perspective 'language is able to transform experience into meaning' (Halliday and Matthiessen 1999: xi). Our knowledge of the transformation is tacit in the sense that it is transparent to the language producer. For example, when asking for a glass of water, my focus is likely to be on my thirst and my request to the listener, more than it is on my use of the indefinite article. In certain social situations I may have more awareness of how I choose to speak, if, for example, I wish to be cautiously polite, but my ability to maintain such attention is limited. Regardless of the context of use, the language used is the focus for understanding the experience construed: 'Instead of explaining language by reference to cognitive processes, we [SFL linguists] explain cognition by reference to linguistic processes' (Halliday and Matthiessen 1999: x).

Language acquisition as a process of 'tacit integration'

Polanyi's TTK does not appear to explicitly align itself with a theory of language. As we have already seen, Polanyi argued that practical knowledge about how to use language is a process of 'tacit integration':

> My view is that the use of language is a tacit performance; the meaning of language arises, as many other kinds of meaning do, into tacitly integrating hitherto meaningless acts into bearing on a focus that thereby becomes their meaning. (Polanyi 1969: 196)

Polanyi suggests that TTK answers Chomsky's questions about how a child acquires the complex rules of grammar. Specifically the theory of tacit integration addresses Chomsky's question regarding how a child can apply the large volume of rules required despite their limited experience:

> . . . we can reply that the striving imagination has the power to implement its aim by the subsidiary practice of ingenious rules of which the subject remains focally ignorant. (Polanyi 1969: 200)

TTK also offers a reply to the general question of how a speaker is able to comprehend and create novel sentences that are not grounded in prior experience. Polanyi argues that this skill is analogous to riding a bicycle. He describes the 'cyclist's striving imagination', responding to new arrays of variables when attempting to balance in different terrain, as akin to 'faculte de langage, which can discover a whole system of tacit grammar' and apply this knowledge instantly to new cases (Polanyi 1969: 200–1).

Tacit knowledge and knowledge management

Eliciting tacit knowledge from employees is a major research agenda in a cross-disciplinary area that has become known as 'knowledge management', both within academia (in fields such as business management and information systems) and professional management practice. Organizations are faced with the perennial problem that when an employee leaves a professional role they take their context-specific tacit knowledge with them (Starke et al. 2003: 210).

The problem is particularly pertinent in relation to IT systems and projects due to the great reliance many firms place on their technical resources.

The kinds of practical knowledge that an employee will have accumulated during their time working in a role typically resists formal operationalization. In other words, they are usually not effectively explicated by methods such as writing a list of procedures, entering information into a database or other attempts at what is usually referred to as 'knowledge codification'. This kind of knowledge defies mechanisms by which other organizational resources are measured, recorded and stored. Without some process for socializing other employees into particular tacit knowledge, the expertise inevitably departs along with the employee.

There are a number of themes that characterize academic discourse on tacit knowledge in the domain of information systems. The most dominant is a tacit-explicit dichotomy rendered in terms of articulation, codification and judgement (objectivity/subjectivity). This perspective casts tacit knowledge against explicit knowledge, with the latter presented as a codifiable and retainable resource (Nonaka and Takeuchi, 1995). However, as we will see, the distinction is essentially a misconstrual of Polanyi's original ideas about tacit knowing.

Most studies focus on the apparent ineffability of tacit knowledge and associated problems in corporate knowledge acquisition and training. Despite the interdisciplinary wealth of research actively studying tacit knowledge (though often, as we saw in Chapter 1, not by that name), most knowledge management studies claim that tacit knowledge is 'below-view' in the sense that its functional structure cannot be mapped. Instead, attempts are made at 'managing ambiguity' (Baumard 1999) and treating tacit knowledge as embedded in other irreducible phenomena, a kind of 'black box' approach.

The misrepresentation of Polanyi

Polanyi is often cited in knowledge management research in order to affirm a distinction between tacit and explicit forms of knowledge. Nonaka and Takeuchi (1995), credited with introducing the concept of tacit knowledge to the information systems community have reconstrued Polanyi's theory in terms of a tacit/explicit dichotomy, in what may be seen as a misreading of the subtleties of Polanyi's work. They distinguish tacit from explicit knowledge along three parameters: objectivity, temporal stance and communication paradigm. On the one hand tacit knowledge is experiential and practical, involved in knowledge production 'in the moment'; on the other explicit knowledge is objective, rational and concerned with past events and artefacts.

Contrary to such binary classification of knowledge, Polanyi asserts a more subtle distinction that gives a larger role to tacit knowledge. According to TTK, explicit knowledge cannot be adequately separated from its tacit coefficient:

> Now we see tacit knowledge opposed to explicit knowledge; but these two are not sharply divided. While tacit knowledge can be possessed by itself, explicit knowledge must rely on being tacitly understood and applied. Hence all knowledge is either tacit or rooted in tacit knowledge. A wholly explicit knowledge is unthinkable. (Polanyi 1969: 144)

However, many theorists take up these ideas as a means of sharpening the divide. For example, Spender (1993: 37) argues that while 'objective knowledge is scientific, abstracted from the knower, the latter [tacit knowledge] is intimately attached to the knower'. Clearly, ascribing this kind of objectivity to scientific knowledge is contrary to the primary project of TTK.

Indeed, problematizing the tacit/explicit dichotomy was part of Polanyi's critique of objectivity in relation to scientific discourse. Dichotomizing objective 'scientific knowledge' and tacit knowledge, presupposes that meaning in science is disinterested, a position that TTK refutes and which has been challenged by the sociology of science. Polanyi argued that the objectivity perceived as inherent in scientific knowledge is a social construct and that scientific discovery instead relies upon tacit knowing:

> . . . the processes of knowing (and so also of science) in no way resemble an impersonal achievement of detached objectivity. They are rooted throughout (from our selection of a problem to the verification of a discovery) in personal acts of tacit integration. They are not grounded on explicit operations of logic. Scientific inquiery is accordingly a dynamic exercise of the imagination and is rooted in commitments and beliefs about the nature of things. It is a fiduciary act. (Polanyi and Prosch 1977: 63)

The distorted reading of Polanyi regarding explicit knowledge that pervades the knowledge management literature appears to have arisen out of disciplinary orientation: the desire of technology-oriented disciplines to situate themselves closer to 'hard science'. This kind of omnipresence view of tacit knowledge challenges the self-presentation of disciplines that conceive of themselves as formal and quantitative. For these disciplines it 'may be somewhat startling to think that analogy, which played such a central role in medieval thought and is so explicit of a technique in humanities scholarship today, should play such an important role in science or in any disciplinary activity that has quantitative techniques and technologies so central to its method' (Day 2005: 63). The TTK, however, is unambiguous in its proclamation that tacit knowledge 'shapes all factual knowledge, [and] bridges in doing so the disjunction between subjectivity and objectivity' (Polanyi 1958: 17).

The ineffability principle revisited

Knowledge management research typically contrasts tacit and explicit knowledge in terms of linguistic articulation. The strong position is that tacit knowledge cannot be articulated in any linguistic form, while the weak position holds that it is difficult to articulate. Almost every study adopts a version of the strong position, with the exception of a handful of studies. For example Busch and Richards (2000) and Busch (2008) argue that tacit knowledge is partially effable, containing a subset of unknown proportions that they refer to as 'articulable tacit knowledge' in a study of 'articulable implicit managerial IT workplace knowledge'. Similarly, Collins allows that some forms of tacit knowledge may be expressed. This 'relational' tacit knowledge involves instances where 'parties could tell each other what they need to know but either will not, or cannot for reasons that are not very profound, such as not knowing what the other party needs to know' (Collins 2010: 91). According to this perspective tacit knowledge may be actively hidden (concealed knowledge), more efficiently retained in expert humans (logistically demanding knowledge), accidently hidden (mismatched saliences) or not seen to be significant (unrecognized knowledge). None of these studies, however, consider the structure and function of language in any but a cursory way. Allusions are made, as is the case with much knowledge management literature, to communicative practices without acknowledging the richness that linguistic analysis might offer in understanding the way language is used.

For those studies adopting the strong position on ineffability the ultimate aim of knowledge elicitation is to 'convert' tacit knowledge into explicit knowledge (Hershel et al. 2001). Tsoukas (2003: 82) argues that this methodological position on 'translation' and 'conversion', concepts adopted from Nonaka and Takeuchi, is fundamentally flawed. He claims that it perverts Polanyi's conception of tacit knowing since it is incommensurable with the specification that tacit knowledge cannot be effectively articulated. Interestingly, Tsuokas' focus on ineffability does not result in an a-linguistic stance on tacit knowing:

> The ineffability of tacit knowledge does not mean that we cannot discuss the skilled performances in which we are involved. We can indeed, should discuss them provided we stop insisting on "converting" tacit knowledge and, instead, start recursively drawing our attention to how we draw each other's attention to things. Instructive forms of talk help us re-orientate ourselves to how we relate to others and the world around us, thus enabling us to talk and act differently. (Tsoukas 2003: 15–16)

Such recursive reorientation of attention is presented as conforming to Wittgenstein's notion that language offers 'reminders' of our existing knowledge. While 'instructive forms of talk' are claimed to have the potential to change the way we approach praxis as a social phenomenon, no protocol is suggested for achieving this end (Tsoukas 2003: 15–16). In mostly adhering to the ineffability principle, the work does not consider analysing talk about praxis. However, as we will see in this chapter, examination of an individual's linguistic patterning offers a way of systematically understanding the latent patterns in their talk and what they can reveal. In this way, linguistic analysis can contribute to a method for meeting the need of people working with technology to, as Tsoukas himself puts it, 'talk and act differently' (Tsoukas 2003: 16). As Sternberg and Horvath (1999: x) note, 'we need to get beyond the "hand waving" that characterizes most current discussions of tacit knowledge … That is we must know more about tacit knowledge than that it is critical and ineffable'.

Knowledge codification and transfer

Numerous studies in the domain of knowledge management and, more generally, strategic management identify knowledge codification as a central issue in communicating knowledge within organizations. These studies refer to the 'transfer', 'capture' and 'dispersion' of knowledge, seeming to adopt the conduit metaphor (Reddy 1979) (see Chapter 1) for describing the knowledge elicitation process. They manifest an 'epistemology of possession', that is, a construal of knowledge as if it were something that a person might own in the way that you can own an object (Cook and Brown 1999). Cook and Brown (1999) suggest that given the social nature of knowledge production, 'an epistemology of practice' would be a more appropriate lens for studying knowledge in the workplace.

Thinking about knowledge, or knowing, as a practice is a central theme in a movement arguing tacit knowledge cannot be captured because it is embedded in socially situated processes (Boland and Tenkasi 1995; Wenger 1998; Stenmark 2001). According to this view we instead need to manage social processes that create the conditions for knowledge to be shared in a social way. These studies suggest that we should create IT services that connect people with relevant experts rather than attempt to externalize and codify their expertise, a kind of 'community-based model' of knowledge management that foregrounds the role of in situ interpersonal interaction (Swan et al. 1999).

Also making use of the conduit metaphor at the heart of the 'epistomology of possession', Schulz and Jobe (2001: 141) suggest that knowledge is codified when it is 'packaged into formats that allow its transmission to other subunits'. Accordingly, tacit knowledge must be codified in order to be dispersed effectively within an organization. This kind of position claims that codification can be accomplished through various semiotic modes such as formulas and reports, and that knowledge can be embedded in physical objects and people factored along a continuum of abstractness (Schulz and Jobe 2001). This continuum positions numbers and codes as more abstract and people and objects as least abstract. Words and text exist somewhere in the middle.

An alternative to the continuum metaphor is a metaphor of transcendence where 'Knowledge codification is a step beyond knowledge articulation' (Zollo and Winter 2002: 342) on a path towards some kind of communicative enlightenment. Distinguishing codification from articulation is a first step in overcoming what Byrd et al. (1992: 123) term 'between obstacles' in communication, that is, the many difficulties in interpreting meanings experienced by interlocutors. This kind of obstacle may contribute to semiotic misalignments between systems analysts compared with users (Zappavigna-Lee and Patrick 2010), and knowledge engineers compared with experts. However, as we will see, approaching language and communication as a social semiotic, and accounting for the stratification of linguistic meaning potential is necessary for any true analysis of communication in relation to knowledge.

Conclusion

This chapter has considered tacit knowledge across a range of fields. Table 1.4 provides the local terms from each discipline loosely corresponding to implicit or practical knowledge. The attributes assigned to tacit knowledge may be summarized as follows:

- Below-view: whether this is figured as unconscious, subliminal, subsidiary or naturalized; the general impetus is to figure tacit knowledge as invisible to attention.
- Ineffable: the strong position is to assert that tacit knowledge cannot be articulated while the weak, less commonly held position is that it is difficult to articulate.
- Practice-orientated: this practice may be described as craft, skilful action, codes, social norms or ideologies.
- Pervasive: it underlies entire disciplines such as science or learning and our experience of the world itself.

Linguistics appears to be the odd discipline out, being the only one to figure language as a way of understanding implicit meaning. However, linguists themselves do not generally figure their analytical practice as uncovering tacit knowledge. The next chapter is an attempt to being to think about our work (and the practical implications of its use in contexts such as the workplace) in this way.

Table 1.4 Locating tacit knowledge in the interdisciplinary literature

Domain	Technicality
Philosophy	Tacit integration
	Phronesis
	Knowing how/knowing that
	Tacit conventions of language, language-games
Sociology of science	Scientific duplication as tacit knowing
	Paradigm (as tacitly enforced)
	Science as craft
Social sciences	Backgrounding, implicit meaning
	Habitus, doxa
Psychology	Implicit learning
	Practical intelligence (subset of)
	Automaticity
Linguistics	Implicit meaning
	Latent grammatical patterning
	Universal grammar

Notes

1 The term 'technologist' is used throughout this book to refer to IT practitioners who work with technical systems in organizations. These practitioners may be software developers or managers.

2 This book will favour the term below-view when talking about tacit knowledge, however, it is difficult not to slip into referring to unconscious knowledge as a more common way of referring to non-focal attention.

2

Under-Representation: A Functional Model of Tacit Knowledge

Introduction: Tacit knowing as a process of making meaning

Grammatical analyses provide us with a tool for understanding tacit language patterns: 'the grammar enables us, unconsciously to interpret experience; and the metagrammar, or grammatics, enables us to reflect consciously on how it does so' (Halliday 2000: 225). Grammatics (Halliday's term for the study of grammar) involves 'language turned back on itself' as a means to uncover latent patterns in the social meanings being made (Firth 1957: 190). The assumption that linguistic analysis can make implicit knowledge more readily visible is at the heart of fields such as Applied Linguistics. An applied linguist endeavours to assist in solving real-world problems by exploring how language is being used in a particular context. For example, this might involve uncovering implicit patterns in the language used by teachers in a classroom and how these patterns contribute to what is sometimes called the 'hidden pedagogy' (Christie and Martin 2008).

In the previous chapter I explained the translation of TTK into Peircian semiotics, an acknowledgement by Polanyi that tacit knowing involves the creation of *meaning*.[1] At the heart of tacit integration is a process of creating meaningful relations ('attending from' something to something else):

> ... There is a significance in the relations of the two terms of tacit knowing which combines its functional and phenomenal aspects ... It is their **meaning** to which our attention is directed. It is in terms of their **meaning** that they enter into the appearance of that to which we are attending from. (Polanyi 1966b: 12, emphasis added)

While Polanyi only went as far as to employ higher-order semiotic analysis when considering tacit integration, I will suggest how higher-order semiotic systems themselves can be analysed in terms of their realization in language. This thesis will require approaching language as a 'social semiotic', that is, as a system of meaning potential that provides a resource for making social meanings in context (Halliday 1973). In other words, I will show what can be illuminated by bringing a functional theory of language to bear on the process of tacit knowing.

The central linguistic process of tacit knowing that I will detail in this chapter is a process 'under-representation'. I focus on grammatical under-representation, however, the patterning might be considered from the perspective of any of the linguistic strata. Because tools for analysing grammar have been highly refined in SFL we will focus on this stratum for analysis. Before dealing in more detail with these tools in relation to tacit knowledge I will further introduce the theory of language underpinning my approach.

The kick-off problem: The predicament of talking about tacit knowledge

Finding an appropriate metalanguage for discussing tacit knowledge is itself problematic. The language that we use to analyse tacit knowledge is fraught both theoretically and empirically in a particular way: the necessity of being grammatical and, at the same time, being faithful to a theory of tacit knowledge as functionally dynamic, in essence, as a process in a context. I have termed this dilemma 'the kick-off problem'. Consider the following utterance:

The function kicks off at three.

Here, kick off is used in a metaphorical sense to convey the idea of commencement. The metaphor likens the idea of kicking a ball as at the start of a football match with the idea of beginning something. The utterance can be paraphrased as:

The function begins at three.

Now, consider the following:

The game kicks off at three.

In this instance the sense of something commencing is present. However, here, a ball may be kicked. We have an instance where the object and the metaphor intersect. The intersection creates a conceptual tension. Another example is as follows:

The football match kicks off at three.

This example may well be literal, but the integration of the expression into idiomatic language makes it uncertain as to whether the usage is literal or metaphorical. The conceptual tension is thus heightened.

With the previous examples in mind, consider the following clause referring to a common kind of tacit knowledge:

I have tacit knowledge of baking.

In this instance, two things are present in a comparable manner to the kick-off example. Rather than the object being a person kicking a ball, the act of knowing how to bake takes this role. Co-present is the knowledge of baking which is our descriptive or metaphoric reference to knowing how to bake. It is a reference that occurs for a particular reason: the difficulty in English of talking about processes without nominalizing them. This is seen in comparing the subsequent clauses:

I have tacit knowledge of baking.

I tacitly know how to bake.

Tacit knowledge is important in baking.

Tacitly knowing is important in baking.

In each of these instances the second option is less favoured. An extended discourse using tacit knowing (the technical term introduced in TTK but largely ignored in subsequent literature) in the subject position would be difficult to sustain grammatically. As we will see later in this chapter, grammatical metaphor is one of the ways in which language has responded to this kind of problem.

Systemic Functional Linguistics

In order to unpack the complexities associated with tacit knowing as a linguistic process, that is, a process of making meaning, be those meanings invoked or inscribed by particular kinds of linguistic patterns, we require a theory of language capable of coping with the semiotic load. The model of under-representation that will be presented in this chapter draws upon the theory of language, SFL, briefly introduced in Chapter 1.

SFL is also a useful tool for use in real-world contexts because it is an interventionist linguistics that has a history of use in different domains, particularly education,[2] where it is used to uncover implicit meanings and so afford the possibility of social and institutional change. The theory has also been used to understand the patterning of discourses in various technical domains such as scientific discourse (Halliday and Martin 1993; Martin and Veel 1998), technocratic discourse (McKenna and Graham 2000) and administrative discourse (Iedema 1997), and to show how specialized knowledge is created within research communities by they way in which they 'utilize different resources from lexicogrammar, discourse semantics, register and genre' (Wignell 1998: 297).[3]

The sections which follow detail the basic principles of SFL necessary for understanding the features of under-representation presented later. SFL is a functional, semantically oriented approach to analysing language as resource for making meaning. Language users exercise choice in the way they deploy this resource within the real contexts in which they operate. Eggins (1994: 23) suggests that SFL is distinct among linguistic theories as 'it seeks to develop both a theory about social process AND an analytical methodology which permits the detailed and systematic description of language patterns'. The following sections explain what it means for SFL to be a theory that is *functional*, *systemic* and *semantic*.

SFL as functional

SFL is a theory of language that is tailored to exploring how meanings function in context. SFL is aligned with the functional tradition in linguistics manifest in the Prague School and arose out of the linguistic school known as Firthian Systemics (Firth 1957). It is a functional theory because it is targeted at answering questions about how meanings operate within the particular contexts in which they are created. In this way it contrasts to formal approaches that position the structure of language as their primary concern. As a method for managing the high dimensionality of language, SFL stratifies language into phonology (systems of sounds/writing), lexicogrammar (systems of wording), discourse semantics (systems of meaning) and context (genre and register) (Figure 2.1). The strata are related to each other in terms of emergent complexity: as patterns of patterns (Lemke 1984). For example, discourse semantics is a higher-order patterning of lexicogrammatical patterns, which are in turn patterns of phonological patterns. SFL adopts the term 'lexicogrammar', as opposed to 'grammar', to accommodate at this strata two types of 'words': content words (the lexicon) and function words (function words). Function words are a closed set of words (e.g. pronouns, prepositions, conjunctions, etc.) that have a grammatical purpose, and thus best considered part of lexicogrammar rather

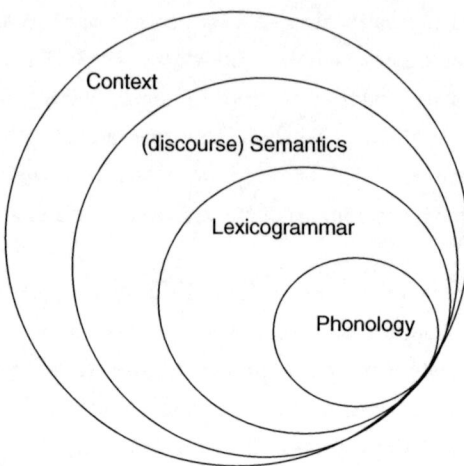

Figure 2.1 The stratification of language according to Systemic Functional Linguistics.

than lexis (Halliday 1989). A 'grammatical description is functional when it is organised around the tasks language fulfils in human interaction and when the categories of description themselves are arrived at on the basis of the semantic consequences of each element of a clause or sentence' (Butt 1996: xvi).

SFL draws its ideas about context from the work of the anthropologist Malinowski who introduced the notion of an ethnographic theory of language. Malinowski argued that 'the real linguistic fact is the full utterance within its context of situation' (Malinowski 1935: 11). By context, Malinowski means phenomena that the anthropologist must describe in order to understand, for example, the meaning of a word in a different culture. The translation of a word that has no equivalent in the language of the anthropologist is made possible by description of its context.

SFL appropriates two broad types of context from Malinowski: the context of culture and the context of situation. The context of culture is a semiotic system, a system of meaning, that may be thought of as 'surrounding' or providing an environment for language, another semiotic system. When using language a person makes choices from the options that the culture makes available to them. They make these choices within a particular circumstance, the 'context of situation'. For example, an IT professional answering a user's question about a system makes choices that are influenced by the culture of the organization about how to address that user. They also makes choices that depend on the particular type of answer they will provide (answering a telephone-based helpdesk question, answering an email, etc.), that is, the context of situation.

Matthiessen (1995: 36) suggests that context is 'functionally diversified', that is, combinations of field, tenor and mode define the way language is used. 'Field' is akin to the popular notion of 'topic', answering the question 'what is happening or what is the text about?', while tenor considers the social relationship of the participants. This social relationship is defined in terms of the roles that the participants occupy and the patterns that constitute their interaction. The final component in this functional combination is mode. Mode deals with the medium facilitating the communication and the rhetorical function of that communication.

According to the theory, language enacts three simultaneous functions, referred to as metafunctions: an ideational function of enacting experience, an interpersonal function of negotiating relationships and a textual function of organizing information (Halliday and Matthiessen 2004). A linguist using this theory will attempt to consider these three functions when analysing any instance of linguistic meaning. The ideational metafunction is about representation. It is used to construe the world of experience, that is, our perception and involvement in the universe. The principle system of the ideational metafunction is the transitivity system. The interpersonal metafunction deals with the social world of interaction. It is about exchange and concerned particularly with speakers and their relationship with listeners. The principle system of the interpersonal metafunction is the mood system. Finally, the textual metafunction organizes these two previous functions to create cohesive discourse.

SFL as systemic

As well as being functional, SFL is a systemic as it arose out of the Firthian tradition in linguistics (Firth 1957). Firth asserted that a distinction needed to be made between structure and system, that is, between syntagmatic and paradigmatic relations in language. Firth's ideas about how the notion of a system might be used to model language were taken up in Halliday's development of system networks. SFL is a systemic theory because it employs these networks rather than modelling grammar as a catalogue of structures. System networks are networks of interrelated options that are organized paradigmatically, in terms of 'what could go instead of what', rather than syntagmatically in terms of structure (Halliday and Matthiessen 2004: 22).

System networks model linguistic choice. The actual choice made is referred to as the instantiated meaning, whereas the other possible choices

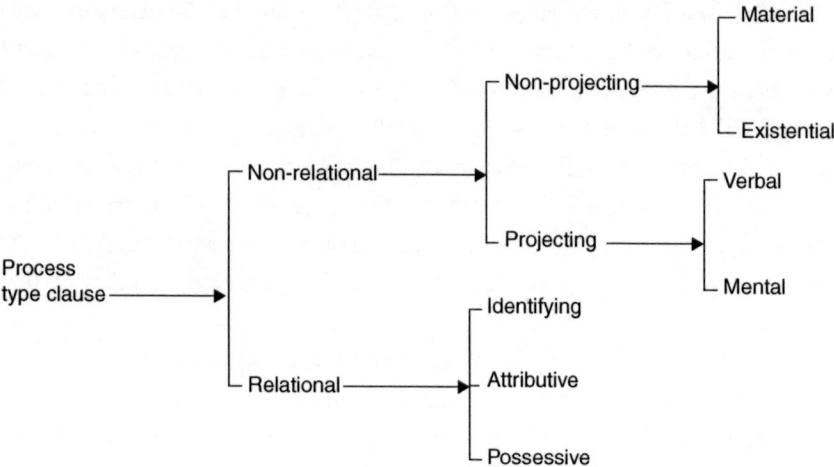

Figure 2.2 A system network for process type based on Halliday (1994).

made available by language as a system is referred to as the meaning potential. For example, Figure 2.2 is a system network for process selection, that is, for describing the happening of goings-on in a particular context. Using this system network, we would describe the process 'built' in the clause 'She built the system' as 'non-relational' (does not set up an abstract relationship between entities), 'non-projecting' (does not project a clause) and 'material' (is a concrete action).

A system network has an entry condition and a set of features. For example, the entry condition for the process selection system network is a clause. A feature from one system might be the entry condition to another system. For example, in the process type system the feature 'non-relational' is the entry condition to a system called projection. In turn the feature 'non-projecting' is the entry condition to a system called 'non-projection type'. As a system network moves from left to right it increases in delicacy. This means that the process type system is less delicate than the 'projection' system which is, in turn, less delicate than the 'non-projection' system. Martin (1987) provides a useful guide to correct system network notation.

SFL as semantic

According to the systemic functional framework, semantics 'is "the way into language" from context – the set of strategies for construing, enacting and presenting non-language as meaning' (Matthiessen 2010: 189). In considering semantics in this way the theory describes language as a social semiotic resource for making meaning (Halliday 1978). Butt et al. (2000) provides a clear outline of what this entails:

> To say language is social implies that a community of speakers share knowledge about systems of sound and writing, about lexicogrammar, about meanings and about situations. To say that language is semiotic implies it is a system of signs which convey meaning about that culture, just as other sign systems such as dress and architecture are shared by a cultural group and constitute that culture. (Butt et al. 2000: 10)

This perspective suggests that the relationship between language and meaning is not arbitrary but culturally produced. The SFL orientation to this meaning is relational: explanation of one aspect of language is always to be conceived with reference to the rest of the linguistic system:

> . . . we can distinguish two main angles of vision: one, focus on the text as an object in its own right; two, focus on the text as an instrument for finding out about something else. Focusing on the text as an object, a grammarian will be asking questions such as: Why is it valued as it is? Focusing on the text as an instrument the grammarian will be asking what the text reveals about the system of the language in which it is spoken or written. These two perspectives are clearly complementary: we cannot explain why a text means what it does, with all the various readings and values that may be given to it, except by relating it to the linguistic system as a whole; and equally, we cannot use it as a window on the system unless we understand what it means and why. (Halliday and Matthiessen 2004: 3)

Employing this kind of modelling strategies means that categorization in systems is not semantically arbitrary, as in traditional grammars, but is based on meaning:

> It makes no sense to ask whether the metafunctions are grammatical or semantic: the only possible answer would be 'yes'. (Halliday and Matthiessen 1999)

Thus when I refer to 'grammar' in this book, we mean lexicogrammar, that is, the overlap of grammar and semantics that occurs by virtue of the capacity of language to make meaning along multiple dimensions concurrently.

Modelling meaning with SFL

SFL adopts particular strategies for managing the complexity of modelling language. The structural dimension of language is organized by rank. Rank is a hierarchical ordering of morphemes into words, words into groups or phases and groups or phases into clauses. In other linguistic theories it is often referred to as *level*. Language may also be thought of paradigmatically as a system. This system is organized in terms of delicacy, that is, level of refinement. Grammar is less delicate than lexis as it makes meaning that is more general.

As a method for managing the multiple dimensions of language use, SFL stratifies language into phonology (systems of sounds/writing), lexicogrammar (systems of wording), discourse semantics (systems of meaning) and context (genre and register). The strata are related to each other in terms of emergent complexity: as patterns of patterns (Lemke 1984). For example, discourse semantics is a higher-order patterning of lexicogrammatical patterns that are, in turn, patterns of phonological patterns.

Instantiation

Instantiation is the principle by which the meaning potential of language is turned into an instance of text. As Eggins (1994: 217) notes, 'it is only by knowing what someone could have meant that we can understand in full the meaning of what they did in fact mean'. The choice the person actually made in the particular context in which they were involved, is referred to as the instantial meaning and may be represented as a cline with potential choices at the system end of the cline and the particular choice made at the instance end. The term cline was coined by Halliday (1961) to refer to a continuum of infinite gradation used as an alternative to a discrete hierarchical representation (Matthiessen 1997). The cline reflects how choices are made from systems of potential mediated by smaller systems available in particular domains. These domains are referred to in SFL as registers.

The clause

Halliday (1994) suggests the centrality of the clause in construing experience, claiming that 'it embodies a general principle for modelling experience – namely, the principle that reality is made up of PROCESSES' (Halliday 1994: 106). According to Halliday, a process has three components:

- the process itself
- participants in the process
- circumstances associated with the process

Within this semiotic space processes are categorized in terms of their meaning into process types. Halliday's categorization of processes into types is perhaps the base level of an ontology of experience. As such it is, as Halliday indicates, 'a resource for thinking with':

> In construing experience this way, the grammar is providing a resource for thinking with. A strict taxonomy of separate process types would impose too much discontinuity, while a bipolar continuum would be precisely too much polarized. What the grammar offers is, rather, a flexible semantic space, continuous and elastic, which can be contorted and expanded without losing its topological order. (Halliday and Matthiessen 1999: 516)

For example 'eat' is classified differently to 'think' as the former refers to a process of physical action while the later a process of mental experience. Halliday conceives of six types of processes: material, relational, mental, verbal, behavioural[4] and existential. I will present some simple examples in the following sections.

Material processes

Material processes are processes of doing, that is, of concrete actions in which an entity does something. The participant role of the entity doing the action is called the actor, while the participant role of the entity at which the action is directed is called the goal. Material processes in their simplest form thus are typically structured: actor + material process + goal (Table 2.1).

Mental processes are processes of sensing, that is, processes in which an entity perceives something. Halliday further divides these into processes of cognition, the institutionalization of affection or perception. The entity which does the perceiving is called the senser (Table 2.2). The thing which is being perceived is called the phenomenon. A simple structure for a clause involving this kind of process is: senser + mental process + phenomenon.

Table 2.1 Transitivity analysis for 'The construction community use service B'

The construction community	use	service B
Participant	Process	Participant
Actor	Process: material	Goal

Halliday suggests that behavioural processes, that is, processes in which a conscious entity performs an action, occupy the space between material and mental processes. They involve an aspect of both psychological and physiological action performed by a conscious entity. The participant roles in this kind of process are a behaver who performs the behaviour and the behaviour itself (though the majority of clauses only have one participant). Behavioural processes are not used in the present study due to the aforementioned semantic, rather than grammatical analysis that is required to identify them successfully that was deemed too complex to undertake in an interview situation.

Verbal processes are processes of saying. The participant roles for this kind of process are of the sayer who performs the verbal action, the receiver to whom this verbal action is directed and the verbiage, the message at the centre of this verbal action. Table 2.3 gives an example of transitivity analysis of clause involving a verbal process of the form sayer + verbal process + receiver + verbiage.

Relational processes

Relational processes are processes of being in which entities are assigned relations to other entities. Relational processes may be attributive or identifying. Attributive relational processes assign an attribute to an entity, while identifying relational processes define the entity[5] (Table 2.4).

Table 2.2 Transitivity analysis for 'I like computers'

I	like		computers
Participant	Process		Participant
Senser	Process: mental: affection		Phenomenon

Table 2.3 Transitivity analysis for 'The users ask the facilitators questions'

The users	ask	the facilitators	questions
Participant	Process	Participant	Participant
Sayer	Process: verbal	Receiver	Verbiage

Table 2.4 'The principle types of relational processes'

Type/mode	Attributive	Identifying
Intensive	The granite is thick.	The engineer is the leader.
Circumstantial	The delivery is on Friday.	Tomorrow is the delivery day.
Possessive	The company has two divisions.	The concept is the CIO's.

Adapted from Halliday (1994: 119).

Table 2.5 Transitivity analysis for 'There are two different types of knowledge management'

There	are	two different types of knowledge management
Participant	Process	Participant
	Process: existential	Existent

Existential processes

Existential processes are processes in which an entity is stated as existing. The major participant role in this type of process is of the existent, that is, of the entity which exists (Table 2.5).

Tacit knowing and latent grammatical patterning

Because tacit knowing involves non-attentive processes, that is processes people are able to perform quasi-automatically rather than with conscious reflection, the field studies in this book focus on spoken discourse rather than on deliberative, written composition. When people speak they are less likely to be aware of their linguistic choices, producing them, as it were, on-the-fly. Because of this the grammatical patterns that people generate in their spoken discourse are also particularly revealing to the project of uncovering tacit meaning. Making meaning with grammar involves making linguistic choices that are much more likely to be unconscious than lexical choices:

> Conscious language achieves its creative force mainly by lexical means; and lexical items are semantically close to experience. Unconscious language depends much more for its creative force on grammar – and grammatical categories are far removed from experience. (Halliday and Webster 2002: 303)

As we 'construe our experience' of the world through language (Halliday and Matthiessen 1999) we reveal our implicit biases, personal preferences and the many and varied assumptions we hold about the social processes in which we are engaged.

The practical knowledge that we develop in life is not divorced from our capacity to creating meaning with language. It forms part of our system of meaning potential:

> . . . once we go outside the language, then we see that this semantic system is itself the realization of something beyond, which is what the speaker can do – I have referred to that as the 'behaviour potential'. I want to insist here

> that there are many ways of going outside language; this is only one of them. Perhaps it would be better at this point to talk in terms of a general semiotic level: the semantic system, which is the meaning potential embodied in language, is itself the realization of a high-level semiotic which we may define as a behavioural system or more generally as a social semiotic. So when I say can do, I am specifically referring to behaviour potential as a semiotic which can be encoded in language, or of course in other things to. (Halliday 1978: 39)

According to this view, 'can say' is a realization of 'can mean' which is in turn a realization of 'can do'. Realization is akin to the idea of embodying or enacting, that is, symbolization. Such a relationship of symbolization is the core of the signifier–signified relation specified in Saussurean semiotics (Matthiessen 1995: 4). However, the arrows in relationship can't be reversed since 'there are other ways of meaning besides saying [and] there are other ways of doing besides meaning ... if you do, you don't necessarily mean (you could be doing something nonsemiotic like burping), and if you mean, you don't necessarily say (you could be writing, drawing, typing etc.)' (C. Cleireigh, personal communication, 30/3/2006). Nevertheless, because of the realization relationship whereby meanings in the culture manifest themselves as meanings in the grammar, tacit knowledge can be analysed via linguistic analysis.

Polanyi cast both knowledge of everyday life and expert knowledge as forms of personal knowledge. Rather that disconnecting the semiotic from the somatic, TTK suggests practical skill shares similarities with what we might think of as more abstract semiotic skill:

> Consider any practical skill. It consists in the capacity for carrying out a great number of particular movements with a view to achieveing a comprehensive result. The same applies to skillful knowledge, like that of a medical diagnostician; he too comprehends a large number of details in terms of a significant entity. (Polanyi and Prosch 1977: 37)

These two forms of knowledge hold in common the essential process of tacit integration:

> In both kinds of skillful knowing we are aware of a multitude of parts in terms of a whole by dwelling in them. The two kinds of skillful knowing are actually always interwoven: a skillful handling of things must relay on our understanding them; and, on the other hand, intellectual comprehension can be achieved only by the skillful scrutiny of a situation. (Polanyi and Prosch 1977: 37)

Hence Polanyi's model allows us to theorize both the physical skill involved in riding a bike and the semiotic skill involved in working with IT systems, of the kind explored in the field studies of this book.

A functional approach

A functional model of tacit knowing considers how we produce practical knowledge in social contexts. Because human experience is complex and multidimensional the model needs to facilitate two concurrent viewpoints: how an individual construes tacit knowledge and how that production is informed by the semiotic resources that are available to them. The functional perspective asks two kinds of questions about a given instance of meaning:

a. What choice has a person made in a particular context?
b. Why did they make that choice and not another?

Considering b requires establishing the potential choices that the person might have made, that is, the 'meaning potential'. Answering the two questions involves understanding meanings that are usually tacit to the language user. In other words, they are unlikely to be able to tell you why they made one choice other than another with anything other than a folk description.

We may consider tacit knowing in terms of its functional relation to articulation. I use Polanyi's terminology 'subliminal' and 'marginal' (Table 2.6) to distinguish between two types of tacit knowledge in terms of patterns of articulation. 'Subliminal' tacit knowledge is peripatetic talk where you say something that you immediately are able to recognize as novel and have the sense of being surprised that you knew it. 'Marginal' tacit knowledge is patterns

Table 2.6 Defining expert knowledge in terms of its relation to articulation

Type of knowledge	Type of articulation
Expert propositional knowledge	When you say something that is within your sense of known experience, that is, when you give an asnwer to a factual question within your sphere of expertise.
Tacit knowledge	
Subliminal	When you say something that is surprising to yourself.
Marginal	When you say something using patterns of language to which you do not attend and which you can recognize when identified by another.

of language that you do not attend to when you talk but which you can recognize when they are identified by someone, such as a trained linguist, who has a metalanguage for describing them.

Under-representation in spoken discourse

The notion that something may be under-represented assumes that talking involves many useful forms of semiotic shorthand and distillation and that we may deploy varying degrees of meaning potential in a given linguistic instance. A related idea developed in work on discourse semantics from the perspective of instantiation is the notion of linguistic 'commitment':

> Commitment refers to the amount of meaning potential activated in a particular process of instantiation – the relative semantic weight of a text in other words. Essentially this has to do with the degree to which meanings in optional systems are taken up and, within systems, the degree of delicacy selected. (Martin 2008b: 45)

For example using a nominalization such as 'requirements' when talking about an IT system (as we will see in Chapter 4) commits less meaning potential about how users express what they want or need to do with that system than an agnate congruent construal. In other words 'when they are reconstrued as things, processes lose their location in time and often also their participants' (Halliday and Matthiessen 1999: 575). Rather than under-representing meaning, a congruent construal enacts the 'the congruent realisations that developed first in the language, [and which] are learnt first by children and tend to occur first in a text (Halliday and Matthiessen 1999: 278).

Thus we might distinguish between argue implicit and explicit styles of speaking in terms of how much meaning potential is instantiated. When an implicit style is adopted by a speaker, 'precise meanings become available only if certain additional conditions are met; the average working knowledge of the language is necessary but not sufficient' (Hasan et al. 1996: 194). Hasan et al. (1996) give the example of the following clause as an instance of maximal implicitness because it does not contain an item that is not implicit:

> They will.

This clause raises the questions: who 'will' and what 'will' they? As Hasan et al. (1996) acknowledge, the 'source of the interpretation of the elliptical verbal group *will* lies in the co-text, i.e. in a part of the accompanying text'. The source of such co-text elaboration may be either exophoric (external to the text and retrieved instead from context), endophoric (preceding the reference) or cataphoric (following the reference).

Aside from adopting an implicit style, a speaker may use various grammatical strategies to condense complex meanings so that they may be referenced and negotiated without needing to be directly elaborated. A resource allowing meaning to be elegantly condensed in this way is grammatical metaphor. Halliday (1994: 342) explains the concept of grammatical metaphor in terms of reference: 'if something is said to be metaphorical, it must be metaphorical by reference to something else'. With traditional metaphor, the reference is to a literal meaning; in the case of grammatical metaphor, the reference is to the less metaphorical variant, the congruent form. While lexical metaphor allows change in the *meaning* of expressions, grammatical metaphor affords change in the *expression* of meaning: 'we are looking at metaphor not "from below", as variation in the meaning of a given expression, but rather "from above" as variation in the expression of the given meaning' (Halliday 1994: 342).

Grammatical metaphor reduces the explicitness of a text:

> . . . one effect of grammatical metaphor is to render many of the semantic relationships implicit: if the happening is construed as a clause, the semantic relations are spelt out in the configuration of grammatical elements, whereas if it is construed as a nominal group they are not, or only partially so . . . On the whole, the greater the degree of metaphor in the grammar, the more the reader needs to know in order to understand the text. (Halliday and Matthiessen 1999: 545)

Resources such as implicitness and grammatical metaphor allow us to under-represent meaning in useful ways so that we can easily talk about highly complex ideas without becoming lost in ongoing elaboration. However, to be useful they also have to be largely tacit so that we do not 'trip over' ourselves linguistically and the flow of discourse can remain seamless. Indeed this is the case for almost all grammatical choices.

An objection at this point might be the case where a speaker is engaging in subterfuge. Clearly, knowledge that is consciously withheld cannot be considered tacit. However, while it may be possible for a person to consciously hide content, it is unlikely that they will be able to control patterns in their grammar. We are not typically conscious of how we use grammar to construe meaning, even though we use language to make complex meanings.

Distinguishing between content and process

In order to respond more fully to the objection raised above it is necessary to distinguish between content and process. Content refers to propositions, what Ryle (1949) refers to as knowing that (see Chapter 1) and what is commonly referred to as an object, namely, knowledge. Process, on the other hand, is, to use Ryle's definition, knowing how: it is the ability to perform a skilful action. Applying this distinction, we define hidden knowledge as content which a novice is not aware of. An example would be a person who is not aware that their bike has a fourth gear. Tacit knowledge is, by way of contrast, a process that the novice can't do. For example, a person may not know how to ride their bike, they are unable to perform the skilful action of riding.

Content is propositional. It is what we say, the semantic dimension of language. How we speak is instead an activity to which we usually do not attend and, as such, is a process realized for example by grammatical patterns. Consider the clause from the previous section:

The user requirements are important.

As a speaker, I will be aware of the content of this utterance: I am talking about functions, commencement and a concrete point in time. I will, however, be less likely to attend to the way in which I have spoken: I have used a nominalization and an attributive relational process. These are phenomena that a linguist could identify but which a speaker does not need to think about to produce meaningful discourse. The grammatical choices are tacit because they are things that a novice can't do (Table 2.7). A novice, in this case, would be a person learning to speak the language. A language-learner will need to think about the grammar in order to produce meaningful sentences. For the novice, the knowledge is at the level of content until it is automatized and they can speak fluently, when it becomes an automatized process.

The different states of knowing and awareness that a person undergoes when learning to do something are usefully summarized in the model in Table 2.8. Unconscious competence is the state of being unaware of both how to do

Table 2.7 Differentiating content and process by way of knowing

Content	What we know (knowing that)	Novice can't 'see'	(hidden) Knowledge
Process	How we know (knowing how)	Novice can't do	Tacit knowing

Table 2.8 Four stages of learning

Unconscious incompetence	
Conscious incompetence	
Conscious competence	Content
Unconscious competence	Process

something and the fact of not knowing how to do it. For example, when learning to drive a manual car, initially, I will not know that I need to press the clutch in when changing gears. I also will not know that I don't know this until the instructor points it out or I stall the car. Conscious incompetence refers to my awareness of my inability, provoked either by the instructor's command or the jolt of the stalling car. Once I have mastered the technique of applying the clutch when changing gears I have conscious competence of this skill. I can perform the skill when I specifically attend to the fact that I need to change gears. Unconscious competence is the state of an experienced driver. This driver will not need to think about whether or not they know how to apply the clutch and whether or not they need to: they will automatically perform the skilful action when they want to change gears.

If we think about this model in terms of content and process it emerges that conscious competence involves both content and process: I know that I need to press the clutch and I know how to do it. Unconscious competence, however, involves only process: I know how to press the clutch and I do it even though I don't need to think about doing it or whether I know how to do it. Moving from conscious competence to unconscious competence is typically achieved practicing a skilful activity through iterative cycles of transforming content into process. This is tacit knowing.

Most interview methods apply content-targeted strategies oriented to ideational meaning at the level of content. The focus of the grammar-targeted method, however, is on process. We may distinguish between content and process in terms of 'saying' as suggested in Table 2.9. Clearly, the content/ process analogy factors out complex dimensions of such language axis (syntagmatic and paradigmatic perspectives on meaning) and stratification (the realization relationship between linguistic strata) so important in systemic functional theory but it is intended merely to highlight the difference between conscious and unconscious language: in Halliday's terms the way that 'grammatical categories are far removed from experience' (Halliday and Webster 2002: 303).

Table 2.9 Distinguishing content and process by way of saying

Content	'What' we say	Hidden knowledge
Process	'How' we say it	Tacit knowledge

Table 2.10 Unpacking 'system', an example of the tacitness of grammar

Turn	Speaker	Talk
1	Information architect	I suppose there are lots of different types of processes that we, that I suppose the system is trying to, manage.
2	Interviewer	So what do you mean by system?
3	Information architect	The content management system.
4	Interviewer	What does that mean? What is the content management system?
5	Information architect	[laughs]
6	Interviewer	You know, what does system mean when you say 'the content management system'? What, what does it consist of?
7	Information architect	Well I suppose at a detailed level it has tools that are so basic things like, you know, if you want to actually publish a story you can press this button and it goes. But then at a higher level there's the way in which it manages the way in which all the processes intersect.
8	Interviewer	What is this 'it'?
9	Information architect	The 'it'? I didn't realize I said 'it' in that sentence!
10	Interviewer	You did.
11	Information architect	[laughs]
12	Interviewer	You talked about 'it' manages.
13	Information architect	The content management system.
14	Interviewer	Ok, yeah, so what is it?

Consider, for example the extract presented in Table 2.10 where an information architect involved in user interface design talks about a system she is working on. In this extract the speaker admits to be unaware of particular grammatical choices she has made when they are pointed out by the interviewer. As she indicates in Turn 9, she was not aware that she was referring to the system in a very general way as an 'it'[6] even though the 'it' was a participant involved in processes of possession (having), action (going) and organizing (managing) in this individual's talk. While the reference is quite commonplace, it interesting to unpack in the discourse of technologists since systems can involve humans, documents and many other kinds of artefacts beyond an instance of software.

A note on the pathologizing of discourse

The project of seeking to unpack under-representation in discourse might be viewed as an attempt to critique the discourse of technologists and people working in organizations. This, however, is not the goal of the grammar-targeted interview method. Indeed the method is oriented towards uncovering meaning that may aid in improving the work life of individuals by helping to share a person's implicit knowledge. Under-representation plays an important role in getting things done with discourse. Being able to condense, elide and imply using language is a useful semiotic trick since elaborating every meaning we produced would result in inefficiency, redundancy and curious interpersonal interactions!

As Martin (2008a) notes it is important to avoid pathologizing features of discourse such as nominalization by putting them in the service of critique alone[7]:

> To be sure, grammatical metaphor affords the kinds of political distortion CDA is concerned to document; there are certainly communicative contexts in which it has been overused (the public documents Plain English movements rail against for example); and people without the requisite amounts of functional literacy are indeed excluded by it. But doing without it would be tantamount to living in an oral culture, without a writing system; and we know too well the fate that awaits cultures of this kind in the face of environmental challenges or, more disastrously, the arrival of invaders with the technology and bureaucracy, both secular and religious, that grammatical metaphor affords. (Martin 2008a: 806–7)

These resources provide us the semiotic flexibility to achieve the various social goals undertaken in different genres. As Martin argues 'we need to take great care in interpreting the role played by nominalization in discourse of various kinds, and to this I would add the need to carefully consider phylogenetic reasoning about why nominalization evolved and how this semo-history relates to the ways it is used' (Martin 2008a: 802). The kinds of under-representation that occur in particular domains allow technicality to be built within those fields. Such technicality is necessary to lessen the cognitive load of talking about complex ideas allowing for more complex ideas to be expressed and developed. This type of semiotic production 'involves turning ideationally metaphorical nominalizations into abstract concepts in a given field, thereby killing off the stratal tension that made the concept thinkable (e.g. condensation, evaporation, transpiration in science); this lightens the discourse-processing demands of a technical discipline, in effect making room for more stratal tension' (Martin 2008a: 808)'.

Rather than vilifying under-representation the approach taken in this book seeks to understand the kinds of meanings that can be uncovered in spoken discourse and what they can reveal about how people work. The aim of making visible these linguistic patterns is twofold: to bring them under scrutiny in relation to the context of the work and to being a process whereby any useful knowledge uncovered may be shared more fruitfully with others. In this sense the analysis is aligned with a movement in discourse analysis known as Positive Discourse Analysis. This is not to say that where language patterns that appear to hinder effective work practices will be ignored, but rather that mere critique of those practices is not enough. Just as language exists for 'getting things done' so too linguistic analysis can play a role in achieving practical change, be it in the workplace or in other areas of social life (Halliday and Webster 2002: 175).

Introducing the grammar-targeted interview method

The aim of the grammar-targeted interview method[8] is to achieve an agnate congruent description of a person's knowledge. In theory, this could be achieved in two ways:

(A) By retrieving context
(B) By 'unpacking' tacit process

Retrieving context would be the case where we had access to the entire cultural and situational context of the individual. Obtaining this would be impossible in practice, although the nearest approximation currently in existence would be ethnography. The alternative approach is to unpack instances of tacit process, that is, activity that is below-view. (B) is a view of context 'from-within' in the sense that we unpack the sepaker's meanings directly rather than look for them in the co-text or context. What we want to achieve is a 'semantically self-sufficient' (Hasan et al. 1996: 195) realization of the speaker's knowledge in the sense that the amount of additional descriptive apparatus that are required to explicate the meaning is minimized. Clearly, this is an idealized goal which will be realized through the 'messy' process of human interviewing in imperfect ways.

Earlier I flagged a distinction between content and process when looking at how we attend to our own language production. In attempting to understand process (how something is said) an interviewer will focus on unpacking grammar rather than on elaborating content. They will thus adopt a different questioning style of a content-targeted interviewer (Table 2.11).

We might think of the elaboration system as defined by SFL as a metaphor for achieving a congruent representation of a speaker's knowledge. We are seeking a grammatical description that provides additional description through *exposition* ('in other words'), *exemplification* ('for example') and *clarification* ('to be precise') (Halliday 1994: 226).

There are a number of possibilities regarding how the relationship of content and the grammar may be theorized in terms of under-representation. While we assume that the metaredundant[9] realization relationship of linguistic stratification is in operation we also suggest that, when using the lens of under-representation on meaning-making, the following relationships between content and grammar are possible:

- **They are *in alignment*** – there appears to be no incongruity between what a person says and how they say it.
- **They are *misaligned*** – there appears to be an incongruity between what a person says and how they say it. For example, an individual may assert the importance of entity X and yet assign that entity minimal agency, instead attributing more agency to entity Y.
- **The grammatical construal *extends* the content.** This means that there are assumptions in the grammar that elaborate those made in the content. For example, unpacking a nominalization may reveal additional participants.

When the grammatical construal aligns with the content of the speaker's talk, 'how' they talk (the patterns on the expression plane) affirms 'what' they say (the patterns on the content plane). For example, a technologist who claims that users are central figures in a system might assign them a large proportion

Table 2.11 Question type differs when addressing content and process

Content	What we say	Hidden knowledge	Question unpacking content – 'what'/'why'
Process	How we say it	Tacit knowledge	Question unpacking grammar – 'how'

of agency when talking about how the system operates in an organization. However, when the grammatical construal misaligns with the explicit construal, the aforementioned technologist might allocate minimal agency to users and instead privilege technical or managerial artefacts. When the grammatical construal extends the explicit construal, additional content is revealed. For example, an unpacked nominalization will reveal processes and participants that are otherwise unmentioned.

The grammar-targeted interview protocol (Appendix A) assumes that trying to understand a person's tacit knowledge is an iterative process. Explicating knowledge that is tacit has been likened to chasing a moving target: as soon as the target is made explicit, it is no longer tacit. While we question the validity of assuming that articulation involves making something explicit, this means we require a dynamic strategic allowing dialogic unpacking of meanings as they occur. The grammar-targeted interview method aims to approach the problem in such dialogic terms, iteratively responding to phenomena in a person's spoken discourse. At the most essential level, the method requires two fundamental processes of the interviewer:

- **Identifying** an instance of a grammatical feature of under-representation in the speaker's talk that is relevant to the topic that the interviewer is trying to understand. The under-represented knowledge is at this point, T1.
- **Probing** this instance by asking the subject a question that prompts the subject to provide a more congruent construal of that feature. At this point, T2, the knowledge is rendered visible, in the sense that it is articulated (though not in the sense that it is codified).

Tacit knowledge at T1, when the subject responds to the initial question, resides in the potential that the subject possesses to achieve further elaboration of their representation. At T2 the subject has made a selection from the system network by responding to a follow-up question by the interviewer. At T2 the meaning made at T1 is reconstrued as a new, hopefully more congruent instance of meaning. The process is iterative as, at T2, there is further potential for tacit knowledge to be elicited in another grammar-targeted question.

The linguistic features of under-representation

This section describes the linguistic features of under-representation that form the basis for asking grammar-targeted questions using the grammar-targeted interview method. These features are derived from SFL, and are an extremely small set of potential grammatical targets. In theory any latent pattern in a person's grammar might reveal useful implicit meaning.[10] There are many potential ways in which a speaker may construe their tacit knowledge in discourse. However, for the purposes of constructing a useful and useable interview method, features that are easy to identify in unfolding talk were selected. They also needed to be easy for an interviewer to unpack with a question in real time. The feature set needed to be small enough, and precise enough, for an interviewer to learn to identify them in the speaker's talk as it unfolded. The features included in the model of under-representation were:

- **Nominalization** (packs up meaning by rendering processes as things).
- **Modality** (packs up meaning by condensing the agent motivating the opinion expressed).
- **Generalization** (packs up meaning through under-specification).
- **Agency** (patterns of agents pack up meaning about power relations in texts).

Table 2.12 provides examples of these features taken from the interview texts. The subsections that follow explain each in feature alongside the kind of question a grammar-targeted interview might ask to unpack them.

Table 2.12 The linguistic features of under-representation

System of under-representation	Feature	Example
Type 1: Nominalization	Action --> thing	We use reinforcing management practices.
	Quality --> thing	Efficiency is the most important factor.
	Circumstance --> thing	Organizational change is our destination.
	Conjunction --> thing	The poor uptake of the system is the cause of the project's failure.
Type 2: Modality	Finite modal operator and/or modal adjunct	We should review this process.
Type 3: Generalization	Non-specific deictic	They reviewed some reports.
	Abstract terminology	This will aid the cost-benefit ratio.
	Generalized participant	Users prefer computers.
Type 4: Agency	Patterns of agency	(Depends on focus of analysis.)

Under-representation type 1: Nominalization

> ... by construing any phenomenon of experience as a thing, we give it the maximum potential for semantic elaboration. ... the more structure that is to be imposed on experience the more pressure there is to construe it in the form of things. (Halliday and Matthiessen 1999: 265, 267)

Nominalization is a structural feature 'whereby any element or group of elements is made to function as a nominal group in the clause' (Halliday 1994: 41). When a procedure or course of action is nominalized, it becomes less contestable. For example, it is more difficult to argue about any component processes and their associated participants. However, those elements are more easily reconstrued as part of other happenings in the discourse. This function is often deployed in the complex relationships generated in technical discourse such as scientific and industrial discourse:

> Processes become things that act on other processes as things, then this relation of 'acting upon' itself becomes a thing. The unfolding of activity sequences are finally re-expressed as parts of composition taxonomies, as criteria for classifying the abstract entities they modify. Instead of a sensually experienced world of unfolding processes involving actual people, things, places and qualities, reality comes to be experienced virtually as a generalised structure of abstractions. (Rose 1998: 263–4)

What was once itself a 'happening' becomes a participant in another happening. This allows more meaning to be packed into the discourse and assists in building technicality. Given the important role of tacit knowledge in being able to skilfully wield technicality in complex fields, the relevance of nominalization to knowledge elicitation is readily apparent.

Other functional structures may be nominialized in addition to processes:

- Making an action into a thing – for example, 'We use reinforcing management practices'. In this clause, 'to reinforce', 'to manage' and 'to practice' are nominalized, forming the nominal group 'reinforcing management practices'.
- Making a quality into a thing – for example, 'Efficiency is the most important factor'. In this clause, the adjectival group, 'efficient', has been rendered as the nominal group 'efficiency'.
- Making a circumstance into a thing – for example, 'Organisational change is our destination'. This clause construes the preposition 'to' as the nominal group 'destination'.

- Making a conjunction into a thing – for example, 'The poor uptake of the system is the cause of the projects failure'. In this clause the conjunction 'so' is realized as the nominal group 'cause'.

Interviewers are most likely to focus on the first kind of nominalization, 'making an action into a thing', because it is the easiest to spot in unfolding talk.

Under-representation type 2: Modality

The modality system construes the region of uncertainty between 'yes' and 'no' (Halliday and Matthiessen 2004). Modality allows a speaker to express attitudes about the propositions and proposals. Halliday (1994) defines two kinds of modality: modalization and modulation. Modalization is the degree of probability or usuality, while modulation is the degree of obligation or inclination. Modality is typically realized by a finite modal operator or a modal adjunct or both.

Modality is included as a feature of under-representation because it typically under-represents agency or cause. For example, an IT professional might say:

I should reassess this requirement.

In this clause the who or what motivating the process of reassessing is effaced. The motivating participant might be retrieved as an authority other than the speaker, or the speaker themselves.

When the interviewer picks up on an instance of modality in the speaker's discourse (that is related to an area of knowledge that the interviewer is trying to understand), they should ask a question probing that instance. For example, an interviewee might say:

We should develop a content management system.

This example contains a finite modal operator of obligation. The interviewer will ask a question of the following form:

Who says we should develop a content management system?

or

Whose rule is it that we should develop a content management system?

This form is chosen over the question 'Why should we develop a content management system?', because the agent is more important than the motivation. The motivation is likely to be a variable with far greater variety in content, less tractable to analysis and contains more unsubstantiated mind-reading of the agent. Identifying the agents is more likely to be stable content. For example:

> Q: Who says …?
> A: The bosses.
> Q: Which bosses?
> A: The boss of the groups involved.
> Q: Which groups are they?
> A: Groups A, B, C …
> Q: So who are their bosses?
> A: Fred, Joe, Mark …

Under-representation type 3: Generalization

Generalization is a form of under-representation that under-specifies meaning. Halliday and Matthiessen (1999: 615) refers to generalization as 'the move from "proper" to "common" as a basic principle for referring'. Generalization functions to make concepts manageable, lessening the semantic burden of excessive detail. Generalizing does not necessarily require abstraction:

> General terms are not necessarily more abstract; a bird is no more abstract than a pigeon. But some words have referents that are purely abstract – words like cost and clue and habit and strange; they are construing some aspect of our experience, but there is no concrete thing or process with which they can be identified. (Halliday and Matthiessen 1999: 615)

Generalization is included as a feature of under-representation as it under-specifies and abstracts meaning. For example, an IT professional who consistently refers only to 'users' embeds a range of assumptions about what it means to occupy the subject position of a user in the context of some configuration of technical artefacts. Referring to someone as an 'end user' would be very different to referring to them as an 'end producer'. Similarly, embedded in a manager's use of the abstract term 'cost' are the ideological positions determining what is valued by this subject. Three kinds of generalizations were considered, outlined in the sections that follow.

Under-specification of a participant

The following is an example of under-specification of a participant:

> A system will solve these problems.

This clause under-specifies the nature and type of 'system'. Are we to assume that it is IT software alone, or are procedures and human workers considered part of the system? An interviewer might ask:

What do you mean by system? Which specific systems will help to solve which specific problems?

Non-specific deictic

Non-specific deictics do not specifically identify their referents instead indicating a class of thing along two dimensions: total/partial and singular/non-singular. They are 'used instead to indicate what quantity of the Head is involved – all, some or none', where it is assumed that we do not need to know the specifics of the headword (Thompson 2000: 182). The following is an example:

I have implemented **some** recommendations.

Here, the speaker has not detailed the precise recommendations that they mean and an interviewer attempting to specify further the nature of the headword would ask a question such as follows:

Which specific recommendations have you implemented?

Abstract terminology

Abstractions are usually domain-specific knowledge about abstract (at an order of experience beyond the material) concepts. For example, a person might say:

This will aid the cost/benefit ratio.

In this example 'cost/benefit ratio' is an instance of abstract terminology that technicalizes more concrete ideas about losing or gaining money. The interviewer might try to elicit the tacit assumptions relating to these processes with a question such as:

How will this cost or benefit the [organization/the users]?

This kind of question aims to elaborate what the speaker means by the processes of loss and gain that are abstracted and associated value judgements.

Under-representation type 4: Agency

Halliday (1994) suggested that two participant roles, medium and agent are central to causality in language. On the one hand the agent causes the process

Table 2.13 An effective clause

They	do	other types of development
Agent	Process	Medium

Table 2.14 A middle clause

The initiative	worked
Medium	Process

to occur, and on the other hand the medium is the participant 'through which the process is actualized, and without which there would be no process at all' (Halliday 1994: 163). For example, in a material process (such as 'do' in Table 2.13) the agent is the actor.

Analysis of agency is referred to in SFL as ergativity analysis. Clauses may be divided into two kinds: those with agents, known as effective clauses (Table 2.13) and those without agents, known as middle clauses (Table 2.14).

The particular configuration of agency employed in a text reveals a lot about the power relations construed. We might consider types of participants who occupy the agent role most often. Tracing the pattern will reveal tacit knowledge about the entities a subject has construed powerful enough to operate upon other entities. As with the other features described, this grammatical distribution will typically not be conscious to the individual.

Under-represented agents will often collocate with modal choices. For example:

The system had to be improved.

Here an interviewer might attempt to retrieve the elided agent (the entity that demands that the system be improved) by asking a question such as:

Who has said the system has to be improved?

Summary of the grammar-targeted protocol

Grammar-targeted questions are designed to prompt the interviewee to reconstrue under-represented meaning in more congruent form. Table 2.15 presents examples of each feature and a grammar-targeted corresponding question. The exact nature of these questions will depend on how the participants in the interview negotiate the interaction and as such is necessarily an imperfect science.

Table 2.15 Summary of features of under-representation and corresponding interview questions

Type of feature	Feature	Example	Question
Type 1: Nominalization	Action --> thing	We use reinforcing management practices.	How do you manage? How do you reinforce?
	Quality -->thing	Efficiency is the most important factor.	What does it mean to be efficient?
	Circumstance --> thing	Organizational change is our destination.	How will you arrive at organizational change? How will you change?
	Conjunction --> thing	The poor uptake of the system is the cause of the project's failure.	How did the poor uptake cause the failure?
Type 2: Modality	Finite modal operator and/or modal adjunct	We should review this process.	How do you know they would review it? Who says that they must always review it?
Type 3: Generalization	Non-specific deictic	They reviewed some reports.	Which reports specifically?
	Abstract terminology	This will aid the cost-benefit ratio.	How does this cost X? How does this benefit X?
	Generalized participant	Users prefer computers.	Which specific users prefer computers?
Type 4: Agency	Distribution of agency	The methodology drives our work.	What do you mean by the methodology?

Knowing when to unpack an instance of under-representation

Under-representation occurs frequently in spoken discourse. It would be impossible to conduct an interview where the interviewee was interrupted as each instance occurred. In addition, many instances are not relevant to the particular type of information that the interviewer aims to elicit in the interview. In other words, the under-representation is not always related to the issue of 'tacit knowledge about X', where X is some particular domain of expertise or issue of concern.

This raises the question of when it is useful to unpack an instance of under-representation. The basic principle is that an instance should be unpacked when the interviewer suspects that the particular grammatical feature is camouflaging meanings related to the specific issues they are seeking to address in the interview. For instance the focus might be on under-representation about knowledge management issues rather than under-representation about, for example, personal relationships, life outside work, etc. According to this criteria the nominalization 'requirement' would be a candidate for unpacking in an interview about requirements analysis, but the nominalization 'marriage' would not (unless it was used metaphorically about some aspect of the system).

The process of identifying relevant instances of under-representation will be considerably quicker for an interviewer who is familiar with a given domain than for an individual who has not been socialized into the particular area of knowledge. The latter will need to spend more time finding out about basic content regarding the field before they are able to begin linguistic probing. They will also have to sample more instances of under-representation to identify the key cases. While probing of grammar will be achieved most efficiently by a domain 'expert', the interview technique remains content-independent since the non-expert is only limited by the time that they can allocate to finding useful grammatical target sites to investigate.

As with all interview techniques, the grammar-targeted method requires that the interviewer is aware of the organizational culture in which the interview is situated. Given the unusual nature of the questioning method, the interviewer may need to spend some time making the interviewee comfortable with the style of questioning and aware that they will be probing material that the interviewee may not have considered likely topics. While grammar-targeted questioning is content-independent, it is not situation-independent, and would be considered inappropriate, for example, in social situations where the questions would appear inquisitorial.

The grammar-targeted interview method allows for a rich description of speakers' tacit knowledge, however, the interviewer needs to possess some skill in being able to identify linguistic features. This may impede its uptake in corporate organizations which do not typically draw upon analytical methods drawn from linguistics. The grammar-targeted interviewer used in the field studies, while not a trained linguist, was familiar with the field. Researchers and practitioners wanting to apply the method would need to develop skills in identifying the linguistic features of under-representation in texts. However, the set of features specified in the interview method are finite, and they have been selected on the basis that they are easy to identify in spoken discourse in real-time. The method has the large advantage that, while linguistic analysis is typically a labour-intensive activity, a limited set of linguistic features means that we leverage the value of linguistic analysis and concurrently profit from the relative speed of targeted interviewing.

Another issue is that tacit knowledge is irreducible (in the sense that there is always residual tacit knowledge left behind after any kind of probing) since we are unlikely to ever produce extended congruent discourse unless explaining something to a child. In light of this problem, the interview technique is intended to be exploratory, rather than exhaustive, and can be used to hone in on particular areas of under-represented meaning depending on the aim of a given interview.

The chapters that follow describe three field studies, the latter two of which employ the grammar-targeted interview method presented here. The first field study (Chapter 3) seeks to more fully introduce the features of under-representation by analysing texts taken from non-targeted interviews about knowledge management in a property services multinational. I then move on to show how to probe these features in grammar-targeted interviewing in chapters describing field studies in two other organizations. The first of these is a study conducted in a media organization looking at the language of requirements analysis. This chapter takes a quantitative corpus-based approach to assessing how the language of the subjects interviewed changes when the grammar-targeted interview method is used compared with a content-targeted method. It seeks to determine whether there is a reduction in under-representation in grammar-targeted interviews compared with content-targeted interviews. The final field study was conducted in a financial services organization during performance reviews of technologists in the IT department. This study adopts a more qualitative, instance-based approach to analysing how more congruent language can reveal tacit knowledge.

Notes

1 Indeed Polanyi authored a book on tacit knowledge titled simply 'Meaning'.
2 See for example work in schools using genre theory (Rose 2012).
3 The particular selections from these resources that a research community makes form the linguistic equivalent of Kuhn's (1962) notion of a paradigm. While they may be specified by a linguist, the selections remain tacit to the language user.
4 The system network for selecting process type is presented in Figure 3.3. This figure omits the process type behavioural which we do not use in the present study because specifying a clause as behavioural rather than material or mental requires semantic analysis beyond the grammatical focus with which we are concerned.

5   The reader is also directed to Eggins (1994: 254–66) for a useful explanation of the
    nature of relational processes.
6   The speaker may be echoing the interviewer's reference choice here.
7   Martin (2008a) directs readers to the following research on the role of
    nominalization in different discourses: Halliday (2004), Halliday and Martin (1993),
    Martin and Veel (1998) and Korner et al. (1992) (science discourse); Coffin (2006)
    and Martin and Wodak (2003) (history discourse): Wignell (2007) (social science
    discourse); O'Halloran (2006) (mathematics discourse); and Martin (1993) and
    Iedema (1995) (administrative discourse).
8   The method is intended to be complementary to existing interview techniques
    and standard aspects of interviewing such as rapport-building, introductory and
    concluding discourse, etc. will be present.
9   Lemke (1995) explains metaredundancy in language as: '... just a way of describing
    how the redundancy, the predictable relation or connection of two things, can itself
    be redundant (i.e. have a predictable connection) with something else' [The basic
    notion was introduced by Gregory Bateson (1972: 132–3) and is closely related to
    his views on meta-communication (messages about messages) and meta-learning
    (learning how to learn); cf. also meta-mathematics (the mathematical theory of
    mathematical theories).] (Lemke 1995: 168–9).
10 The following areas of ideational indeterminacy identified by Halliday and
    Matthiessen (1999: 549) are likely to be fruitful areas for exploring under-
    representation:
    (1) Ambiguities ('either a or x'): one form of wording construes two distinct
        meanings, each of which is exclusive of the other.
    (2) Blends ('both b and y'): one form of wording construes two different meanings,
        both of which are blended into a single whole.
    (3) Overlaps ('partly c, partly z'): two categories overlap so that certain members
        display features of each.
    (4) Neutralizations: in certain contexts, the difference between two categories
        disappears.
    (5) Complementarities: certain semantic features or domains are construed in two
        contradictory ways.

Misaligned Agency: Tacit Knowledge in Knowledge Management

Introduction

Differences in the way people construe the same situation can be very helpful in understanding their implicit assumptions, particularly in semiotically complex environments such as the workplace. This chapter presents the first of three field studies conducted in IT departments, and explores how managers, technologists, knowledge managers and users in an engineering/property services multinational talk about their experience of knowledge management processes and technology. The focus is on four texts taken from interviews conducted with these participants. The chapter examines each text in terms of the types of under-representation (nominalization, modality, generalization and agency) that were introduced in Chapter 2.

The instances of under-representation identified in the texts are examples of the kind of lexicogrammatical sites targeted by the grammar-targeted interview method used in the two other field studies. The general aim is to provide the reader with some familiarity with these features as they occur in real discourse before unpacking them interactively in interviews in Chapters 4 and 5. We begin by considering why tacit knowledge has become such an important issue in knowledge management and how the field as reconstrued (perhaps misconstrued) Polanyi's TTK.

The organization that hosted this field study was engaged in knowledge management processes aimed at helping its employees to effectively utilize its human and technical resources. 'Knowledge management' is the technical term used in management discourses to refer to initiatives aimed at retaining and deploying the expertise of employees in light of the potential that new technologies afford for storage, manipulation and reuse. If we were to unpack the nominal group into a more congruent form it might mean something akin to 'managing what people in our organization know'. 'Knowledge management' often collocates with the term 'competitive advantage' and general meanings about 'leveraging organizational knowledge' as if it were a financial asset. The term is a nominalization, embedding participants and processes about what it means for 'someone to know something' and what it means for 'someone to manage something that is known by someone'. This embedding masks ideological positions relating to where the knowledge originates, how it is transmitted and stored, and what counts as meaningful information in an organization.

Tacit knowledge and technology in a property services company

We now turn to a field study of tacit knowledge in a real organization. This study investigates tacit knowledge in the knowledge management practices of a property services multinational operating in building construction and management. There is evidence of attempts within the organization over the last 20 years to retain some forms of knowledge such as patterns in construction defects that have been archived over time. It was only in the last 10 years, however, that knowledge management had entered management discourse in the organization. The current knowledge management programme in place in the organization involves two initiatives introduced in the Construction and Development areas of the business respectively. Each initiative produced a knowledge management system and associated processes.

The study involved four main classes of speakers associated with these knowledge management systems: technologists, business analysts, knowledge managers and users (Table 3.1) and focused on how these different participants talk about the knowledge management systems that they used in their work. The aim of the linguistic analyses was to reveal the tacit assumptions about knowledge management these speakers held.

The IT group, 'Strategic Global Solutions', serviced the two business communities in this study, as well as the business globally, and was comprised of a chief information officer (CIO), three business analysts and a team of developers (Table 3.1). The CIO adopted a strategic role, identifying which systems should be, in his terms, *put across* the various businesses in Organization X globally. His role involved formulating implementation plans for the delivery of these systems

Table 3.1 Subjects interviewed

Service A	Service B
Chief information officer, Global Services	
Three business analysts, Global Services	
Two knowledge managers	Two knowledge managers
Knowledge sharer	Three facilitators
	Community of practice leader
	Community of practice member
Five users	Five users

in the different regions. The business analysts worked with business users, that is, employees working in any of the organization's business areas. The analysts' work involved attempting to transform the business users' needs into terms that the development team could understand in order to build systems. The most senior business analyst with the most developed knowledge of the business had been with the organization for more than 10 years, and occupied the additional role of project manager. The analysts were situated at a crucial point in the two subcultures as semiotic systems, effectively acting as translators of meaning from the world of business into the IT domain. As mediators at the point of intersection of two discourses, these analysts had the potential to radically redirect the meanings made in the two different communities.

Twenty-four semi-structured individual interviews were conducted by the researcher with these speakers. Each interview was approximately 1 hour in duration. The interviews with the business analysts were conducted in person. However, since the organization was a multinational, most of the other participants were located outside Sydney and these interviews were conducted via conference call. The goal of the interviews was to encourage the participants to talk freely about their work and their experiences surrounding Services A and B. While it is never possible to interview a subject without influencing their language to some degree, strategies were employed to minimize the impact of the interviewer's speech on the grammar of the subjects. The strategies were the following:

- The ideational content of the speaker's response was used as the basis for the subsequent question.
- Questions were open-ended (e.g. 'Tell me about knowledge management in Organization X') to encourage speakers to form their own orientation to the topic.

However, despite these measures, it is acknowledged that the influence of the language of the researcher and the nature of the interview genre are unavoidable confounding variables in interview-based field research.

Extracts from the transcribed interviews with four of the subjects (the CIO, a user, a business analyst and a facilitator) were sampled for linguistic analysis. The sampling strategy was qualitative and aimed at detecting phases of discourse where the speakers were talking about an area of their work in which they were proficient and which contained interesting examples of under-representation. The size of the text excerpts used in this chapter is relatively small compared to the interview lengths as instance-based SFL analysis is very detailed. In order to understand what is happening grammatically from a more global perspective, a more quantitative, corpus-based approach is used in the next chapter. However, it is important to begin at the local instance level to gain insight into the kind of meanings that are embedded in the grammatical patterns encountered. It is also important to begin with undirected interviews, rather than interviews were grammar was deliberately probed, to ascertain whether the features of under-representation occur in (relatively) free talk.[1]

Two communities: Project management and construction and development

The Property Solutions sector of the firm consisted of two parts: one side of the business dealt with project management and development, and the other focused on construction. Construction was concerned with building, while development focused on adding value to property investments by managing redevelopment projects. Culturally, the two communities were very different and approached knowledge management in very different ways.

Knowledge Management Service A

In the wake of a large and successful development in the UK division of the business, a need for some form of knowledge management in the organization became apparent to senior management who believed that 'the substantial lessons learnt' should be retained in the corporate memory. Since the development community's core business was to locate opportunities to develop property, their knowledge management concerns were deemed to centre upon both researching current markets and learning from past ventures. In addition, because documented information played such a central role in this process, an online knowledge base was created for storing information (though a human-based service point was also provided).

A major requirement expressed by the community involved in this project was a place to store documents and retrieve people who had particular information. The knowledge managers translated this need in terms of entities and relationships, generating a topic-based ontology as a map of organization resources with content focused around construction, development and management of properties. Following this initial categorization, there was some consultation of users regarding the scope and naming of categories in the knowledge base. Each geographical region of the company was provided with its own instantiation of the knowledge map and corresponding database. The developers hoped to integrate these versions of the system if they were able to overcome difficulties in translating between regional differences.

Service A also included a 'Help Point': a phone number which was set up to assist users working on projects to find relevant knowledge. 'Knowledge sharers' were put in place to address the major areas in which requests occurred. The 'expert' knowledge sharers' role was to interact with the business user to share their insight into an issue and any relevant documentation. The general aim was to 'convey best practice in order to speed up the progression of current projects'. Service A also incorporated a programme known as 'Technical Skilling' designed as a forum for individuals to share their expertise and interests. The ultimate aim was to promote the available 'skillsets' within the organization and showcase the range of projects which were running at a given time.

Development managers tended to avoid using IT systems, preferring instead to liaise with people. This group of users more frequently accessed the Help Point rather than the online system. Project managers, by way of contrast, frequently made use of the online system, reporting that they felt it assisted them in adopting a systematic approach to high-risk financial decisions by making key documents readily available.

Knowledge Management Service B

The construction community, by way of contrast, was characterized by people wanting to connect quickly with other members of the organization to solve immediate and practical engineering problems. Engineers of every discipline were employed in this sector of the business and the drive was towards finding answers to specialized construction problems among the diversity of expertise available rather than retrieving pre-existing artefacts from a knowledge base.

Members of this community wanted their questions to be answered quickly often while they were out of the office on a job.

The construction industry in general is extremely fragmented, manifesting a multitude of different practices and regulations. The diversity and global distribution of the construction sector of the organization meant that any knowledge management system would have to deal with intersecting and divergent discourses. In particular polysemy and synonymy would be issues for any organization-wide ontology that might be used in a traditional knowledge management system for this community. For instance disambiguating the names used for a particular material was a major issue for global construction. Clearly determining that you have the correct material no matter your geographical location is vital to quality control and safety.

The concept of knowledge management at the time this study was undertaken was very new to the construction services industry. Projects in this industry were typically run on a fast track schedule with a high rotation. The time constraints involved in completing a project meant that 'best practices' were often not collected for future use. In addition the sector worked with fairly low profit margins. Owners of ventures were characteristically unwilling to incur further expenses that might benefit future clients but potentially offer little return to their own project.

The practices of the construction community were thus substantively relationship-focused. This community relayed a significant part of their knowledge through oral communication. The written mode was avoided in part due to the nature of the construction environment which was often inhospitable to portable devices. People wanted to solve construction problems on site by drawing on the experience of people who had worked with a particular material or design. Such past expertise was usually acquired by contacting a person who had dealt with a similar issue directly by phone.

The designers of the knowledge management service developed for this community felt that as the organization currently did not have a culture in which best practice was collected, the next best thing was to create a 'just-in-time' service. Instead of investing time and money in cataloguing knowledge as it was acquired, a 'demand-side' system was created which centred upon establishing a process to quickly find answers to questions without any pre-categorization or pre-processing. Knowledge Management Service B was hence a phone-based service designed to connect people with experts, offering three subject positions to participants: seeker, facilitator and sharer. A seeker was an employee looking for an appropriate person to offer advice on a query. Seekers relied on the mediating capacity of a facilitator to find an appropriate sharer with the specialist knowledge.

The role of facilitators was described by a manager as in-between a switchboard operator and a librarian. They acted as a clearinghouse or research desk by putting individuals seeking answers to questions in contact with individuals with the relevant expertise. During this process, facilitators have carte blanche access to the company's knowledge resources and employees have been instructed to assist them in any way possible when approached. In each region the senior business managers were available to act as 'pointers' to direct facilitators to the most appropriate sharers, with one facilitator jokingly describing themselves as 'the first and last line of defence'.

There were three facilitators located in headquarter cities in the company's three regions. The facilitators collaborated via weekly conference calls to discuss cases and pass on those that required expertise from a particular region. Facilitators were trained for their role as intermediaries by external consultants in areas such as 'listening skills' and 'customer service issues'. This training involved activities such as role-playing how to deal with questions and communicate by telephone.

The organizational logic behind the development of the facilitator positions was efficient use of the organization's disparate resources. These resources included project history databases; safety, legal and accounting databases, cost history and estimating systems, physical lending libraries and subscriptions to a variety of financial and research services. The logic of mediated access, however, meant that the facilitators became a 'knowledge bottleneck' in the organization since the number and nature of the queries that could be answered was limited.

Facilitators logged the calls that they receive in System B. This log included a description of the question and which sharer was chosen to resolve it. Each sharer was given a profile within the system. Sharer's profiles were comprised of self-descriptions consisting of fields composed of keywords and free text. The 'Types of Project Experience' field used keywords defined by the system. The hope was that when the number of questions in the system reached around 10,000, it would itself act as a useful resource for locating a useful sharer. At the time of this study the facilitators' throughput of cases was approximately 30 per week and they had processed approximately 2,300 cases. The questions tended to be fairly diverse with one facilitator estimating that of these total cases, only about 1 per cent would involve questions that have been asked twice.

The degree of effort required to answer a question varied substantially with the quickest taking a few minutes and the slowest taking a month. The complexity of a query was not the sole factor contributing to the length of the response. Facilitators found that while it was usually relatively easy to locate a sharer within the business, explaining the problem to the sharer, obtaining their agreement to help and getting them to call back was often a time-consuming process.

One facilitator indicated that he believed there were ten primary types of questions asked by seekers. The top three of these would represent approximately 60 per cent of the volume of questions. The project-orientated nature of the business meant that the most frequent kind of question was related to past experience on particular project types. The next most common question was a 'building element' question about a particular aspect of the design of a building. Questions relating to the organization's relationships with clients formed the third most frequent type. These were typically seekers putting a proposal together for a particular client and wanting to know the company history with that client.

There was substantial debate within the facilitator team about whether questions should be categorized by keywords, a function which had been dropped from the logging tool. The search facility offered by the system was not particularly sophisticated and significant expenditure would be needed to create a more nuanced tool. One facilitator cited the example of searching for 'the size of the curtain wall market'. This search required the system to determine that 'market size' is a component of 'strategic procurement'. In addition all the usual problems faced by search engines were applicable and part of the reason the service remained human rather than automatic.

Detecting patterns of under-representation in texts

The following sections explore four spoken texts extracted from the interviews. These texts are excerpts where the subjects talk about topics relating to their work in knowledge management or their use of the organization's knowledge management services. They were sampled qualitatively on the basis that they deal with knowledge management issues that the speakers foregrounded as important in their work. We explore how their grammar packs up meaning through under-representation and how this might relate to the problem of understanding a person's tacit knowledge. The focus is on the four areas of under-representation identified in the previous chapter, namely, nominalization, modality, generalization and agency.

Under-representation in Text 1

Text 1 is an extract from the interview with the Global Services CIO. In this extract he talks about how to create the kind of 'cultural change' in the IT department that he believed was necessary for the organization to successfully embrace knowledge management services that his department have developed. Readers familiar with management discourses will quickly recognize the tendency towards nominalizations that realize the so-called management 'buzzwords' such as 'knowledge sharing company' that were in-vouge at the time.

Table 3.2 Text 1, the CIO talking about cultural change in Organization X to accommodate knowledge management

Turn	Speaker	Talk
1	Interviewer	So how are you trying to create that cultural change?
2	CIO	It's messages from the CEO, it's **compensation,** it's lots of **communication** and you often find that in fact that's the secret to it. You have to have messages from the CEO, lots of **reinforcing communication,** lots of **activity** and some demonstrated, as part of the **communication, demonstrated cases** where people have found value through the programme and then you need to have some technology to support it as well. So I don't think there is a magic formula in any organization. I really think that you have to match your approach to the style of organization you are and, in this case, we felt we had to have a **bottom up approach** and **topdown approach. Topdown approach** is simply the CEO saying, 'We're going to become a **knowledge sharing company** and we are going to be known as a company with a **high knowledge worth,** if you like'. So LL is a company you want to deal with because their level of **knowledge** is superlative. That's probably the wrong word. It's the highest, seen as the highest in the market place and has a **competitive advantage** and the **bottom up approach** is simply having a programme in place that has **procedures.** We have phone calls, phone numbers to call if you a have a question. We have **facilitators** who will try and resolve an answer and we have a system that is being developed to first of all support the **facilitators** who are trying to put **knowledge seekers** in touch with **knowledge sharers,** but also we will eventually develop that into a **self-service tool** so that people can actually go straight into the system and try and find things first off and if that fails then go to the **facilitator.** That's how we scale up. So that's the **bottom up approach** and then there are **reinforcing management practices** such as **rewards** for **knowledge sharing** and **knowledge seeking.** So if you have demonstrated that you have actually gone out into the company to network through the programme and get some expertise expert advice which allows us to either get more business or do something better it will count for the employee's **performance** within the company.

The sections which follow explore separately each of the four kinds of under-representation that unfold in Text 1 in turn.

Nominalization in Text 1

Nominalization was a resource that allowed the CIO to condense meanings about how the organizational culture needed to change for a knowledge management service to be used effectively in assisting employees with their work. Examples of nominalizations about knowledge management in the discourse of the CIO included:

> Knowledge sharing, knowledge creation, knowledge programme, core competence, best practice, expertise location, collaboration.

Aside from what it means 'to know', these nominalizations pack up meanings about how the speaker construes what it means 'to share', 'to create', 'to organize', 'to be competent', 'to practice', 'to locate' and 'to collaborate'.

Instances of nominalization in Text 1 appear in **bold** (Table 3.2). The bold type provides a visual snapshot of the unfolding of nominalization in this text. Each of these instances may be thought of as a 'target site', the unpacking of which would provide insight into how the speaker construes the process of creating 'cultural change'. The unfolding might also be thought of a 'cascade of under-representation' as the CIO talks about 'cultural change' with the various instances of nominalization not only contributing to local meanings about specific aspects of organizational change, but also to wider meanings in the text about knowledge management as construed by the CIO.

Taking the nominalization 'cultural change' as a starting point, we can begin to trace how tacit meanings about knowledge and management build up as the text progresses (Figure 3.1). A congruent realization of the term 'cultural change' would be:

> Something or someone changes the culture.

In this clause both the agent and the medium are visible (Table 3.3). However, the speaker instead chose to talk about 'cultural change', leveraging the expansive capacity of the nominal group but, in turn, obscuring participants. Rather than talking about 'how change happens', 'who makes change happen' or 'to whom change happens', the CIO talks about 'what cultural change is' as a metaphorical substitute.

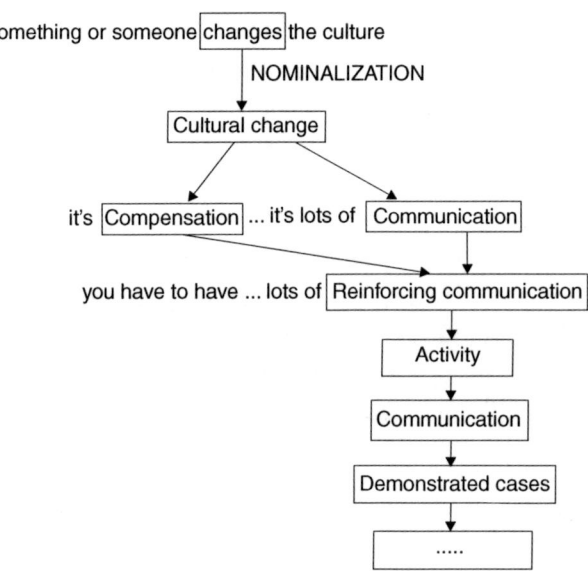

Figure 3.1 The cascade of under-representation in Text 1.

Table 3.3 Experiential analysis of clause 'Something or someone changes the culture'

Something or someone	changes	the culture
Agent	Material process	Medium

For example, the CIO says:

It's messages from the CEO ...

A literal reading of this clause would be:

Cultural change is messages from the CEO.

However, the metaphorical implication is that

Messages from the CEO cause cultural change to happen.

Similarly:

Compensation causes cultural change to happen.

and:

Communication causes cultural change to happen.

In these latter two instances, the agents are nominalizations that embed more congruent structures that involve participants who are involved in processes. The under-representation of these participants appears part of the way the CIO constructs 'cultural change' as an abstract concept rather than a lived experience. Factors contributing to this construal from the context might be the social construction of executive management and its focus on high-level documentation and budgeting. In this way, the grammar is useful to the CIO because it allows him to leverage meanings drawn from these executive domains. It assists him in operating and getting things done in the social context of his work environment, however, it also renders opaque important meanings about managing people.

Some instances of nominalization are partially unpacked by the CIO himself. For example, he says:

> Topdown approach is simply the CEO saying 'We're going to become a knowledge sharing company . . .'

Here, the nominalization 'topdown approach' is elaborated as a verbal process of saying. The sayer is the CIO, however, the receiver is elided. Theses types of elisions create a sense that 'cultural change' is organizational (in the ideational sense) rather than interpersonal: that is about a change in states rather than a change in relationships. Most clauses in the text pack the participants doing the knowledge managing into nominalizations. Where participants are directly employed, they are relegated to embedded clauses, for example:

> ||You have to have messages from the CEO, lot's of reinforcing communication, lots of activity and some demonstrated, <<as part of the communication>>, demonstrated cases [[where **people** have found value through the program.]]||

The embedded clause (marked in square brackets), 'where people have found value through the program', involves an actor, 'people', that is the agent in a material process of finding. The embedded clause functions as a qualifier in the nominal group. Here 'people' seem to function as entities that describe the type of organizational artefact the CIO is interested in, more than as entities who are animate and involved in the relationships that form the culture of the organization.

Similarly, towards the end of the text, the CIO says (nominalization in bold):

> . . . and then there are **reinforcing management practices** such as **rewards** for **knowledge sharing** and **knowledge seeking**.

This clause contains four nominalizations. At the most basic level, these nominalizations embed seven processes: to reinforce, to manage, to practice, to reward, to know, to share and to seek. An unknown number of participants are involved in these processes. Rather than a congruent instantiation where participants are acted upon and cause things to happen, the grammar uses nominalization to construe complex concepts as existing or having relationships with other things. Figure 3.2 shows the distribution of the nominalizations in Text 1, classified by the type of process that is nominalized. Material processes were the dominant category, followed by mental processes and verbal processes. The actions, thoughts and talk of people involved in and experiencing knowledge management in the organization are packed up in these categories.

The grammatical focus on abstract relationships is also seen in the tendency towards relational processes in process type selection (Figure 3.3). The most common type of relational process used is the identifying relational process (Figure 3.4), that is, processes that specify the identity of a participant, as opposed to attributive relational processes which define the participant's attributes. This appears part of the aforementioned tendency of the speaker to portray cultural change as if it is something that exists rather than acts, as a destination rather than a journey. The implication of this tacit construal of organizational culture is that this CEO may be less tuned to the interpersonal meanings that are the partners to the kind of ideational change that he wants to see in the culture. Theses grammatical choices tacitly construe such change as commodity-driven rather than interpersonally motivated.

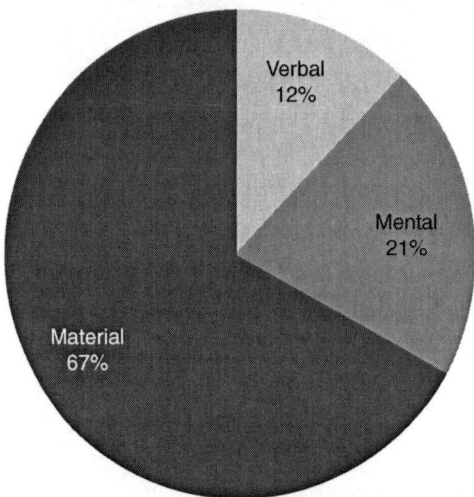

Figure 3.2 Nominalizations in Text 1 classified by process type.

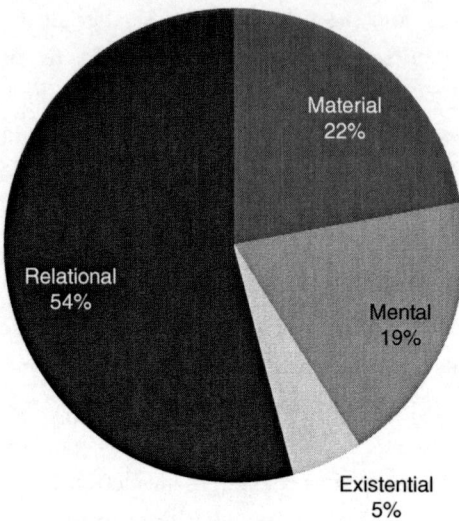

Figure 3.3 Types of process in Text 1.

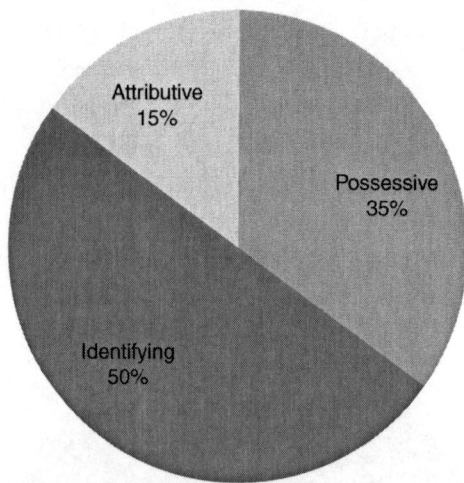

Figure 3.4 Types of relational processes in Text 1.

Modality in Text 1

The majority of instances of modality in Text 1 are of modal 'obligation' (e.g. 'must', 'need' and 'should'). The modal choices involve a generic 'you' (Table 3.4). The grammatical choices made construe the acquisition of certain phenomena as creating conditions that permit the culture to change:

You **have to** have messages from the CEO ...

Table 3.4 Examples of modality in Text 1

				Type of modality
1	You	**have**	to have messages from the CEO ...	Obligation
2	And then you	**need**	to have some technology to support it as well	Obligation
3	.... I really think you	**have**	have to match your approach to the style of organization you are	Obligation
4	We felt we	**had**	to have a bottom up approach and a top down approach	Obligation
5	That's	**probably**	the wrong word	Probability
6	You	**often**	find	Usuality

In this clause a modal operator (have to) signals obligation regarding the generic 'you'. However, the theoretical participant who has imposed this requirement is elided. Obfuscating who or what has instigated the obligation has the rhetorical impact of construing the proposition (that messages from the CEO are needed) as fact rather than opinion.

The implications of this kind of camouflaging of the agent motivating statements about cultural change is that these statements may be taken for granted, that is, taken as part of the 'background' of the knowledge management service rather than as what managers would term a 'critical success factor'. In simple terms, the reasons why 'you have to have messages from the CEO' are not presented as available for discussion. However, such discussion may be critically important as failure of the knowledge management service to align with the organizational culture will mean users may not make optimal use of the service because it does not conform to they way they approach their work activity (as we will see later in this chapter).

Generalization in Text 1

Table 3.5 gives instances of generalization by under-specification, non-specific deictic or abstract terminology in Text 1. For example, the CIO says:

It's messages from the CEO.

Here, messages is an instance of under-specification since the 'circumstance of matter', that is, what the messages are about, and the receiver, that is, to whom the messages are addressed, have been elided. The ellipsis is part of the way the speaker summarizes complex content. However, the type of features he chooses to

Table 3.5 Examples of generalization in Text 1

				Type of generalization
1	It's	**messages**	from the CEO	Under-specification
2	You need to have	**some**	technology to support it as well	Non-specific deictic
3	To be known as a company with	**high knowledge worth**		Abstract terminology
4	So that	**people**	can actually go straight into the system	Under-specification
5	Do	**something**	better	Non-specific deictic

condense or foreground are significant when trying to understand tacit meaning in the text about what the CIO means when he talks about communication in relation to cultural change.

The motif of commodification, that we have already seen realized via nominalization, continues as the CIO talks about requiring 'some technology'. The non-specific deictic 'some' construes technology as, to use a favourite IT analogy, something that can be take 'off the shelf' as if it were a packaged object.

Agency in Text 1

Tracing patterns in agency in a text can reveal how it distributes power over semantic domains. A large proportion of clauses in Text 1 contain no agent (43%) and 19 per cent of agents are categorized as impersonal you, that is, they are about a generic rather than specific participant (Figure 3.5). Thus the events in the text seemingly occur on their own, or, where there is an agent, it is not a specific individual. The pattern appears to be of tempering responsibility. In addition, when this tendency in agency is considered with concurrent patterns in nominalization and generalization, a tendency to sidestep specificity, and reduce accountability, is apparent. The non-specific deictic allows the speaker to economically skip over details and keep the discourse progressing efficiently. However, what are the implications of presenting technology in this way? What kinds of phenomena are subject to this kind of shorthand in the CIO's discourse and why? We can only answer these questions by looking at more text, or, as we will see later in this chapter, asking a question that probes the features itself.

If we now turn to consider how the meaning on the content plane are realized on the lexicogrammatical patterns on the expression plane we see an essential

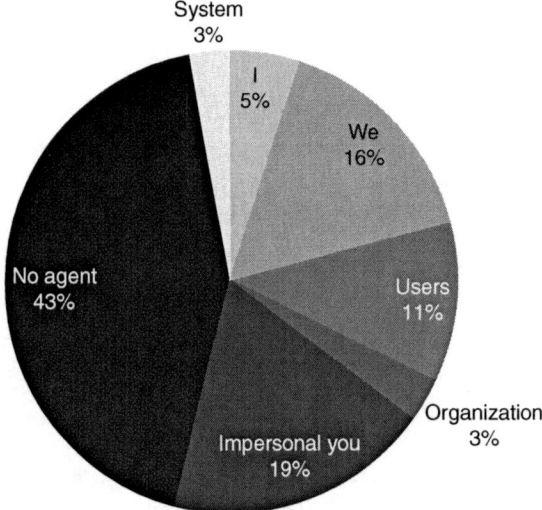

Figure 3.5 Distribution of agency in Text 1.

contradiction between content and grammar. For example compare the explicit orientation of the text to cultural change with the pattern of agency that has been identified. The CIO asserts that cultural change is necessary in his organization in order for knowledge management practices and services to be successfully adopted by employees. However, he dissipates responsibility through a tacit grammatical pattern where the agent causing the change is camouflaged. The contradiction between emphasizing that the organizational culture should be changed, and a grammatical structure that hides the agents who would carry out this change suggests that there is a high likelihood that the cultural change will not be achieved under his governance.

As knowledge management services are typically expensive to create and support, the organization should make sure that the various stakeholders in the services have 'ownership' of the service not only in terms of the technological infrastructure and personnel, but also in terms of ownership of the responsibility to ensure change occurs. Part of establishing such ownership is ensuring that the messages that are sent to employees do not involve internal contradictions between content and grammar of the kind manifest in Text 1. As the 2500-year old history of rhetoric suggests, the below-view patterns in a message are more likely to have an impact on the listener than the content alone. Thus, for the CIO to produce statements about knowledge management that are going to be effective at motivating employees, he should ensure that he aligns key (though tacit) dimensions of his grammar with the message he wishes to convey.

Under-representation in Text 2

Text 2 is a technologist talking about a knowledge management system that he was involved in developing for users in Organization X (Table 3.6). In this extract, he discusses the 'development methodology' that he used to build the system. The under-representation in this text is about how this technologist construes the

Table 3.6 Text 2, Technologist 1 talking about the development of System X

Turn	Speaker	Talk
1	Technologist 1	So to consolidate all the requirements and make everyone agree on what we are going to build for the next release, sometimes it takes time, more time than actually the development effort. For example, we may take 1 month to get the user requirements and to build it we may take a week or two.
2	Interviewer	So was it a linear process or was it prototyping?
3	Technologist 1	We don't believe in heavy documents. So we only, we have a process there, but it is only a light weight process. So it's the 'good enough' process that means, as long as we know what we are going to do, then that's it. We stop there. We don't, for example, we don't try to tell how long the field length is.
		And then the principle is we build whatever we build, but we give the users something that they can see. So it is not really a prototype. A prototype is something that you may throw away or try to get them to understand. The user requirements . . .
		What we do is more an iterative approach. Doing it you involve the application. So we implement it a little bit and then put it into production and they can do feedback on that, the potential system, that we change and so on.
		System X. We've finished the iteration. When we first developed version one about 20 to 24 months ago, when we first released version one, we had three iterations. Basically, we had three attempts to deliver the solution and afterwards every 2 months we have a maintenance release to capture what their need is and we implement every 2 months and then we give a new release. Now, the System X program is release 1.6. We have had six maintenance cycles already and we stopped the maintenance cycle, I think, 8 months ago. So, because the users don't have many new ideas to add into the existing program, but they have new ideas totally . . . but they are not effective for putting into the existing platform. The biggest challenge for us, in thinking of stopping the maintenance release and building a new one, is the technology we use and the way that we organize our knowledge base or knowledge map.

relationship of the users to the system produced. As the following sections will detail, the technologist draws on the grammatical resources of nominalization and generalization to control the subject positions that are available to the users during the system development. He also uses agency to maintain his semiotic power over the system and its users.

Nominalisation in Text 2

The nominalization in Text 2 was typically about aspects of the procedures that the technologists used to develop the system. These were largely material processes about creating and sustaining the system (Table 3.7). An exception was the nominalization 'user requirements'. This nominal group is about 'users needing to do things with a system'. It embeds interpersonal processes about understanding and satisfying groups and individuals in the organization who are not necessarily familiar with the type of technology being introduced. Under-representation of this type is the focus of Field Study 2 conducted during the requirements analysis phase of a project (see Chapter 4). The grammatical choice to condense these processes into the nominal group 'user requirements' positions accounting for the users' needs as a background to system development rather than its ultimate focus. The term 'user requirement' allows those needs to be referenced with semiotic brevity but if we look elsewhere in the text, for example at the distribution of agency, we see how the subject position of the user is restricted. Importantly, the technologist's grammar reveals a tacit construal of system development as being about technical and managerial artefacts that can be controlled more than it is about people.

This revelation is incongruent with propositional content elsewhere in the interview where the technologist asserts the importance of understanding the users to providing a successful system. The incongruity between grammar and content suggests an incongruity between what the technologist believes he is

Table 3.7 Examples of nominalization in Text 2

Nominalization	Nominalized process	Process type
Requirements	To require	Mental
Release	To release	Material
Development	To develop	Material
Feedback	To feed back	Material
Iteration	To iterate	Material
Maintenance cycle	To maintain, to cycle	Material, material

doing (in the process of system development) and what he is actually achieving. Identifying this type of mismatch is critical to preventing the kind of user resistance to the knowledge management system that technologists and users alike went on to describe elsewhere in the interviews.

Modality in Text 2

Text 2 contains minimal modality as its focus is on what the technologists have done rather than the vagaries of why they should do, or the opinions of users on how they should do it (Table 3.8). Thus probing modality is unlikely to be fruitful in uncovering under-represented meaning. One example of potential interest, however, is the final instance regarding providing the users with permission to give 'feedback'. The modal operator used in this clause may be probed to determine how the technologist knows that the users feel comfortable about giving feedback to the technologists and how he knows if they understand how to describe their experience of the system in terms that are meaningful to the technologists.

Generalization in Text 2

The generalization in Text 2 was typically under-specification (Table 3.9). For example, when the technologist says 'heavy documents', he does not specify what the documents are about, who wrote them or to whom they are directed. Similarly, when he refers to a 'light weight process', he does not reveal what he means by a 'process', who is doing the process and how you know when it is 'light'.

The implications of this kind of generalization is to do with the amount of scope for personal judgement in determining completion that the generalization affords. For example, determining when something is 'good enough' (instance 1 in Table 3.9) centres upon what 'good' means to an individual (for a theory of evaluative language using a Systemic Functional framework, see Martin and White (2005)). The under-specification removes accountability of the technologist to the users because there exists no standard measure of 'goodness' to which

Table 3.8 Examples of modality in Text 2

Talk			Type of modality
1		**make** everyone agree …	Obligation
2	… we	**may** take 1 month …	Probability
3	… they	**can** do feedback …	Obligation

Table 3.9 Examples of generalization in Text 2

Talk			Type of generalization
1	So it's the	'good enough'	process	Under-specification
2	So we implement it	a little bit		Under-specification
3	And make	everyone	agree	Under-specification
4	We don't believe in	heavy documents		Non-specific deictic
5	But it is only a	light weight process		Under-specification
6	So because the users don't have	many new ideas	to add into the existing program	Under-specification
7		sometimes	it takes time	Under-specification
8	The	technology	we use	Under-specification

they can appeal. In essence, the reduced precision allows the technologist greater control over how the IT services they produce are critiqued. This type of under-representation is the focus of the third field study on performance reviews.

Agency in Text 2

The pattern of agency in Text 2 privileges the technologists as the creators of the system over the users as its recipients. On the one hand it is unsurprising that a technologist talking about their work activity would construe themselves as the main class agent performing the action. If, however, the pattern of agency is maintained when the technologist is talking about different topics, such as the opinions of the users about the system, that pattern becomes more marked and a potential target site for probing. The dominant agent in Text 2 is 'we' (Table 3.10). The processes in these clauses are mainly material (1, 2, 6, 8, 9 in Table 3.10).

Text 2 seems to minimize the agency of users. The users as agents are often relegated to embedded clauses with the technologists an agent in the main clause either providing something or trying to make something happen, for example:

we give the users [[something that [[[**they** can see]]]]]

Users are given permission to act rather than acting on their own initiative. The final two instances position the users as agent in relation to negative polarity (don't have, not effective). This pattern throughout the agency in the text seems to suggest a view of users as less important than technologists in the development process. In understanding the pattern the nominalization 'feedback' would need

Table 3.10 Examples of 'we' as agent in Text 2

1	For example,	**we**	may take 1 month to get the user requirements
2		**we**	may take a week or two
3		**we**	don't believe in heavy documents
4		**we**	have a process there
5	As long as	**we**	know what we are going to do
6		**we**	stop there
7		**we**	don't try to tell how long the field length is
8		**we**	build whatever we build
9	But	**we**	give the user something that they can see

to be unpacked in order to gain insight into how the technologists construe the process of the users providing information and opinion that can be used in creating the system. A similar pattern of agency is seen in Chapter 4 when the subjects in that study talk about tracing user requirements for a content management system.

Under-representation in Text 3

Text 3 (Table 3.11) is a user talking about her experience of working with a knowledge management system. This user, a lawyer working for the organization, described the main part of her role in the organization as confirming that 'the legal intent reflects the commercial understanding' between parties on development projects. In this extract she describes the ways in which the system failed to meet her knowledge management needs. As we will see, this user manifests a very different distribution of agency in relation to the knowledge management system to that of the technologist detailed in the previous section.

Nominalization in Text 3

The nominalization in Text 3 is focused around the semiotic entities that are key to this user's work. This text tends to nominalize verbal and mental processes (rather than the material processes that characterized the previous texts). The speaker does much of the work herself of unpacking the dominant nominalization in the text, 'information' (Table 3.12). The user is cognizant of the different discourses that system designers and users deploy and the impact that the different language of these speech communities can have on the kinds of keywords that are used as labels for the 'information' contained in the system:

... in actual fact, yes, the information is there. It is just that I keyed in a word that, you know, is colloquial to my project but certainly wasn't colloquial to the person who originally put that document on.

Unlike Text 1, there is no pronounced misalignment between the content and grammar. In addition, the speaker tends to self-unpack (exemplified

Table 3.11 Text 3, Subject 1 talking about her experience of using System X

Turn	Speaker	Talk
	User 1	System X would be so much more effective to me if the search engine was tailored to the way I think. What I mean by that is, whenever I type in a keyword that I think will find me the information, it will say, 'No, item not found' because what has been keyed in by the original people who set up the System X databases, probably they didn't have the sort of practical understanding of what those documents were, what that information was. So they wouldn't use the same sort of language that we use. For example, these dreadful professional services agreements. Nobody calls them professional services agreements. We call them PSAs or appointments for short. If you type in PSA or appointment, it will not come up with any information. So you think, 'There is nothing on this database, I had better go an ask someone else', when in actual fact, yes, the information is there. It is just that I keyed in a word that, you know, is colloquial to my project but certainly wasn't colloquial to the person who originally put that document on. This is why I don't tend to use System X, because whenever I key in a word, 'Oh, there is nothing on this database', and I can't be bothered, I don't have the time to go through each of the topics on the off chance that I might find something. You have to learn how they have set up the categories and learn the topics they have set up. The categories and the topics might not have any relevance in the way we speak at work or how we refer to things.

Table 3.12 The nominalization 'information' in Text 3

1	Whenever I type in a keyword that I think will find me the	**information**	
2	They probably didn't have the sort of practical understanding of what those documents were, what the	**information**	was
3	It will not come up with any	**information**	
4	When in actual fact, yes, the	**information**	is there

above), meaning that it is unlikely for a question probing the nominalization 'information' to elicit tacit knowledge regarding how this user interacts with the system. She has done a lot of this unpacking work herself in the congruent activities sequences relating to using the system (Table 3.13).

Modality in Text 3

The modality in Text 3 is mainly about the probability of the system being able to meet the user's needs ('System X **would** be so much more effective to me if . . .'), and supposition about the developers of the system (e.g. 'they **probably** didn't have the sort of practical understanding of what those documents were') (see Table 3.14 for examples). Probing modality is likely to uncover assumptions this user has made about whose responsibility it is to determine what the system should do. Indeed in this text the user herself begins by spontaneously unpacking the first instance of modal under-representation (Table 3.14):

> What I mean by that is, whenever I type in a keyword that I think will find me the information, it will say, "No, item not found" because what has been keyed in by the original people who set up the System X databases, probably they probably didn't have the sort of practical understanding of what those documents were, what that information was . . .

Table 3.13 Examples of nominalization in Text 3

Nominalization	Nominalized process	Process type
Information	To inform	Verbal
Understanding	To understand	Mental
Agreements	To agree	Verbal
Search engine	To search	Material

Table 3.14 Examples of modality in Text 3

	Talk			Type of modality
1	. . . System X	**would**	be more effective if . . .	Probability
2	. . . . the categories and the topics	**might not**	have any relevance . . .	Probability
3	. . . they	**probably**	didn't have any sort of practical understanding . . .	Probability
4		**. . . certainly**	wasn't colloquial to the person who originally put that topic on . . .	Probability

Again this self-unpacking reveals the user's awareness of the role of interpretation in how information is packaged by a system. The unpacking is, however, incomplete, itself producing additional under-representation such as the nominalization 'practical understanding' (condensing a range of assumptions about how someone can achieve a working knowledge of someone else's documents). Probing this nominalization may reveal this user's tacit expectations regarding how a technologist 'should' go about trying to understand both what she does in her work and how she invests the artefacts with which she works with meaning.

Generalization in Text 3

Text 3 displays a tendency towards non-specific deictic (Table 3.15). We might expect this kind of patterning in the discourse of someone who is talking about a field into which they are only partially apprenticed. However, this individual is not a naive user, being able to identify the semiotic discord between the system design ('the categories and the topics') and the discourse of her work practice:

> The categories and the topics might not have any relevance in the way we speak at work or how we refer to things.

The under-representation by generalization in this text pivots on non-specific deictic structures relating to determining criteria about the system's usefulness (does it contain 'something' or 'nothing'). Part of this assessment relates to the language that should be used in the system. Should the system designers use identical terminology to the users? How do they negotiate the space between folksonomy (where multiple users may deploy different keywords for the same phenomena) and more formal taxonomy of the kind usually demanded by an information system?

Table 3.15 Examples of generalization in Text 3

	Talk			Type
1	System X would be	**so much more**	effective to me	Non-specific deictic, under-specification
2	There is	**nothing**	in this database	Non-specific deictic
3	I had better go ask	**someone else**		Non-specific deictic
4	I might find	**something**		Non-specific deictic
5	How we refer to	**things**		Non-specific deictic

Agency in Text 3

Text 3 construes the speaker as the dominant agent doing the semiotic work when performing a search (Table 3.16). Instances where the system is an agent collocate with various kinds of failure such as 'not finding' or 'not coming up with' a search result. The grammatical patterning throughout the interview with this speaker construed the system as a passive tool. It was more often in the medium role in clauses than in the agent role. If we look at the social context of the knowledge management system, we see that this grammatical choice is echoed in the behaviour of the users in Organization X by their tendency to not use the system. The technologists termed the tendency of users to avoid using the system 'user resistance'. While the nominalization 'user resistance' positions the users as the locus of resistance, Text 3 contrastingly locates the system as resistant.

A previous study with the same data (Zappavigna-Lee et al. 2002) suggested that the ergative patterning of users and technologists in relation to the knowledge management system was very different and might be thought of as in misalignment. There was a general tendency in the users interviewed to cast themselves as an agent and the system as an inert medium. By way of contrast the IT professionals manifested the opposite tendency, instead of mostly casting the system as an agent.

There are very practical implications resulting from this difference in how the two groups construe the system. The tacit nature of the misalignment of perspectives about how 'active' the system is in the process of getting work done may mean that the two groups are unable to communicate their problems about the system with each other. If at a fundamental, below-view level they have differing semiotic models of what is going on, then refining the higher-level complexities of phenomena such as the nature of the ontology defining the entities in the system will be much more difficult to negotiate. The misalignment suggests that it may be useful to probe the nominalization 'user resistance' to understand how the technologists construe the users' tendency to avoid using the system. On the other hand we might probe the user's modality to better understand how we would know when a satisfying change has been made to the knowledge management system.

Table 3.16 Examples of 'I' as agent in Text 3

1	Whenever	I	type in a keyword
2		I	had better go an ask someone else
3		I	keyed in a word
4		I	don't tend to use System X
5	Because whenever	I	key in a word
6		I	might find something

Under-representation in Text 4

Text 4 is a facilitator talking about her work role (Table 3.17). As detailed earlier, facilitators performed the function in Service B of locating experts within the organization to answer engineering and project management questions. The questions were typically in the domain of construction engineering where expertise was widely distributed and often on different continents.

Text 4, as we will see, provides few obvious target sites for questions aimed at unpacking under-represented meaning about knowledge management. However it is included here as a reminder that, while under-representation occurs frequently in spoken discourse, not every instance of under-representation is always directly relevant to the aim of a particular interview, in other words not everything that a speaker says needs to be unpacked. Instead the interviewer should be selective about the instances that they choose to probe. For an interviewer familiar with a particular field it will be easier to avoid unnecessary probing. While the grammar-targeted questioning method is inherently portable and field-independent it still must be used with common sense[2] in mind.

Generalization and agency were not particularly prominent resources with which Text 4 condenses meaning about the knowledge management service. Thus the sections that follow treat only nominalization and modality.

Nominalisation in Text 4

The term 'facilitator', used to describe the interviewee's work role, is itself a nominalization, condensing what it means for 'someone to cause something

Table 3.17 Text 4, a facilitator talking about her role

Speaker	Talk
Facilitator	My role as a facilitator. There are a few components about that. One of them is, as questions come into System Y from the Americas, it is my responsibility to log the calls and find the person with the knowledge who can help the person out with the question or request for knowledge or insight or whatever they happen to be looking for. I also help Asia Pacific and Europe. We have a global handout sheet so it is my responsibility to check the handout sheet every day and help them find people in Americas who can help out with questions being asked in those two regions.
	So answering questions is one priority. Another is talking with people, going to project sites, getting the word out about System Y, because it is fairly new service that Organization X has implemented so it's still a big challenge just to communicate what it is and to talk to people, to get to talk to people one on one and trying to generate questions as well as talk to people.

to happen on behalf of someone else'. This nominalization is significant in the context of the organization as the people requiring help often came from different discourse communities, be they different areas of construction engineering or different countries. While 'facilitate' is a material process, negotiating the differences among these communities requires mental and verbal processes of understanding and communicating and where nominalization occurs in this text it is mostly packing up processes about such interpersonal negotiation (Table 3.18). For example, 'request for knowledge' condenses how the facilitator construes verbal processes of asking and responding to questions. It also condenses mental processes of knowing and determining who knows something and whether they know it well. The tendency of this facilitator in the overall interview towards using verbal processes when talking about her role represents an alignment between the professed aim of mediating between people as a facilitator and the patterns in her grammar.

Modality in Text 4

The modality in Text 4 is minimal and is generally about the potential of the 'sharer' to assist the 'seeker' (Table 3.19). Two instances of modality are embedded clauses with modal operators modifying the nominal group 'people'. The key attribute of 'people' is their potential to help, however, the characteristics which endow them with this capacity are elided. An interviewer might seek to pursue

Table 3.18 Examples of nominalization in Text 4

Nominalization	Process	Process type
Facilitator	To facilitate	Material
Questions	To question	Verbal
Responsibility	To be responsible for	Material
Request for knowledge	To request, to know	Verbal, mental
Insight	To see into	Mental
Handout	To hand out	Material
Service	To serve	Material
Challenge	To challenge	Mental

Table 3.19 Examples of modality in Text 4

Talk			Type of modality
...knowledge that	**can**	help the person out with the question	Obligation
...people who	**can**	help out with questions being asked ...	Obligation

under-representation about how a facilitator knows that someone is likely to be a useful sharer. It is likely that tacit knowledge or 'intuition' plays a role in finding a sharer quickly given the time constraints of the process and the geographical dispersion of potential sharers.

What can we learn from these patterns of under-representation?

The instances of under-represented grammar uncovered in the extracts in this field study have been highlighted to show the potential that probing might afford an interviewer. I have not undertaken a detailed reading of the texts as only small samples have been considered here. What such probing might reveal will be explored in the two chapters that follow. Having noticed under-represented features in an interview, there are a number of courses of action that may be taken by an analyst trying to understand the tacit meanings these features embody. Two of these are:

- To look for patterns of other under-represented grammatical features that contribute to the case being made for the current instance. This is the general principle in SFL of accounting for both local and global patterns.
- To seek a means of probing the particular instance itself. As transcribed text cannot talk, this requires human intervention! One strategy is to ask the subject targeted questions that unpack the grammatical feature of interest.

A possible objection to probing a user's talk is that people will often tell you things that bear little relation to how they actually behave (while maintaining vehemently that they do behave in a certain way). However, it is precisely for this reason that we look to their grammar both in deciding what to probe and in interpreting the unpacking. The field studies in the two chapters that follow leverage the value of the kind of linguistic analysis presented in the present chapter with the relative speed afforded by real-time questions in interviews.

Notes

1 We are bound, however, by the problem that no text occurs in a vacuum, and to this extent, all texts are influenced by the context in which they are produced.
2 Note that common sense refers to addressing a particular interview goal, not to applying a common-sense, folk model of language.

4

Whose Requirements? Tacit Knowledge in Requirements Analysis

Introduction

This chapter focuses on a form of tacit knowledge commonly found at the heart of technology projects: how to negotiate and translate meanings about the things people need to do with a system in light of the available technical resources. We might imagine a technologist embarking on the requirements analysis phase of a project enjoying the following line from the Rolling Stones:

> You can't always get what you want, but if you try, sometimes you might find, you get what you need.

The chapter presents the results of a field study conducted in an Australian media organization with a team of technologists working on a Content Management System (CMS) redevelopment project.[1] The study consisted of 4 months of interviews with these subjects by two independent interviewers: an experienced systems analyst,[2] who conducted content-targeted interviews, and an interviewer trained in the grammar-targeted interview method (described in Chapter 2).

The analysis presented here comprises both qualitative and quantitative dimensions. On the one hand we consider two corpora of transcribed interview texts, annotated for features of under-representation. These corpora contain the speakers' responses to the content-targeted interviews and the grammar-targeted interviews respectively. Statistical analysis of the annotated corpora was used to identify whether there was a statistically significant change in the language of the participants in relation to the interview method used. The essential question was whether the grammar-targeted interview method reduced the amount of under-representation in the texts, having unpacked key instances. Following on from this general statistical approach was more qualitative consideration of the meanings made in the interviews, with particular attention given to instances where tacit knowledge was revealed via unpacking under-representation. Thus, we are able to report on tacit knowledge in two ways: in terms of covert linguistic patterning that can be assessed quantitatively, and in terms of qualitative examples of particular instances of tacit meaning-making construed by the speakers.

Preamble: What is a 'requirement' in the technical discourse of IT professionals?

'Requirements analysis' is the technical term used within IT practice and research referring to the procedures that technologists undertake to understand what the users need to be able do within a business area in order to create technical systems that can support this work. The standard term for referring to the object of requirements analysis is a 'user requirement' or simply, a 'requirement'. The terms sit at the juncture between the experiential and the technical; between the users' work activity and the technical artefacts of developers and analysts. Halliday and Martin (1993) describe the way in which meanings are gradually packed-up in discourse as distillation. The technical discourse of requirements analysis has distilled this meaning in order to bridge the semiotic gap so that experiential meanings about user doing things can enter into their technical discourse about IT systems and their design (Figure 4.1). In the distillation shown the processes of 'a user needing to do something' has been nominalized and reconstrued as simply a 'requirement'.

In the distillation of 'a person needing to do something by using a system', the users, their needing and their ownership of their needing, as processes (though this is difficult to express without falling into nominalization ourselves), are gradually effaced. Figure 4.2 shows how the modifier of the thing shifts from a possessive to a classifier, and is then omitted. The resultant term, 'requirement', is ambiguous regarding just whose need is being referenced. It could be a 'system requirement', defined by the technology, or a 'user requirement', specified by the users. The present field study will detail the tacit nature of such semiotic reconstrual by the a technical project team, and point to examples were knowledge is under-represented by the types of grammatical choices that are

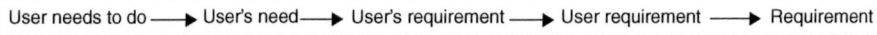

User needs to do ⟶ User's need ⟶ User's requirement ⟶ User requirement ⟶ Requirement

Figure 4.1 The distillation of a requirement in technical discourse.

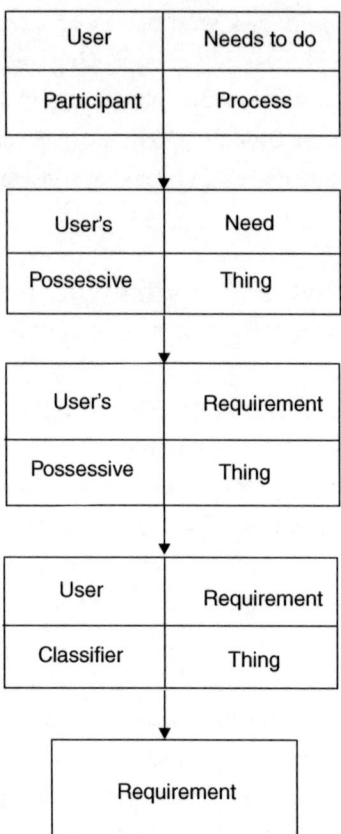

Figure 4.2 Analysis of the nominal groups in the distillation of 'user needs to do'.

made by the speakers. It will also discuss the consequences of assumptions about working with technology that are uncovered with the grammar-targeted interview method and the problems these assumptions can create.

The host organization

The host organization was a major broadcasting corporation in Australia. The study was conducted within its New Media division, an area of the firm producing systems used for generating and managing multimedia content. The subjects were working on a project to redevelop a CMS used by journalists and other content producers. CMS are systems for managing the processes involved in generating, syndicating, storing and publishing data and are commonly used to manage publishing process in the media.

An existing CMS had been in place for 5 years and, while it had been developed by an external consultant, was supported and maintained in-house. The project manager described the system as having reached 'technical end of life'. In light of this apparent technical demise, the project aimed to determine whether the existing system should be modified, a new system developed in-house or an external package purchased. The decision-making process was referred to as the 'make, buy or reuse' strategy. In order to come to a conclusion about what to do the project team gathered what they termed 'requirements' from stakeholders and users. As we will see in this chapter, talk about 'requirements' was a key area of tacit knowledge relating to how the team negotiated the endeavour of trying to understand the meanings made by the user community in relation to the potential system the technologists might produce.

The participants

The CMS project team consisted of four members: a project manager, an information architect and two individuals with software engineering experience, Technologists 1 and 2 (these participants are introduced in the section that follows). The team members have been working on the project for different durations, precipitating the problem of establishing common frames of reference. The project, however, has little reference material other than deliverables and business cases. The project manager himself acknowledged that he tends to assume a level of knowledge that might be incommensurable with the differing levels of familiarity with the project workings among team members. For example, Technologist 2 had been involved with an earlier phase of the project and recommenced work in the current phase after a long period elsewhere in the organization. Similarly, the information architect did not commence work on the project until a year after its inception.

The project manager responsible for the CMS project reported to the controller of Capital Projects, the project director and the project owner. He had several years experience working on technology projects in Australia and internationally. The main challenges he identified in his role were budget control and maintaining 'quality' both in light of the budget constraints and the opinions of stakeholders. Another key area of concern for this manager was 'knowledge transfer'. He claimed that despite regularly achieving apparent consensus in meetings, his team left the meetings with different understandings of what had been agreed and in general had problems in communication about the project status, documentation and deliverables. He found it challenging to assess whether his team had 'processed' descriptions of existing work and determining ways to reference verbal material was also an issue. The group intended to construct an intranet to assist in the dissemination of information among team members, however, this did not occur during the 4-month study.

The project employed two specialist technical professionals: Technologists 1 and 2 hereon. Technologist 1 had 10 years commercial experience in new media, ranging from the design of websites to complex knowledge management systems. During this time he had been a programmer and requirements engineer. His educational background was in instructional multimedia, focusing on graphic design, animation and video production. In terms of his current role on the project, Technologist 1 was in charge of analysing requirements from a technical perspective and managing the technical information needed by the project. The 'requirements analysis' which he undertook involved meetings for users to determine their technology needs. He believed himself to be a good communicator and thus enjoyed his interaction with users. The social aspect of this interaction provided a release from the relative isolation of writing code.

Technologist 2, with more experience in business analysis and who was undertaking an MBA, was more involved in the 'make-buy-reuse' decision analysis. He had commercial experience as a software designer and in generic web technologies. His educational background was a degree in law and an honours degree in critical and cultural theory and he believed that this interdisciplinary background both provided him with a better understanding of user and business concerns, and aided him in logical and statistical analysis.

Technologist 2 had been with the organization for 2 years during which he had worked quite closely with Technologist 1 whom he felt shared similar commercial experience despite a different academic background. He thus believed they have a good understanding of each other's perspectives. He felt that he probably has very different assumptions to the project manager and information architect due to the differences in their work experience. He believed it would be interesting to deal with an information architect who does not have an IT background.

Technologist 2 was involved in a precursor project to the CMS redevelopment but had not been involved in the inception or requirements analysis phase of the current project. As he had missed the first 9 months of the project, he had to familiarize himself with the existent documentation in order to gain an understanding of the project's current status. His main activities were working in the area of documenting the existing system. Technologist 2 also spent time responding to vendors' questions about the Expression of Interest document regarding the CMS that was released into the public domain.

The information architect was the most recent recruit to the project. She had a graphic design background and a liberal arts degree, giving her a different skillset to the other project members. The information architect described her main concern as the 'usability' of the system in terms of what the users 'want and need to do' in the system. Thus an important part of her role was attempting to specify a user interface that would meet the needs of this community as governed by discoveries made in the requirement analysis.

The interviewers

The two interviewers conducted blind interviews, that is, they were not aware of the content or nature of each other's interviews. The interviewer conducting the grammar-targeted interviews (hereon the grammar-targeted interviewer) was an Information Systems academic currently working in computational linguistics. Before becoming an academic he worked as an IT consultant. The interviewer also had a background in psychotherapy and hypnotherapy practice. While he was not a linguist by training, he had experience in linguistic analysis through his research in computational linguistics and pyschotherapy. The grammar-targeted interviewer was trained in the grammar-targeted interview protocol that was developed by the researcher (Appendix A). Due to his background in IT consulting he was familiar with conducting interviews with people in organizations.

The content-targeted interviews were conducted by an experienced systems analyst (hereon referred to as the content-targeted interviewer). He complemented his long and ongoing career in IT consulting with academic work in Information Systems. The interviewer was asked to draw upon this experience and to employ the interview strategies he would use as a consultant in the content-targeted interviews.

The interviews and data sampling

Both the content-targeted interviews and the grammar-targeted interviews covered the same topic areas so that the interviews could be meaningfully compared. Each interviewer was provided with the same written interview topic description before each interview (see Appendix B). There was no specific interview protocol for the content-targeted interviews other than the specification that the content-targeted interviewer should apply the interview technique that he has developed in his experience as a systems analyst and that he should follow the topic guide. The interview protocol used in the grammar-targeted interviews focused on unpacking features of under-representation and is provided in Appendix A.

Each subject was interviewed by each interviewer every month over 4 months, producing a total of 32 interviews. For a pair of interviews with a subject the first was conducted by the content-targeted interviewer and the second by the grammar-targeted interviewer within the next week. The interview types were not alternated. While alternation would reduce the effect of interview sequence in a traditional experiment,[3] in the present field study, with an object of study as complex as language, alternating would be unlikely to significantly minimize this effect because the interviews are texts unfolding over time rather than self-contained events. This means that discourse produced in the first interview will impact discourse produce in, for example, the fourth interview, even if the interviews were alternated. We do make some attempt to control for content from the first interview influencing content produced in the second interview by matching the topic areas in which questioning was to occur.

The grammar-targeted and content-targeted interviews were transcribed by the researcher and divided into clauses. A staggered sampling strategy was employed to reduce the impact of the logogenetic window selected. A sample of 150 clauses was selected from each interview: 50 clauses from the beginning, 50 clauses from the middle and 50 clauses from the end. Where the interview contained less than 150 clauses the entire interview was used. The 24 samples formed a total corpus of 3,096 clauses.

Annotation and statistical analysis of under-representation in the corpus

Five kinds of linguistic annotation were performed on the corpus of clauses conforming to the model of under-representation introduced in Chapter 2. The linguistic analysis was undertaken using Systemic Coder (O'Donnell 2002), a software tool that allows a user to code a corpus using system networks to represent the annotation schema. The program allows you to define a system network of features, segment your text into units and then apply the features in your system network to the units.

Given the focus of the analysis on grammatical patterning, for the purposes of this corpus annotation, the main unit of analysis was the clause. A clause corresponds to the folk notion of a simple sentence. For example, *I built*

Table 4.1 Linguistic annotation undertaken on the corpus

Linguistic analysis undertaken	Type of under-representation	Features of interest
Nominalization analysis	Type 1: Nominalization	Nominalized process
Modality analysis	Type 2: Modality	Finite modal operators, modal adjuncts
Generalization analysis	Type 3: Generalization	Abstract terminology, non-specific deictic and under-specification
Agency analysis	Type 4: Agency	Agents
Process type analysis	N/A	Processes

the system is a clause. A complex sentence can contain multiple clauses. For example, *I built the system and they didn't use it.* This sentence contains the additional clause *and they didn't use it.* Halliday (1994, p. 106) proposes that the clause is central in construing experience, claiming that 'it embodies a general principle for modelling experience – namely, the principle that reality is made up of PROCESSES'. A process might be thought of as the heart of the clause. In lay terms, a process is a verb, that is, something that happens such as 'eating', 'thinking', 'saying' and 'playing', or something that 'is' such as 'being' or 'existing'. Processes are important to this study as they are the common content that is made tacit by various lexicogrammatical con- structs such as nominalization. Within systemic functional grammar complexes of clauses are the highest-ranking unit in lexicogrammar, where rank refers to a hierarchy of units (Matthiessen 1997). Below is an example clause boundary analysis of an extract of the fourth grammar-targeted interview with Technologist 2. The | symbol is used to indicate a clause boundary. Each clause contains a process, that is, a verb of doing, being or sensing. These processes are identified in bold:

> I **think** | by **involving** them | you **would have** | they **would go back** to their various departments | they **would talk** about the process with their colleges | it **would be** a better way of informing the general user population of what processes we're going through | and they**'d feel more involved** | which I **think** | is very important | and I **think** | that kind of feeling **is** something that has been left out of this project.

Clauses may also be embedded. For example, consider the following clause:

> that kind of feeling **is** something [that **has been left out** of this project].

In this instance, the main process is 'is'. However the nominal group in this clause contains an embedded clause, marked with square brackets. This embedded clause modifies the 'something' to tell us the particular kind of something that it is.

We investigated the effect of interview type on the tendency of subjects to use under-representation in their interview responses. For each feature of under-representation we tabulated the level of that feature for each subject in each interview, working with a total of 3,096 clauses. We performed a repeated measures ANOVA, with the three rounds of interviews forming the repeated observations for each subject. Our interest was in determining the within-subjects effect. A repeated ANOVA was performed because the same subjects were interviewed multiple times (see Appendix C). We also wanted to account for the possibility that there will be a level of under-representation that varies according to the person rather than the interview type.

The below-view stratum of requirements analysis

The tacit dimension of requirements analysis activity on the CMS project, uncovered through grammar-targeted questioning, involved competing notions of what it means to need (realized in the technologist's discourse as 'requirements'), to organize ('systems'), to communicate ('knowledge transfer') and to act ('workflow'). These issues rarely competed explicitly and a large body of knowledge that the speakers had about these areas remained tacit.

As the speakers spoke about their work activity, the role their language played in rendering activities of the domain of experience into the domain of the technical became apparent. The experiential was tacitly reconstrued (Halliday 1998) as technical in their talk. To reconstrue is to ' "reconstruct semiotically": that is, replace one semiotic construction by another' (Halliday 1998: 185). This means that the speakers replaced a way of talking about what they were doing as 'experiences' with talking about what they were doing in terms of 'technical artefacts'. The knowledge about how to do this reconstrual was tacit for the speakers and it is the under-representation inherent in this type of reconstrual that the present chapter seeks to analyse.

The requirements analysis activity in which the team were involved was the central focus of the phase of the project that was analysed in this study. The team adopted a Rational Unified Process (RUP) methodology for managing this activity. While this methodology specified terminology that the team used when talking about requirements analysis, the terminology, as used by the technologists, contained many assumptions about both working with technology and working with people. Examples of these assumptions are given in this chapter, ordered by the type of under-representation to which they correspond. As the following sections elaborate, the assumptions were not in consistent alignment with the explicitly stated aims of the project team. In addition, the content-targeted interviews did not uncover this type of inconsistency, leaving most instances of under-representation uncontested.

Unpacking nominalization in the interviews

There was less nominalization in the speakers' responses to the grammar-targeted interview questions than the content-targeted interview questions (Figure 4.3). The results of the repeated measures ANOVA indicate that this difference was significant ($F(1,11) = 48.8$, $p < 0.001$). The result suggests that the grammar-targeted interview technique has successfully unpacked instances of nominalization. It will be shown that the more congruent discourse that has been generated in the grammar-targeted interview responses elaborates the tacit meanings that were embedded in such nominalizations.

The significant difference in the amount of nominalization between the two interview corpora indicates that the speakers are talking about their experience in different ways. The smaller amount of nominalization in the grammar-targeted interviews indicates that there are less instances of 'packed-up' meaning via this grammatical choice. Since the interviews covered the same topic areas,

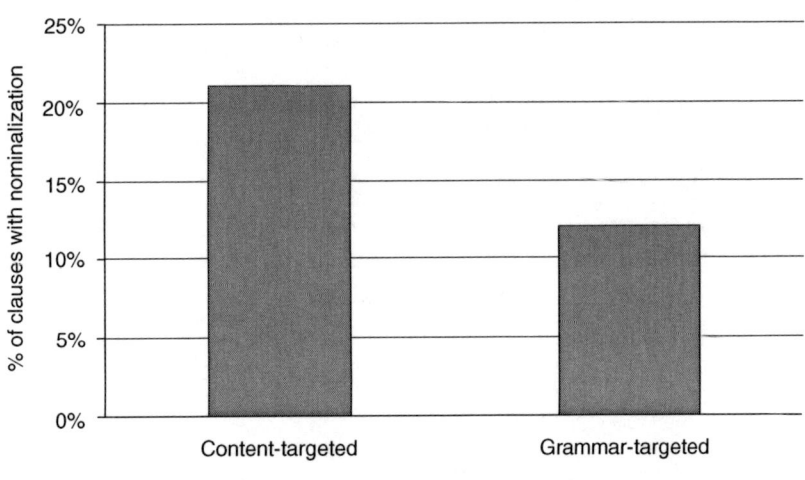

Figure 4.3 Comparing nominalization in the grammar-targeted and content-targeted interview styles.

the difference also suggests that the meanings embedded in nominalizations in the content-targeted interviews have been more often elaborated as congruent processes and participants in the grammar-targeted interviews. The more congruent discourse seen in the grammar-targeted interviews favours constructions of the following form:

participant + process

(e.g. We evaluated the vendors by interviewing them)

This choice was favoured over forms in which nominalized processes act as nominal groups causing or involved with other processes such as the following:

nominalized process + process

(e.g. Vendor evaluation resulted in various recommendations)

The two major kinds of nominalization present in the interviews were technical nominalization and managerial nominalization. Technical nominalization was nominal groups about artefacts and procedures to do with technical systems, and managerial nominalization was nominal groups about artefacts and procedures to do with managing phenomena in organizations (Table 4.2).

The following sections detail three examples of instances of nominalization that occurred in the content-targeted interviews that were unpacked in the grammar-targeted interviews:

- Nominalization 1 – *requirement*
- Nominalization 2 – *tracing* and *traceability*
- Nominalization 3 – *knowledge transfer*

Table 4.2 Examples of nominalization occurring in the content-targeted interviews that were unpacked in the grammar-targeted interviews

Nominalization type	Example
Technical nominalization	Non-functional requirements
	Vendor evaluation
	Open source solution
	Traceability model
	Requirements management plan
Managerial nominalization	Documentation
	Communication
	Knowledge
	Deliverables

Nominalization 1: Unpacking 'requirement'

The CMS team members all used 'requirement' in the interviews as a technical term central to their activity on the project. For example, in the fourth content-targeted interview, Technologist 2, responding to a question asking him to summarize the team's work, figures the work in terms of acting upon 'requirements' (Table 4.3). In this extract, 'requirements' are things that are subject to the technologists' processes of 'gathering' and 'signing off' and have attributes that suggest when they are 'ready to go'. The term 'requirement' was, however, undefined in the project glossary. The absence of the term in the glossary suggests that the team members consider it part of their everyday discourse rather than a term necessitating precise definition. Hence 'requirement', as a concept seems covertly to have moved from the technical realm of defined terminology in the project to the experiential realm of tacit knowledge. It forms part of the habitus[4] in which the team resides.

References[5] to 'requirements' pervade all the content-targeted interviews with the four subjects, both in cases such as the above where they are mentioned as part of a project summary, and cases were specific details about the system are being explained. Because the terms appear part of the project habitus and the larger context of IT discourse in general, into which the content-targeted interviewer himself was socialized, the term at no stage in the content-targeted interviews is questioned by the interviewer or elaborated by the speakers.

By way of contrast, the grammar-targeted interviews situate the term 'requirements' as a definite locus of inquiry. The term is probed through questions of the type:

What does it mean to (process e.g. 'do') X?

The speakers responded with their particular construal of 'doing X', where participants, often camouflaged agents, and embedded processes were uncovered

Table 4.3 Technologist 2, Content-targeted Interview 4

Turn	Speaker	Talk
1	Content-targeted interviewer	So, Technologist 2, we start off with a very standard question: summary of the project in your opinion. So what has happened so far?
2	Technologist 2	What's happened so far? Well, we have gathered requirements to an initial sort of point that have been signed off and are sort of ready to go.

(e.g. Table 4.4). There was typically a shift in construal when a grammar-targeted question was used, with the speakers rendering concepts from the technical domain into the experiential domain. This might be thought of as reversing the type of 'reconstrual' introduced in Preamble: What is a 'requirement' in the technical discourse of IT pr. The reconstrual was made grammatically by a move from nominalization to configurations of processes, participants and

Table 4.4 Unpacking 'requirement', Technologist 1, Grammar-targeted Interview 3

Turn	Speaker	Talk
1	Interviewer	To, to move onto requirements which is a lot of what this is about? What's your understanding of the differences between a requirement and a feature?
2	Technologist 1	A requirement is a capability of the system. A feature I think is, is more what the system must do in order to fulfil a need. So requirement can be a feature, it can be a need, it can be – let's see what else could it be – a problem. That kind of thing as well as a requirement to me is an overall desire I guess pretty much.
3	Interviewer	So it's any type of description about what you want the system to do?
4	Technologist 1	Yes.
5	Interviewer	So, so what's a use case compared to a requirement and a feature?
6	Technologist 1	A use case more is how the, well how a feature works or part of a feature. So it's essentially, to me it's a scenario. You start at one point and you get to an endpoint and then you've got deviations in that, in that path. So that, that to me is a use case and a feature really is the, is more, just, just what the system should do but it doesn't contain how it should do it and that where the use case comes into, into play.
7	Interviewer	Right, so what's the difference between a requirement and a request?
8	Technologist 1	Well to me, as I said, a requirement is an overriding thing so it is a request. Sorry, a request is a requirement. I mean, going into a more detailed level, from what I can see there's a request and then there's a problem which is 'I want to be able to drink my cup of coffee'. My problem is that I have hardly any coffee left so my need is to, I need to go and make some coffee and that kind of thing so that's a more. A request is just, to me, something that someone wants pretty much so it doesn't necessarily mean that it's, it's what they need. Because I don't think I need another cup of coffee! [laughs]

circumstances. This means that rather than under-representing concepts as nouns, a convenient shorthand for encapsulating technical processes, the subject construes them as actual happenings involving entities acting upon other entities. For example, when the grammar-targeted interviewer asks Technologist 1 to explain his use of the term 'requirement' the subject begins his response with the following construction:

requirement + relational process + nominalization

(e.g. requirement + is + a capability of the system)

However, after probing of the speaker's grammar by the interviewer there is a shift to the following construction:

requirement + relational process + embedded clause

(e.g. There's a problem which + is + I want to be able to drink my cup of coffee)

The embedded clause 'I want to be able to drink my cup of coffee' elaborates the agent ('I') and processes ('wanting', 'being able to' etc.) packed up in the nominalization in the previous example (Table 4.4, Turns 2 and 8). In this instance the unpacking is metaphorical. The speaker places himself in the position of the user and employs the example of making a cup of coffee as an analogy for a user needing a system to perform a function. In subsequent unpacking of this type in the interview, we discover that the subject believes that a user wanting something does not necessarily equate to their needing it. The general shift in language that occurs as the under-representation is unpacked in grammar-targeted interview 3 with Technologist 1 may be represented on a continuum of experientiality and technicality (Figure 4.4). The 'experiential' end of the continuum is that of events involving actors. Grammatically, it is populated by processes, participants and circumstances. The 'technical' end of the continuum is increasingly characterized by semiotic artefacts and abstractions.

These artefacts are rendered grammatically through nominalizations and generalizations. Halliday and Matthiessen have noted this kind of movement away from meaning experiential that is at the heart of generating technicality:

Almost all technical terms start out as grammatical metaphors; but they are grammatical metaphors which can no longer be unpacked. When a wording becomes technicalised, a new meaning has been construed – almost always, in our present-day construction of knowledge, a new thing (participating entity); and the junction with any more congruent agnates is (more or less quickly) dissolved. (Halliday and Matthiessen 1999: 286)

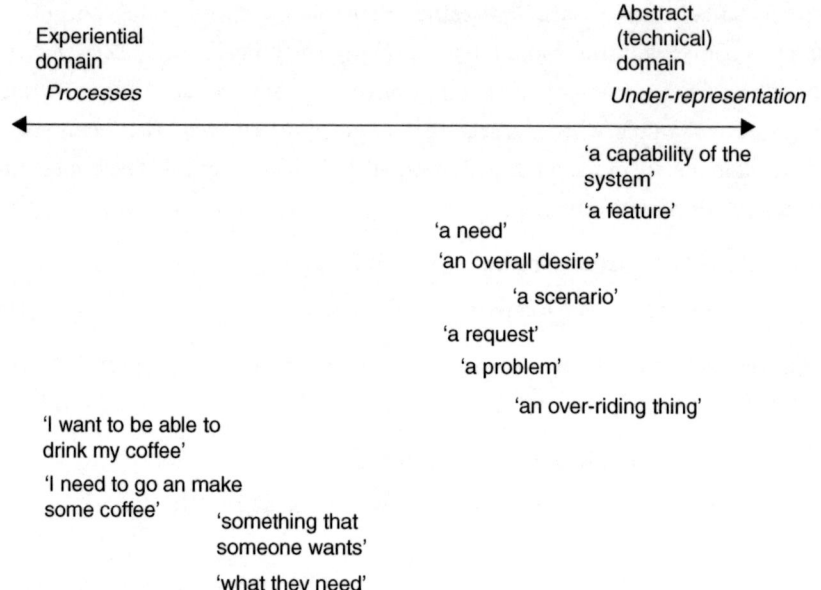

Figure 4.4 Locating a description of 'requirement' on the experiential-technical continuum [Technologist 1, grammar-targeted interview 3].

It is in this act of dissolution that tacit knowledge is produced. While the meaning 'cannot be unpacked' in the discourse itself, that is, we cannot directly retrieve the tacit knowledge without considering co-textual patterns, we can unwind the process and retrieve the 'more congruent agnates' by asking questions that probe the grammatical metaphor as we will see in the further examples on grammatical probing of interviewee's talk explored in this chapter.

In contrast to the grammar-targeted interviews, the term 'requirement' was not deconstructed in the content-targeted interviews. For example, when the information architect uses this nominalization to make claims about the extent to which her analysis accounts for 'what the users need to do with the system', the interviewer does not seek additional description about what this means (Table 4.5). The term 'requirement' is, in this instance, taken for granted as a shorthand for talking about meeting these needs. While on the one hand such shorthand reference is a useful and necessary semiotic resource for the technologists, it may camouflage ways of thinking about the users that are less than optimal. These include trying to contort the descriptions made by the users to fit the 'system requirements' rather than adjusting the system specifications accordingly.

Table 4.5 Information architect, Content-targeted Interview 3

Turn	Speaker	Talk
1	Information architect	We've got a lot clearer understanding of our requirements now. We were in the process of gathering requirements and analysing them when we started, so now I'm very confident in the requirements that we've got and I believe that it fulfills the needs, I think …
2	Interviewer	OK. [changes topic]

The notion of a 'requirement' was also embedded in nominal group complexes. One such nominal group complex was 'requirements management plan'. This was a document developed by the CMS team to assist them with the requirements analysis phase of the project. It is defined in the CMS glossary as follows:

Requirements Management Plan

Describes the documents, requirement types, and attributes; and information and control mechanisms for measuring, reporting, and controlling changes to the software requirements.

The definition of the plan makes no reference to users. Instead the classifier 'software' is applied to the headword suggesting that the requirements 'belong' to the technology. As this glossary definition is intended to be the definition upon which the group as a whole agrees, the implication is that the group agrees that users are not participants not involved in the process of understanding requirements. This is unproblematic in the sense that the users do not make the plan or contribute directly to the management of the requirements analysis, however, it is deeply problematic in the sense that understanding the users' description of what they want/need the system to do is the aim of managing the 'requirements' in the first place. Thus, failing to mention the users in the definition is a failure to specify the goal of the plan.

The nominalization 'requirements management plan' is shown in its most congruent form in Figure 4.5. Packed-up are a series of ideas that remain tacit because they are under-represented in the form of nominalizations (Figure 4.5). The processes under-represented include the following (with strategic areas of organizational management upon which they have the potential to impact are included in brackets):

- Who are the people who need something? (User base of the system)
- What is the something that the people need? (User satisfaction)

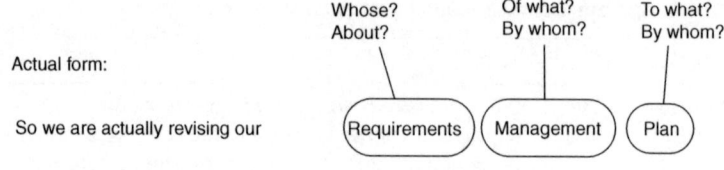

Figure 4.5 Unpacking the nominalization 'requirements management plan' in Clause A.

- Who are the people managing? (Resource allocation)
- Who or what is the thing being managed by the people doing the managing? (Domain specification)
- Who is doing the planning? (Resource allocation)
- What is the plan about? (Project goals)

As this list suggests, while what is under-represented may at first appear trivial, the strategic areas of the project upon which they impact are anything but inconsequential.

What kind of tacit knowledge about 'requirements' was unpacked?

The tacit knowledge about 'requirements' that was unpacked via the grammar-targeted questioning technique is summarized in Table 4.6. The sections which follow treat each instance in turn.

Instance 1: Requirements are aligned as attributes of the system

The question of whether a 'requirement' is mental process undertaken by a user or an attribute of a system remained tacit in the content-targeted interview because the nominalization remained unpacked. It was unclear whether it meant the things that the people using the system would need to be able to do, or the attributes that the developers wanted the system to have. The former construction, 'requirement as a need performed by a user' involves a mental process of needing where the 'user' is the senser and agent (Table 4.7).

Here the developers need to understand the user's perspective. The latter construction, 'requirement as an attribute of the system' is an identifying relational process where the system has particular qualities that the developers inscribe upon it (Table 4.8).

Table 4.6 Tacit knowledge explicated in the grammar-targeted interviews and corresponding grammatical evidence for the item 'requirements'

Tacit knowledge	Grammatical evidence
1. Requirements are aligned as attributes of the system	– Large proportion of agency assigned to technical artefacts – Small proportion of agency assigned to users – Clauses containing relational identifying processes where a 'requirement' is the token and an aspect of the system is the value
2. Requirements are constructed as things rather than processes	– Nominalization of the concept that a user needs to do something. – Technical artefacts rather than mental processes of 'needing' are unpacked from the nominalization 'requirement'
3. There is a problematic relationship between requirements and requests	– Both processes of 'needing' and 'wanting' are unpacked from the nominalization 'requirement'

Table 4.7 Transitivity analysis of 'The user needs the system'

The user	needs	the system
Senser	Mental process	Phenomenon

Table 4.8 Transitivity analysis of 'A requirement is a capability of the system'

A requirement	is	a capability of the system
Token	Relational process	Value

For example, there were many instances in the interviews where requirements are defined by the interviewees as being attributes of the system rather than properties that the users need (see Appendix E). The technologist often located a 'requirement' as part of the system rather as something owned by the users. For example the project manager classifies a 'requirement' as 'a functional or non-functional aspect of the system' (Table E3 in Appendix E). After the project manager has defined 'requirement' in this way, the interviewer seeks to distinguish the speaker's use of the term from the technical term 'user requirement'. The latter term positions the 'user' as the classifier and 'requirement' as a thing in the nominal group. However, the project manager claims that 'user requirement' is not a term he uses and that, if he were to use the term, it would either constitute a separate entity or be a subset of 'requirement'. This distinction seems to

Table 4.9 Unpacking of 'requirement' in Grammar-targeted Interview 4

1	A feature was functional	**requirement**	of the system
2	A	**requirement**	is a capability of the system
3	In the RUP you end up with your	**requirements**	document which is your use cases and your supplementary specifications
4	And then I suppose the implementation of each	**requirement**	in the software project
5	A	**requirement**	is a, a functional or non-functional aspect of the system, aspect that must be performed by the system

suggest that the project manager tacitly construes 'requirements' as things more closely aligned with the technical demands of the system than to the human demands of the users. The implications of this type of grammatical choice is that the technologists may focus less of their attention on understanding the users because they perceive 'requirements' as so closely aligned with the system that they talk about them, as we have seen, as if they were part of the system.

At the level of content, these distinctions might seem arbitrary. However, the grammar has important implications for how the activity of attempting to decide how to satisfy the users' request for an improved CMS is addressed by the project team. Making the speakers aware of the way they are talking about 'requirements' will allow them to consciously reflect upon these implications. In other words, it will allow them to decide whether they are talking about 'user requirements' or 'systems requirements'. If the users are not adequately consulted, the system that is developed is likely not to be useful to them. In this way, grammatical choices that point to a less than optimal focus on the users are likely to be early warning signs of project pitfalls.

Instance 2: Requirements are constructed as 'things' rather than processes

The speakers consistently made the grammatical choice to construct 'requirements' as 'things', although each speaker's specific construal was idiosyncratic. The speakers' use of the term manifests many of the characteristics of Reddy's (1979) notion of the conduit metaphor, introduced in Chapter 2. 'Requirements' are specimens inside which the users' needs reside and upon which the technologists act. Table D1 in Appendix D details the processes occurring in clauses about 'requirements' and whether, in these instances, the 'requirement' was an agent or a medium. As this table shows, 'requirements' typically occupied the participant role of medium rather than the role of agent. As such, they were things that were acted upon by the technologists, rather than things that caused action to occur. In some cases 'requirements' were constructed as the evasive 'other', almost enemies of the technologists that had to be subdued. For example, in grammar-targeted interview 4 the project manager talks about 'the way that requirements would be captured' (emphasis added). In this clause the 'requirements' are the goal of a material process often used to describe seizing a prisoner (capturing). Later it is shown that this representation points to potential difficulties.

Instance 3: *The problematic relationship between 'requirements and 'requests'*

One of the team members, the information architect, in elaborating 'requirements', raised the issue of the difference between a 'requirement' and a 'request'. The subject was flagging what can be considered a parallel nominalization to that of a 'requirement', that is, the nominalization of the process of 'someone wanting to do something' (Figure 4.6). In fact, the contemporary term 'requirement' derives from the verb 'require' which has its origins in the Latin 'seek to know, ask' the sense of which we now find in the word 'request' (Harper 2001).

The information architect was the only subject to explicitly identify that there was a difference between a 'requirement' and a 'request' in the first round of interviews (Table 4.10). In response to grammar-targeted questions by the interviewer, she produced answers where she suggested that this difference had implications for the kind of processes the team should adopt in understanding 'what the users need to do with the system'. She indicated that while the other team members had acknowledged her position about the difference between a 'requirement' and a 'request', this had not necessarily changed their practices. An explanation for this is that these speakers held an understanding of 'requirements' was tacit, while the information architect had explicit awareness of the problem.

Correspondingly, the team members' practice could only change when they addressed the tacit assumptions manifest in their language. Approaching 'requirements analysis' in terms of 'what the user's want' rather than 'what the

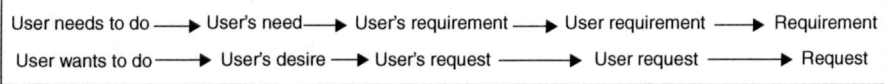

Figure 4.6 The distillation of a requirement and a request in technical discourse.

Table 4.10 Unpacking, 'requirement', information architect, Grammar-targeted Interview 1

Turn	Speaker	Talk
1	Information architect	Well, I, the others will disagree with this but I believe that we have literally just asked the stakeholders 'what do you want?' So and we haven't done enough analysis of that. We haven't worked out what do they need as opposed to what do they want
2	Interviewer	So your user investigations are not attempting to establish requirements?
3	Information architect	Yes they are
4	Interviewer	So where do they fit with this stakeholder request document?
5	Information architect	They're going to feed into it. So we're actually revising our requirements management plan

user's need' is easier as the latter perspective requires an additional layer of analysis. However, failing to understand 'need' represents a failure to prioritize the various aspects of the system that may be implemented. It is thus more likely, that if the technologists are conflating 'user requirements' and 'user requests' that they will create a system that does not optimally distinguish between 'requirements' that are critical and those that are optional.

The IT consequences of the tacit knowledge unpacked from the nominalization 'requirement'

Construing 'requirement' as an attribute or aspect of the system means that the project team are more vulnerable to perpetuating a technocratic perspective on requirements analysis. This type of approach to system development focuses on the attributes of the system rather than fulfillment of human needs as the goal of requirements analysis activity. As such, it is unlikely to produce a system that is optimally aligned with those human needs. Similarly the construal of 'requirements' as things rather than processes, while useful in the sense that they are more readily ported to abstract models, means that the requirements analysis becomes more focused upon stable technical artefacts rather than dynamic human processes. In addition, the conflation of 'requirements' and 'request' means that there may be confusion over which parts of the users' descriptions are critical and which reflect desires for the system that are optional. Confusing the two is likely to be an expensive exercise if a critical component is overlooked in the place of an optional component.

Nominalization 2: Unpacking 'tracing' and 'traceability'

The previous sections have dealt with the speakers' understanding of the technical artefact 'requirement'. We now address the process in which these artefacts are embedded: the activity of performing 'requirements analysis'. The speakers employed the nominalization 'traceability' to describe the potential of a technical artefact to enter into a relationship with another artefact in requirements analysis. They referred to establishing relationships between artefacts as 'tracing'. The way the speakers use the term 'tracing' makes and restricts various subject positions, that is, potential roles that people or things may occupy in requirements analysis. The nominalization 'traceability' assumes that 'something or someone can trace something to something or someone'. This section will discuss the ways in which the subject position of the user is marginalized by the language the technologists use.

Construing the user's opinions as objects in 'tracing'

The speakers used the terms 'tracing' in both the grammar-targeted and content-targeted interviews, however, it was only in the former that the interviewer asked what the speakers meant by the term. The nominalization was probed by questions such as:

What does it mean that X traces to Y?

or

What does tracing mean for you?

In the fourth grammar-targeted interview with Technologist 1 the subject revealed that tracing for him involved an interpersonal activity of 'taking someone's thoughts and concepts' (Table 4.11, Turn 2). The subject initially claims that he does not know how he performs this activity. However, with probing from the grammar-targeted interviewer he is able to elaborate this as an activity involving processes of recording, listening, trying to work out, concentrating, taking, pausing and doing (Table 4.12). Despite the interpersonal character of these processes, probing the grammatical choices that the technologist made suggested that he views the process of 'understanding the ideas and opinions of users' as a process of extracting a tangible artefact. This is seen in his choice of the material process 'taking' in 'taking people's thoughts and concepts' rather than a mental process of understanding (2).

Table 4.11 Unpacking 'tracing', Technologist 1, Grammar-targeted Interview 4, Part 1

Turn	Speaker	Talk
1	Interviewer	I remember in an earlier meeting we had you talked a lot about tracing. I'm just interested to know what you understand by tracing now because you've got that perspective of all of the work you have done over a period of time.
2	Technologist 1	I think for us now that we have got to the use case level it's, I mean, for me tracing has always, as you've mentioned, it's very important to me because I want to take what someone has mentioned in the first beginning and make sure that it gets delivered in various, in whatever form it needs to get in, in the product. So tracing would be to me taking someone's thoughts and concepts and making sure that those thoughts and concepts were translated through every step of the requirements.

Table 4.12 Unpacking 'tracing', Technologist 1, Grammar-targeted Interview 4, Part 2

Turn	Speaker	Talk
3	Interviewer	How do you 'take people's thoughts and concepts'?
4	Technologist 1	Good question. I don't know.
5	Interviewer	It seems fundamental to your requirements management plan.
6	Technologist 1	Yeah it is. I mean, I've done a similar thing to you where I've recorded interviews and so I've found that actually really valuable because what, when, when I'm listening to someone and asking them things I'm not necessarily, well I'm trying to work out exactly how to do that but I don't want to concentrate on how to do that at, at that point and so by recording it I'm able to do that later on so taking what someone says then and recording it and then listening to it afterwards and trying to like pause it at a certain point and working out the various things that you can do in that concept there and that's, that's the kind of knowledge transfer that I've had between the person and us.
7	Interviewer	So that's your, that's your collection process. Then how from the point at which you have collected it, how do you then place that into the communal space so that it's available to everyone communally and they can use it?
8	Technologist 1	We've put that on a network drive so, all those, all those interviews are available essentially on the intranet.

However, the activity of 'finding out' something from the user is rendered as an act of possession. As the subject elaborates his meaning, 'what someone says', that is, the object of his practice, becomes an 'it' that is the medium of processes of recording, listening and pausing. The interviewer takes up the speaker's use of 'it' and asks how the 'it' can be shared. The subject responds by saying that they have 'put that on a network drive'. The assumption in the grammar here is that a person's 'thoughts and concepts' can be 'taken' and 'put' on a technology platform as if they are objects which do not require interpretation. This assumption reduces the level of critical analysis that the technologists are likely to apply to the statements the users make about their requirements and, in turn, reducing the likelihood that the system built will effectively address those statements.

If we move from this instance-level perspective to look at how the participants construe 'tracing' across the corpus, we see that there is systematicity to their construal that suggests a way of thinking about tracing that is tacit in their talk. The majority of the processes used in place of 'tracing' were material processes that are metaphorically relational (Table I.1 in Appendix I). The 'materiality' of these processes suggest action in the physical world but their metaphorical 'relationality' signals the part that they play in the construction of the high-level technical abstractions of requirement analysis. For example, consider the process 'to cover'. In its material sense 'to cover' means to physically lay one thing over another, as in the following:

'I covered my eyes with my hands.'

The meaning is, however, relational when 'cover' is used as follows:

'It really means that one requirement artefact covers off or covers the scope of the one it is tracing to.'

In this second example from the project manager's discourse, the meaning of 'cover' is to do with one participant 'dealing with' or 'addressing' the other. This is relational in the sense that it is about an abstract relationship rather than a tangible action: the 'requirement' does not literally place itself over the scope. Such construction of users' opinions as things (Table 29–1) and use of metaphorical relational processes to talk about 'tracing' appear to be part of the way the project team's grammar operates to solidify their analytical approach. By tacitly rendering the perspective of the users as passive objects they provide themselves with stable artefacts to act upon. Alternative ways of approaching the same activity would be to render the user's opinions as dynamic or fluid.

Talking in this way would involve a different grammatical patterning. Instead of relational processes of abstraction, mental and verbal processes of negotiation would dominate.

The privileging of this 'relationality' seems to be part of the way the technologists maintain power in requirements analysis. In fact, the information architect acknowledges the importance of processes of justification in the team's work practice (Table 4.13). In this extract it appears that the needs of the users are the primary focus of the decision making as she repeats the term 'need', however, if we look at the way she talks about 'tracing' the picture becomes more complex. For example, the information architect refers to the importance of being able to 'map' stakeholder needs to features, however, the way she attributes minimal agency to the users in her grammar effaces the ownership that users and stakeholders have of their requirements.

Tracing is about being able to justify requirements analysis decisions

The information architect acknowledged explicitly that traceability is about the team being able to justify their requirements analysis decisions (Table 4.14). In fact, if we look at the grammar that the team members used to talk about 'tracing', it confirms that 'tracing' is about justifying the relationship of technical

Table 4.13 Unpacking 'tracing', information architect, Grammar-targeted Interview 3

Turn	Speaker	Talk
1	Interviewer	In our try in our attempt to understand the processes going on here, there is one expression that comes up quite a lot which is tracing. What do you understand by tracing?
2	Information architect	I guess it goes back to that derivative requirements. Basically if a requirement is derivative of another requirement, you need to know exactly, you know, where it derives from. That's how I understand tracing.
3	Interviewer	So what does tracing express?
4	Information architect	It expresses the. I don't know how to express it further. [laughs] Well, I suppose it traces back to the source in the end.
5	Interviewer	So traces what to the source?
6	Information architect	A requirement, a derivative requirement to an original requirement.
7	Interviewer	A requirement. OK, so it doesn't, it doesn't then trace an original requirement to a user request?
8	Information architect	An original requirement is a user request.

Table 4.14 Unpacking 'tracing', Part 2, information architect, Grammar-targeted Interview 2

Turn	Speaker	Talk
1	Information architect	The use cases have just been formulated but they are still being formulated. So it's been the feature list and the non-functional requirements which kind of occupy a space in the supplementary specifications.
2	Interviewer	So how is that different? I don't understand the difference.
3	Information architect	The difference between?
4	Interviewer	Between using a model for decision making and using that model for decision making.
5	Information architect	It's just the traceability. That's all.
6	Interviewer	So it's all about how you are able to justify your decision.
7	Information architect	Yeah, that's right, that's right.

artefacts. The team refer to 'tracing' at the surface or overt level as if it is a material action but use processes that are, from a subsurface or metaphorical perspective, relational: in simple terms they dress up the inactive as active. The construction of users' opinions as things and use of metaphorically relational processes to talk about 'tracing' is part of the way the project team's grammar operates tacitly to solidify their analytical approach. It is part of their genuinely held belief that they are engaging in work activity that is analytical and rigorous. By tacitly rendering the perspective of the users as objects they provide themselves with stable artefacts to manipulate.

The consequences of thinking about 'tracing' in this way are that the masking of relationality as materiality allow the team to avoid negotiation with the users and stakeholders over requirements. The privileging of 'relationality' seems to be part of the way the technologists maintain power in requirements analysis. It allows them to pay 'lip-service' to interpersonal negotiation with the users while effacing the role of users in requirements analysis. On a practical level this was seen by the way the project team involved only a small group of a large population of users in their analysis, that is 5 out of a total of 500.

Figure 4.7 shows how the team conceive of tracing as a binary mapping between 'requests' and 'features' of the system. However, as this figure visualizes, these artefacts occupy different domains of meaning-making. Alternative ways of approaching the activity of tracing would be to render the user's opinions

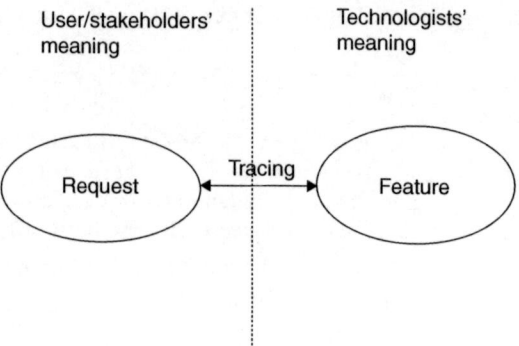

Figure 4.7 Tracing between two kinds of meaning.

as dynamic or fluid. Instead of relational processes of abstraction, this would necessitate mental and verbal processes of negotiation.

The IT consequences of the tacit knowledge unpacked from the nominalization 'tracing'

The technologists construed the users' opinions as objects that could be inserted into various technological 'boxes'. This reduces the level of critical analysis that the technologists are likely to apply to the statements the users make about their requirements and, in turn, reduces the likelihood that the built system will effectively address those statements. Similarly, the technologists construed 'tracing' as about being able to justify requirements analysis decisions through relational processes of abstraction rather than material processes of action. This grammatical signalling of a tendency towards inaction is likely to reflect a project that will exceed its budget in terms of time and hence costs.

Nominalization 3: Unpacking 'knowledge transfer'

The nominalization 'knowledge transfer' occurred in the content-targeted interviews when the speakers were talking about how they shared ideas in the project team. This is one instance where the content-targeted interviewer does attempt to unpack a nominalization in the second interview with the project manager (Table F.1 in Appendix F). The interviewer asks the following question:

> How is, sorry, what is being transferred amongst team members and how it is being transferred?

The project manager begins his response with an anaphoric reference to 'it'. Most likely the reference is to 'knowledge transfer' in the question in Turn 1. The reference could also be to the 'what' in the 'what is being transferred' or the 'how' in the 'how is it being transferred?'. The interviewer has adopted a passive construction in these last two questions so the agent doing the transferring is undefined, as is the person to whom the transfer is being made. Such ambiguity prompts the project manager to clarify the agent himself in the questions in Turns 2, 4 and 6.

As the discourse hinges on this under-represented 'it' the utility of the project manager's description is questionable. Further under-representations in the response compound the problem. For example, the project manager describes the 'it' as potentially being 'better'. The question of 'better than whom or what' is left under-represented. The issues that prevent this betterment are in turn under-represented. The project manager then proceeds to discuss the processes involved in updating the stakeholders on the knowledge that the project team have produced. This precipitates further under-representation through generalization and nominalization (e.g. 'stuff', 'features', 'non-functional requirements', 'use case model', 'task analysis', 'project governance', etc.).

The corresponding phase discussing how knowledge is transferred in the project in the grammar-targeted interview begins in a similarly general manner to the content-targeted interview (Table 4.15). However, the interviewer goes on to probe the grammar of the speaker's response to hone in upon specific issues. For example, the grammar-targeted interviewer tries to unpack what the subject means by 'discussing' as a way of understanding how he transfers knowledge (Turn 5). Turn 4 reveals the central position that the nominalization 'requirements', already unpacked in Nominalisation 1: Unpacking 'requirement', holds in how this subject construes communicating with the stakeholders. This is an example of the way key under-representations often intersect. The task of the grammar-targeted interviewer is to identify these key under-representations as efficiently as possible. As the section which follows will elaborate, the project manager's construal of 'knowledge transfer' centres upon the nominalization, 'clarity', as he explains his understanding of when he knows that he has 'made something clear' to someone else.

'Clarity' is a tangible commodity that can be exchanged

The nominalization 'clarity' is central to the way that the project manager conceives 'knowledge transfer'. The project manager indicates that the questioning strategy that is part of his notion of 'discussing' is below-view in the sense that

Table 4.15 Unpacking 'knowledge transfer', project manager, Grammar-targeted Interview 2

Turn	Speaker	Talk
1	Interviewer	What other things have you been doing on the project, on the CMS project?
2	Project manager	On the CMS project. I have been, I have been discussing with the IT stakeholders and the New Media stakeholders getting them, pre-briefing them on some of the aspects of the, the evaluation that we've done and trying to elicit their real needs in terms of selection criteria that they may have which they is in there minds but is at this stage at this point a little undocumented.
3	Interviewer	So this is what discovering hidden, unexposed materials that you think are relevant to decision making?
4	Project manager	Yeah, well I think they're just requirements that they have. They are quite high-level business requirements and but they're requirements that they may not usually need to voice because they're because they they're not there is no conflict and they just usually are met by the way that they go about their business but in this particular instance where there needs to be a decision made in terms of spending, you know, a reasonable amount of money to, to make an investment in a vendor package or go down the open source route. Where there is now conflict. I think those issues need to come to the surface and be discussed. So I've just been trying to work out exactly what they are.
5	Interviewer	Ok, how do you actually go about doing that? I mean you have said discussing. But what does discussing actually entail?
6	Project manager	I ask questions about what they're, you know, what they're really trying to achieve or why they have reservations about going down a particular route and just try and get to the route cause of why they think the particular scenario that they have in mind is appropriate and why they, what had led them to believe that is the appropriate scenario.
7	Interviewer	Do you know anything about that questioning strategy that you use to do that? Or is it all automatic?
8	Project manager	No it's all automatic.

it is 'automatic' (Turn 8, Table 4.15). Having established that the subject is not directly aware of how he achieves consensus among stakeholders, the interviewer proceeds to unpack this idea in more detail (Table 4.16). The subject reveals that the mechanism by which he determines the stakeholders' perspectives involves establishing 'clarity'. The interviewer begins to unpack this by probing for the participants associated with obtaining 'clarity' (Turn 3, Table 4.17).

Table 4.16 Unpacking 'clarity', project manager, Grammar-targeted Interview 2

Turn	Speaker	Talk
1	Interviewer	So all of this is oriented around arriving at your selection criteria?
2	Project manager	Yes all of this is about trying to, trying to just get some clarity around both people's perspective because at the moment they're, they're not aware of each other's perspective and they and I think they would both have their own view.
3	Interviewer	So who is it that then needs the clarity?
4	Project manager	Well I'd like to bring them just to get the views debated and to the surface so that they could be properly appraised by the steering committee and the project owner and the project director so that they have all the information in, in front of them basically.
5	Interviewer	Ok so who needs the clarity?
6	Project manager	Ultimately, the project director and the project owner.

Table 4.17 Unpacking 'clarity', Part 2, project manager, Grammar-targeted Interview 2

Turn	Speaker	Talk
1	Interviewer	So what is the event that tells you that clarity has been reached?
2	Project manager	I don't know if you could ever say that ultimate clarity has ever been reached. You, we would just be attempting to get more clarity than we had but the, the event that would tell you that clarity has been reached is that you have a set of selection criteria which you think covers all the arguments that have been raised.
3	Interviewer	Who's the you you've been talking about?
4	Project manager	Myself.
5	Interviewer	Right so you're the one who needs the clarity.
6	Project manager	No, I'm attempting to find the clarity to provide to somebody else.
7	Interviewer	Ok, so clarity is something you give someone else?
8	Project manager	Um clarity is something you give somebody else. Clarity is something that you try and uncover I guess, and, I mean, I'm just trying to make things clear so that people understand the issues, and I've got, I don't think it's clear at the moment, and I'll have a gut feeling as to when I think it is.
9	Interviewer	Ok, ok, right. So your criteria for having sufficient clarity is your gut feeling?
10	Project manager	I would thinks so.

As the probing for these participants continues the project manager uses the following construction:

Agent ('I')+ mental process

(I'm attempting to find) + participant (the clarity) + circumstance (to provide to someone else)

At this point clarity still remains packed-up as a concept. The interviewer responds by seeking to confirm whether the project manager is in fact the agent or the medium associated with the process of obtaining clarity. In his response the project manager uses the construction that follows:

Agent ('I') + mental process

(I'm just trying to make things clear)

Here the 'clarity' that was previously a participant is now a process of 'making things clear' (Turn 8, Table 4.17). The project manager confirms that the criteria for 'having sufficient clarity' is tacit, being the product of 'gut feeling' (Turn 9). These ideas about 'making things clear' are effaced in the discourse produced in the content-targeted interviews as they remain condensed in nominalizations such as 'communication', 'discussion' and 'agreement' and other forms of under-representation.

The grammar used by the project manager indicated that 'clarity' is a participant in processes of possession and transaction such as 'to get', 'to provide' and 'to give'. For example, the project manager says:

We would just be attempting to get more clarity than we had.

This is a view of 'clarity' as a tangible gift that can be exchanged. The project manager 'gives' or 'takes' the clarity 'to' or 'from' the stakeholders. This is the compulsive rather than collaborative sense of 'make' in 'making things clear'. It also makes 'clarity' appear an objective 'thing', 'feeding into the selection criteria' and allowing the project manager to assert completion or exhaustivity about when 'clarity' is achieved. The consequences of thinking about 'agreement' in this way is that the possibility of interpersonal negotiation about meaning between the members in a meeting is reduced. In response to grammar-targeted probing by the interviewer, the project manager acknowledges that the aim of 'making things clear' is about the mental process of understanding. In a similar way to the example of' tracing', the project manager 'dresses-up' what has been construed as relational and static as interpersonal and active. In other words, at the content level, his talk about 'clarity' seems to be about accounting for the opinions of the stakeholders, however, the grammar he uses reveals that 'clarity' is part of a motif of commodification in the project manager's talk. In very simple terms, this is a representation of achieving consensus as a person giving another person a pre-packaged version of their own 'clarity' on a particular issue. In this way the project manager is 'attempting to find the clarity to provide to somebody else'. Such a view is in line with a mathematical model of communication.

The IT consequences of tacit knowledge unpacked from the nominalization 'knowledge transfer'

The general IT consequence of tacit knowledge about 'knowledge transfer' remaining embedded in under-representation is the possibility that interpersonal negotiation about meaning between people associated with the project is reduced because consensus is viewed as a commodity. This means that 'clarity' is viewed as something that you can 'give' to someone as if it were an object. This has the potential to effect an IT project in a number of ways:

- The project manager controls the point at which clarity is reached. This may not be the same point needed by others, hence his performance may be seen as inadequate by his supervisors.
- Likewise the project team members may feel inadequate and proceed to work with less than adequate understanding without voicing it.
- Likewise users and stakeholders may feel inadequately understood and so passively refuse to cooperate with the project and ultimately resist using the system that is produced.

Unpacking modality in the interviews

There was less modality in the speakers' responses to the grammar-targeted interview questions (18%) than in their responses to the content-targeted interview questions (22%). However, the difference was not significant ($F(1,11) = 2.22$, $p > 0.05$). A possible reason for the lack of significant difference is that the grammar-targeted interviewer did not tend to unpack modality in favour of unpacking the other kinds of under-representation. This may be because it is more difficult to notice instances of modality in spoken discourse or because the speakers happened to not embed meanings relevant to knowledge management in modal structures.

In addition, the way modality was distributed in the two interview corpora was relatively consistent. Modals of probability were the most often selected type (12% in the content-targeted interviews and 10% in the grammar-targeted interviews). This means that they spend more time talking about the likelihood of events or actions than, for example, obligation about events or actions. It is evident that the change in interview method has had little effect on how the speakers chose to construe probability, usuality, obligation and inclination in their discourse.

Table 4.18 is an example of how modality was unpacked in the grammar-targeted interviews. At the end of Turn 2 the information architect refers to things that the members of his team 'have to do'. The modal operator 'have to' signal obligation and the entity demanding this obligation is under-represented. The interviewer attempts to unpack the under-representation by

Table 4.18 Unpacking 'have to do', Information Architect, Grammar-targeted Interview 3

Turn	Speaker	Talk
1	Interviewer	So how do you perceive the twists that have gone on since we last met?
2	Information architect	Yeah, interesting to say the least. I can't say I didn't expect them actually because I knew at one point that the senior management would take a look at what we've done and and start to make some decisions and I knew that in ways we've done things in a longer time frame than we should of. So in that sense the money's running out. So, you know, from the management side of things they'll say well we've got this amount of money left. So there's various things that we have to do in order to get ourselves a CMS.
3	Interviewer	When you say, 'we took more time than we should have', by sort of whose rules?
4	Information architect	Partly some of my rules. I guess with the . . . It's, I guess, with the added benefit of hindsight, looking at the things we've done, the processes we've followed could have been improved and shortened pretty much and also, I guess, when I think about the actual length of the project when it was first initiated it was 18 months and that kind of thing. So we had 18 months to do something and that kind of thing as well and we're – what is it now? – a third of the way through just about, sorry, no two thirds of the way through. So I guess it's those sort of things.
5	Interviewer	So it's very much your own internal assessment criteria you are using there.

questioning the identity of this entity in Turn 3. The response which follows in Turn 4 reveals the information architect herself as the entity dictating what has to be done. Whether this self-attribution of agency is important is not pursued by the grammar-targeted interviewer who goes on to pursue other matters.

The approach in Table 4.18 may be contrasted with the general approach in content-targeted interviews which did not typically ask questions about expressions of obligation or necessity when they occurred. For example, a visual snapshot of unpursued modality is provided in Table 4.19, an extract from the second interview with the project manager. Modal operators and modal adjuncts are indicated in the extract in bold type. In each of these cases the agent, be it a person, a rule or a mechanism that causes the speaker to hold an opinion about

Table 4.19 Instances of modality, project manager, Content-targeted Interview 2

Turn	Speaker	Talk
1	Interviewer	That's spot on actually. I would be doing the same. The question then, that is in addition to what you are doing is are you looking at the challenges of customizing the package to suit your use cases or and slash or changing the business processes to suit the package?
2	Project manager	I think that's something that we are going to **have to** look at when we see how these packages are implemented. We have discussed that and we realize that we **could** dream the use case model and design the perfect interface but that work we assume is already been done to a certain extent for the purposes of general content management by these vendors and that they **would have,** you know, we spent a fair amount of money on that already and we realize that it's possible to come up with a couple of designs that **would** do the same thing so, we're not necessarily going to go to the design how we **should** think it **should** really work and customize it exactly to that. We will look at what the vendors have and do some testing and if the testing comes out ok, then we will just go with that so the purpose of testing against the scenarios is to see how difficult it is to custom ... to configure the package to work with scenarios. So our assumption is that if its quite difficult and we run into all sorts of problems getting it to work for one workflow or one particular start to end scenario, then it is **probably** going to be difficult to configure it for all the scenarios.
3	Interviewer	Do you see your team working on the package to configure it to fit the scenarios or to modify it?

probability, usuality, obligation and inclination is omitted and the following issues are left undeconstructed:

- Why the team has to pursue customization.
- Why the speaker believes he could dream up a perfect use case model.
- Why the speaker believes that the vendors have spent a lot of money perfecting their use case models.
- Why the speaker believes they could produce equally useful use cases designs.
- How the speaker knows how the use case would work.
- How the speaker knows the package will be difficult to configure.

While the instances of under-representation highlighted are candidates for grammatical probing, whether an interviewer will attempt to unpack a particular instance will depend on the general aim of the interview and the kind of tacit knowledge they are interested in eliciting.

The unpacking of modality in the interviews did not in general reveal below-view phenomena that was deemed important to the knowledge management issues covered in the interviews. Typically the hidden agents unpacked were the speaker themselves rather than tacitly held opinions or worldviews. This may be a function of the domain or could indicate that, while in principle, such tacit knowledge might be embedded in modality, in practice, it is difficult to elicit from people in interviews.

Unpacking generalization in the interviews

There was less generalization in the grammar-targeted interview responses than the content-targeted interview responses (Figure 4.8). This means that the subjects were more grammatically specific in the grammar-targeted interviews, using less instances of under-specification, non-specific deictic and abstract terminology. A repeated measures ANOVA indicated that the difference was significant ($F(1,11)=145.48, p < 0.001$).

Unpacking 'system': Elaborating what it means to organize

The speakers all used the term 'system' to describe the artefact to which their requirements analysis activity aimed to contribute. The 'system' is the object of the 'make-buy-reuse' strategy that the team aimed to specify. 'Making', 'buying' and

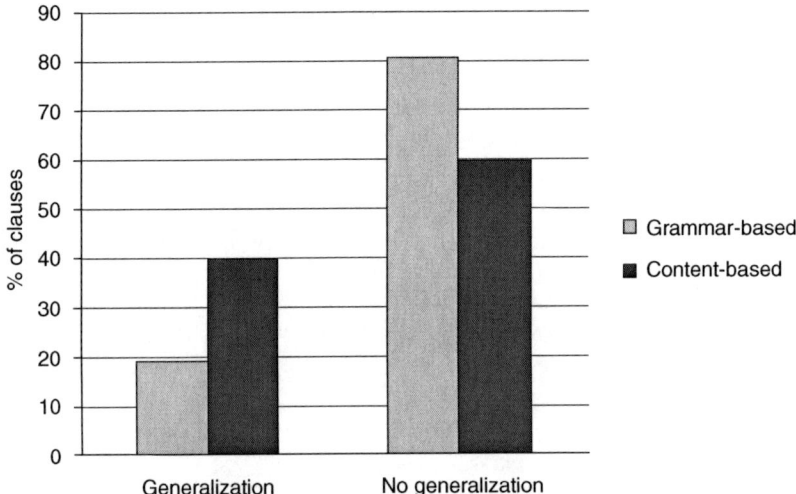

Figure 4.8 Generalization compared by interview type.

'reusing' are all material processes. An assumption in favouring this process type is that the 'system' is a tangible entity that can be involved in physical actions: it can be bought, it can be made and it can be reused. On one level, this is intuitive, as a system involves physical things such as computers and cables. However, on another level, a system is a semiotic environment, involving configurations of complex, often symbolic meanings, with which users interact.

'System' is originally from the Greek 'systema', meaning an organized whole (Harper 2001). The technical discourse of the project team seems to retain this Greek notion of completeness by the way the term is so pervasive in technologists' discourse as to be transparent. For example, if we return to the example where the information architect referred to the system as 'it', we see that when probed, she has difficulty explaining just what this 'it' is (Table 4.20). Her description distinguishes between the 'system' and its users, arguing that 'no system can have intelligence'. As the interviewer suggests in Turn 11, the information architect has presented a view of the system as purely technological rather than as a complex of people, processes and technology.

Unpacking the information architect's tacit understanding of the generalization reveals an incongruity between content and grammar in the speaker's talk. The incongruity is between the speaker's explicitly professed preoccupation with the users and the relationship with users embedded in the way she talks about the 'system'. While she claims that the users are the focus of her use case analysis, her grammatical construal of the 'system' for which she is creating

Table 4.20 Unpacking 'system', information architect, Grammar-targeted Interview 2

Turn	Speaker	Talk
1	Interviewer	You talked about 'it' manages.
2	Information architect	The Content Management System.
3	Interviewer	Ok, yeah, so what is it?
4	Information architect	Well I suppose it is a method of communication more than anything else so I guess at the end of the day no system can have intelligence it's the people involved, people who are using the system who have the intelligence.
5	Interviewer	So a system is something that gets used by people.
6	Information architect	Yes.
7	Interviewer	And in this context what is it?
8	Information architect	[long pause] Well, it manages content.
9	Interviewer	So what's the 'it'?
10	Information architect	[long pause]
11	Interviewer	The way you are talking about it to me sounds like you're talking about technology, you're talking about software or software and hardware. It sounds to me but I don't really know whether that's truly what you mean.
12	Information architect	Well, yes that's the case that is the case.
13	Interviewer	In this context.

these use cases is of a purely technological construct. This incongruity points to under-representation that may be significant in establishing whether the subject is working effectively towards her explicit objectives.

Such a construal of 'system' as a technical object rather than a social complex of people, artefacts and processes occurs frequently in the content-targeted interviews. However, the interviewer does not directly question whether a 'system' involves people, although he asks many questions about its technical components. The speakers often construed the 'system' as something tangible that they may be 'given' (Table 4.21). This may be interestingly compared with the grammatical analysis suggesting the lack of specificity about what a 'system' is. Casting the system as concrete yet vaguely defined is an example of incongruity between content and grammar. As was previously discussed, such instances of incongruity are important sites indicating potential problems in how an aspect of the project is being conducted. The capacity for this type of incongruity to surface below-view issues will be taken up in more detail in Field Study 3.

Unlike the rest of his team, the project manager displays explicit awareness about the poor definition of the 'system' and its scope (Table 4.22). He acknowledges that the team has used 'system' to cover a very broad range of phenomena. The lack of specificity has reduced the extent to which performance can be guaranteed as there are differences of opinion as to the scope of the performance metrics. Here we see the impact of the under-represented 'it' on the more tangible world of performance measurement. It is also an example of how

Table 4.21 System as a technical object, Technologist 2, Content-targeted Interview 4

Turn	Speaker	Talk
1	Technologist 2	It's sort of hard when the project director's away on holidays, but it certainly looks like we're going to **get** a system, which at one stage really it didn't, given that the prices I think came back from the vendors from the expression of interest were sort of seen to be outside the budget of the project.

Table 4.22 Unpacking 'system', project manager, Grammar-targeted Interview 2

Turn	Speaker	Talk
1	Interviewer	What is a system?
2	Project manager	A system? This is another interesting definition that's come up because we, we were using the, the word system to describe really everything. Well, I think we were using it in the more general term as in the interface, the client, the server and applications and interestingly then the datanet group assumed that the system included everything that was part of that hosted the applications, communicated the data between the various sites in the ABC so that can include the WAN which is the routers, the modems, the this, the thats, the PCs, the cards that are in them and absolutely everything to do with the people using the system wherever data travelled. So of course when they were trying to guarantee the performance of the system they were identifying a whole bunch of areas where they probably couldn't guarantee particular performance. Whereas we were talking about other areas. So, yes, we have settled on the system being their definition which is everything to do with the actual CMS.

what is tacit for one person may be explicit for another person even where they are working within the same habitus.

Table 4.23 summarizes the unpacking of each of the speaker's tacit definition of a system in the fourth round of grammar-targeted interviews. As this table indicates, technical artefacts are participants in all the speakers' definitions but only the project manager and information architect include people in their definition. Three interviewees provided multiple definitions.

The relative lack of human actors in the project team's talk about 'system' is echoed in the project glossary which defines the term as follows:

System

An interdependent group of objects, and procedures constituted to achieve defined objectives or some operational role by performing specified functions. A complete system in terms of the CMS project includes all of the associated equipment, facilities, material, computer programs, and firmware to the degree necessary for self-sufficient use in its intended environment.

This definition is based [on] the definition in the IEEE Standard 1233 – IEEE Guide for Developing System.

Table 4.23 Unpacking 'system' in Grammar-targeted Interview 4

Speaker	Elaborated form	Participants
Project manager	System + identifying relational process + selection of technical artefacts	Technical artefacts
	People + material process + system	People, technical artefacts
Information architect	System + attributive relational process + attribute	Technical artefacts
	People + material process + system	People, technical artefacts
Technologist 1	System + identifying relational process + selection of technical artefacts	Technical artefacts
	System + identifying relational process + circumstance of location	Technical artefacts
Technologist 2	System + identifying relational process + technical artefacts and business artefacts	Technical artefacts, business artefacts

Table 4.24 Agents in the Content Management System project glossary definition of a 'system'

Agent	Type
An interdependent group of objects, and procedures	Technical artefact
A complete system	Technical artefact
This definition	Textual (reflexive)

This definition makes no reference to human actors or a user. The references to the system and its components as interdependent, complete and self-sufficient are in accord with the Greek etymology. However, if we look at the grammar by which this notion of wholeness is constructed, a fundamental absence becomes visible: the users of the system are missing. The agents in this text are technical or reflexive in nature and do not allow for user autonomy (Table 4.24). At the content level, the definition is doing a lot of work to show exhaustivity, however, it fails to make reference to the very people for whom the system was built.

The consequences of tacit knowledge unpacked from the generalization 'systems'

The implications of the technocratic view of the 'system' displayed by the speakers are that the technologists may manifest a bias towards technical rather than socio-technical solutions to the problems they will encounter as they continue with their requirements analysis activity. This means that they may fail to produce a satisfying system for the user base. The incongruity found in, for example, the information architect's language about the system suggests that the project team members are not necessarily aware of this type of tacit technical bias. An alternative construal of 'system' would be as a socio-technical complex involving people, processes and technology rather than a purely technical construct.

Unpacking agency in the interviews

The types of agents identified in the grammar-targeted and content-targeted corpora were technical artefacts, managerial artefacts, technologists and users (Table 4.25). In general, agency distribution was dominated by the categories, technologists, and, technical artefacts, while the category, users, was allocated minimal agency. The pattern in agency parallels the assertions made in the

Table 4.25 Classification of agent types in the interviews with examples

Agent type	Explanation	Example
Technical artefact	Participants about technology or attributes of technology. This included phenomena such as systems, processes associated with systems and parts of the system development lifecycle.	The full implementation of the system The requirements Workflow A vendor package
Managerial artefact	Aspects of management practices of control and regulation, such as documents and recommendations.	The recommendation The submissions The outcome of my document The project owner
Technologists	People working with technology such as the members of the project team and other developers in the organization. Most often the agent was a reference to the speaker or a collective reference to the team as 'we'.	We I The team The project manager
Users	People using the system such as managers and their employees.	User X The manager

previous sections about how the users were marginalized by the project team's approach to requirements analysis.

There was, however, a difference in how these agents were distributed in the grammar-targeted interviews compared to the content based-interviews. A chi-squared test on the distribution of agency in the two interview types showed that the difference in distribution was significant (Chi = 29.05, $p < 0.001$). There were 1,100 clauses that contained agents in the content-targeted corpus and 1,537 clauses containing agents in the grammar-targeted corpus. The relatively small amount of agency attributed to users (7%) remained consistent in both the content-targeted and grammar-targeted interviews (Figures 4.9 and 4.10). In addition, the technologists and their artefacts occupied the major distribution of agency in both types of interviews (24% and 33%).

The tacit choice made by the speakers to allocate a large proportion of agency to the category 'technologists' and a relatively small proportion of agency to the category 'users' represents a particular perspective on what it means to conduct requirements analysis. It echoes the technocratic view of requirements analysis activity, suggested in previous sections. For example, while the observer who

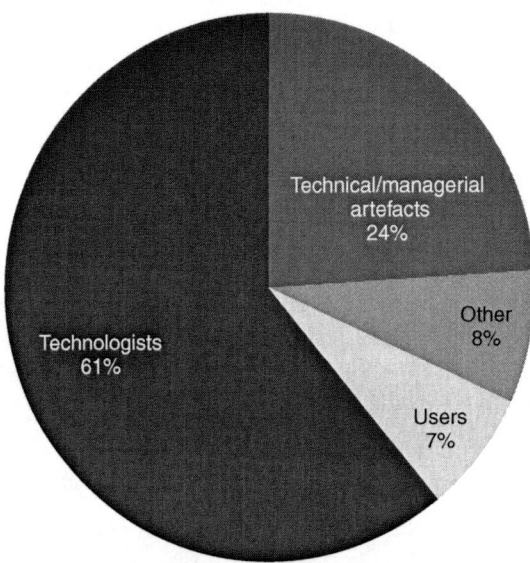

Figure 4.9 Distribution of agency in the content-targeted interview corpus.

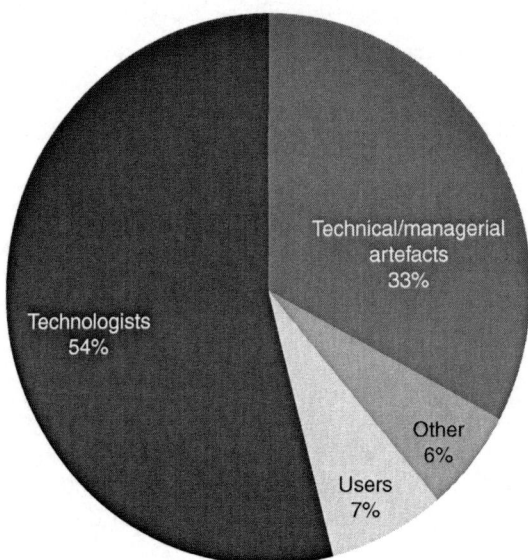

Figure 4.10 Distribution of agency in the grammar-targeted interview corpus.

has not been socialized into the discourse of the project team may assume the primary focus of a 'requirement' is the users, analysis of the team's talk shows that this is not a position which the grammar that they use can unambiguously sustain. Their grammar suggests that 'requirements analysis' for them is less about imbuing users with a sense of involvement in the system than it is about justifying the relationship of technical artefacts. While it may seem logical that the technologists are the agents performing the analysis, a more user-focused perspective on requirements analysis might produce talk by the technologists where the users are agents telling the analysts what they need or expressing opinions on the system. These would be constructions of the type 'The users think X' or 'The users typically do X' rather than the dominance of constructions of the type 'We (the technologists) did X and produced artefact Y' or 'Artefact Y suggests that we should do X'. It is clear that some degree of shorthand reference to technical abstraction is necessary when working in complex semiotic contexts, however, one would still expect that when such shorthand is unpacked, the more congruent construal would reflect underlying assumptions about the importance of understanding the user community.

The tendency to allocate most of the agency to technical artefacts was unpacked in many examples in the grammar-targeted interviews. For instance, in Interview Round 3 the grammar-targeted interviewer unpacked Technologist 2's understanding of the nominalization, 'requirements management plan' (Table 4.26). In Turn 2 of the technologist's response 'RUP', is an abstract authority that occupies the role of agent in the verbal process of 'saying' ('RUP says'). Similarly, in other sections in the interview, the RUP is the agent dictating the gathering and analysis of requirements. The implication here is that if the project team are constructing 'requirements' as being more about systems than they are about users, they may not have dealt optimally with the user base and thus compromised the success of the project. In this way, the incongruity

Table 4.26 Unpacking 'requirements management plan', Technologist 2, Grammar-targeted Interview 3

Turn	Speaker	Talk
1	Interviewer	Ok. So what then is a requirements management plan?
2	Technologist 2	Well that's a document that the RUP says you have to have [laughs] which, well it's essentially, as it says, a plan for the, managing the capturing, documentation and then I suppose the implementation of each requirement in the software project. Really it, I don't know, whereas we should have made the decision of whether we are going to buy or build before we even started down this whole sort of highly managed process I've been of the opinion the whole time that the RUP really is for a pure software development environment, because it's really slowed things up a lot.

of assigning users a small proportion of agency, despite explicitly stating that requirements analysis is about users, means that the project team may not be doing what they say they are doing.

In fact, in this field study it was the case that the project team were not doing what they, at the level of explicit content, said they were doing. In the final interview, after probing by the grammar-targeted interviewer, Technologist 2 admitted that the project had only had detailed discussions with a handful of users of the existing system when the user body numbered in the vicinity of 500. This is an example of how probing grammar can uncover tacit assumptions that may have important implications for the success of IT projects. If the project team does not effectively engage with the user base they run the risk of producing a system that most do not want to use. They may privilege their technical artefacts to the extent that the artefacts have little concrete relationship with the experiential world of the users.

The consequences of tacit knowledge about 'systems' explicated through unpacking patterns in agency

Assigning more agency to participants in the semantic domain, 'technical artefacts', than to, 'users', has particular consequences in an IT project. On the one hand, the tendency may appear common sense given that requirements analysis is largely a semiotic activity in which technologists attempt to understand the meanings about work and working with technology that the users produce and translate those meanings into 'systems requirements'. However, requirements analysis is also a social and interpersonal activity in the sense that finding out about the users means engaging with them on some level, be that interviews, questionnaires or group sessions. If a substantial amount of such activity had occurred, and if the technologists' deeply held conviction about requirements analysis involved a commitment to understanding the user community, it seems logical to find instances in the project team's talk where they refer to the users' opinions and descriptions in clauses that construct the users as agents. By instead positioning themselves, and their technical artefacts, as the dominant agents, the project team assigns themselves more semiotic power but they run the risk of producing technical systems that have little relationship to how the users operate. This means that these systems are more likely to be deemed inadequate by the users, resulting in expensive 'user resistance' (people deciding not to use the system).

The difference in the language used by the two interviewers

The previous sections have focused on how tacit knowledge was uncovered by probing the speakers' grammar and how their language differed in the content-targeted and grammar-targeted interviews. We now briefly describe the differences in the language used by the interviewers themselves. While both the grammar-targeted and content-targeted interviewers covered the same topic areas they approached the activity of formulating questions in different ways.[6] The interviewer conducting the grammar-targeted interviews adhered to the grammar-targeted interview protocol (Appendix A), while the interviewer carrying out the content-targeted interviews used his experience as a systems analyst to formulate questions.

Putting aside interrogatives, there was a difference in the type of declarative clauses used by the interviewers in the two interview methods. The content-targeted interviewer typically produced more scaffolding and propositions than the grammar-targeted interviewer (examples are shown in Table 4.27). The scaffolding in this interviewer's discourse was indicative of his experience as an interviewer as he managed the progress of the interview to increase the comfort of the subject. The propositions were typically clauses dealing with his personal opinions and experiences regarding such projects. This discourse had the potential to influence the responses of the speakers in various content

Table 4.27 The IT consequences of tacit knowledge elicited by unpacking patterns of agency

Clause type	Explanation	Example
Dependent clause	Set the context for a question.	'So when you arrived at your ten [criteria] was that consensual as well?' (Grammar-targeted interviewer)
Propositions	Makes a statement about a fact the interviewer holds true.	'There are some projects that are tightly controlled by the the senior most stakeholder' (Content-targeted interviewer)
Referencing clause	Makes reference to the language of the subject.	'When you say requirement, [what do you mean?]' (Grammar-targeted interviewer)
Scaffolding clause	Provide explanatory commentary on the progress of the interview.	'I am now going to ask you some more questions' (Content-targeted interviewer)

areas about technology. By contrast the majority of the declarative clauses in the grammar-targeted interviewer's language were dependent or referencing clauses. The dependent clauses were typically used by this interviewer to ground the question in the context of the interviewee's experience (i.e. something be something that the interviewee had mentioned earlier in the interview). Similarly, the referencing clauses pointed anaphorically to specific parts of the interviewee's co-text, usually directly prior to the question.

These differences suggest a fundamental distinction between the content-targeted interview method and the grammar-targeted interview method as they were applied in situ. A major difference is what happens in the interview when the interviewer isn't asking a specific question such as, 'What is X?' The content-targeted interviewer appears to use a top–down approach where the interviewer makes propositions introduced with scaffolding where needed and assesses the interviewee's reaction to the proposition. In contrast, the grammar-targeted interviewer applies a bottom–up approach using the interviewee's grammar as a starting point for questions rather than additional propositions. Obviously, the differences between the two interview methods involve shades of grey and, at times, where the grammar-targeted interviewer needs to switch topic or find additional content, he will use propositions in conjunction with his questions.

In response to a questionnaire about their experiences of the interview method, each of the subjects suggested that the questioning process had been beneficial to improving their work practice because it caused them to ask questions about material that they assumed was 'beyond question'. This was phenomena such as the assumptions underlying how a 'requirement' is defined, seen as too obvious to deconstruct, yet integral to performing requirements analysis. The following is an example of the type of comment made:

> The grammar-targeted interviewer's questions made us better assess the way we worked as a team, and the fundamentals behind the day-to-day requirements our project attempts to address.

These 'fundamentals behind the day-to-day requirements' appears to be phenomena that is taken as give, occupying the position of doxa or the 'the universe of the undiscussed' (Bourdieu 1977: 168). If the interviewer is already socialized into the discourse of IT, such phenomena may be so naturalized that they do not consider asking specific questions about, for example, what a requirement is, and the subject does not consider elaborating. Instead the utterances pass between the interviewee and interviewer taken as given. A less under-represented discourse shifts the emphasis from justifying abstract relations between artefacts to finding ways to account for such 'day-to-day' practice of users in their functional contexts. In turn, it shifts focus to unpacking the parts of discourse where meaning that is 'obvious' to an expert, but hidden for a novice, resides.

Conclusion

This chapter has presented the findings of a field study in which the grammar-targeted and content-targeted interview methods were compared. The results showed that there was less under-representation in the grammar-targeted interview responses than the content-targeted interview responses. These results were statistically significant for nominalization, agency and generalization, with insignificant results for modality. Specific examples of the tacit knowledge elicited from the probing of the under-represented grammar were given along with the IT implications of uncovering this knowledge. The main instances of tacit knowledge that were uncovered through the grammar-targeted interview method along with the corresponding IT consequences are summarized in Table 4.28.

Under-representation in language can be extremely useful in efficiently getting things done. It can also serve in technical discourses to separate 'those who have the knowledge from those who are left outside' (Halliday 1993: 78). This chapter has shown how it may also divert the technologists themselves from their goal of providing systems to the users that help them perform their work well. Perhaps a more congruent language will enhance communication between technical and non-technical personnel and prompt technical staff to give proper focus to agency in the development of information systems. Hence we propose that 'systems requirements' might be avoided and forms such as 'users' requirements for system description/design/development' be favoured. The participant (the users) made visible in this expression is paramount in construing the meaning that what is required is 'owned' by the users and the purpose or goal of what is required is 'for' system description, design and/or development but only in the sense that it can assist the user community.

The field study which follows moves from the corpus-based approach adopted in this chapter to a more instance-based analysis of the unpacking of under-representation by the grammar-targeted interview method. The type of incongruity between grammar and content found in the present study is elaborated in the following study.

Table 4.28 Summary of tacit knowledge about requirements analysis that was elicited in the grammar-targeted interviews

Type of under-representation	Tacit knowledge	IT consequences
Nominalization	A 'requirement' is an attribute of the system.	Technocentric approach to system development, that is, a focus on the attributes of the system rather than fulfillment of human needs as the locus of importance in requirements analysis activity.
	A 'requirement' is a thing rather than a process.	The focus of requirements analysis is on stable technical artefacts rather than dynamic human processes.
	Conflation of 'requirement' and 'request'.	The facets of the system are not optimally prioritized, meaning that those which are critical and those which are optional may be confused.
	'Clarity' is a tangible commodity that can be exchanged.	The possibility of interpersonal negotiation about meaning between people associated with the project is reduced because clarity is something that you can give to someone as if it were an object.
Modality	–	–
Generalization	Systems are technical constructs rather than social-technical complexes.	The project team may manifest a bias towards technical rather than socio-technical solutions to the problems they will encounter as they continue with their requirements analysis activity. This means that they may fail to produce a satisfying system for the user base.
Agency	Technologists and their artefacts have more power than users in requirements analysis.	The technical artefacts that the technologists use in their requirements analysis have little relationship to how the users operate. This means that the system that is ultimately produced is more likely to be deemed inadequate by the users.

Notes

1 A less detailed account of this work is provided in Zappavigna-Lee and Patrick (2010).

2 Systems analysts work in IT system design and (re)development in organizations. They usually are involved in gathering software requirements from users and

producing technical specifications. A common part of their role is liaising between different groups such as IT vendors and technical teams.

3 The present study acknowledges the limitations in validity that arise from not controlling for interview sequence. However, it does not claim to be a controlled experiment and instead is intended to be exploratory in nature.

4 See Chapter 1 for an explanation of Bourdieu's theory of habitus.

5 Appendix D provides a transitivity analysis of clauses containing the term 'requirements'.

6 The grammar-targeted interviewer noted that he had to restrict his questioning to what he thought would yield the most useful comment as time availability of the interviewees was limited. In real life he would have pursued various types of unpacking 'more actively'. Likewise, without permission to 'intervene' in the project, the interviewer couldn't press the interviewees too closely on some issues as he would have liked to get to the bottom of their meanings.

5

Working Well: Tacit Knowledge in Performance Reviews

Introduction

Performance reviews involve assessing the work of employees, usually through interviews with managers. The process calls to mind the following lines from 'Yes Minister', the popular BBC TV series:

> 'How would you say I'm going, Humphrey?' Jim would ask. 'Alright, Minister' came the cheerful reply from his cabinet secretary.
>
> 'But is alright, alright?'
>
> 'Well', (came the measured response this time), 'alright is, er, alright'. ('Yes Minister', www.imdb.com/title/tt0751817/)

This third study of tacit knowledge considers the meanings made during performance reviews. It was undertaken for over 6 months in the IT department of an insurance and financial services company in Australia and consisted of interviews by two different classes of interviewers: managers working in the department, who conducted content-targeted interviews, and an external interviewer trained by the researcher, who conducted grammar-targeted interviewers. This field study builds upon the method employed in the first and second field studies. Here, however, we focus further upon detailed analysis of specific instances where under-representation was unpacked. Such focused, instance-based analysis affords insight into how the speakers' grammar operates to construe particular experiences of work and 'working well'.

The study aims to make visible tacit knowledge held by the participants involved in performance reviews. The interviews were conducted during a performance review process that the department undertakes with its business analysts throughout the year. The process operates by managers and stakeholders critiquing the work of business analysts, who in turn critique their own performance. These interviews are referred to as the 'content-targeted' interviews because they deal with participants' experience of work without directly applying strategies to uncover tacit meaning.

Three types of relationship between grammar and content, as defined in Chapter 2, occur in this study:

- The content and the grammar misalign.
- The content and the grammar align.
- The grammar extends the content.

We focus on the first and the last types of relationship between grammar and content, using grammar-targeted questions to unpack the tacit knowledge to which these relationships point. For example, we seek to uncover, in the case of misalignment, the tacit knowledge held in the grammatical patterns that contradict the explicit construal. Similarly, where the grammar extends the content, we seek to make visible the elaboration.

Host organization

The interviews took place within the context of an informal performance review process that the IT department of Organization Z conducts at various times each year to assess its business analysts working on internal and external projects. This informal process feeds into a more formal performance review conducted once a year to specify bonuses, calculate pay-rises for the next year and determine how to improve employee development.

In order to understand the nature and scope of the in-house performance review process in the host organization, prior to conducting parallel grammar-targeted interviews, the researcher undertook an informal interview with the head of the IT department who was in charge of the appraisal process. The interview revealed that the managers running the appraisal process were faced with problems arising from what we may term the 'below-view' stratum of performance reviewing. These problems centred upon difficulties in eliciting, understanding and calibrating appraisals made by the interviewees due to the absence of a protocol for dealing with tacit meaning in the organization.

A central problem that managers face in undertaking performance reviews was that they often received very general answers from stakeholders to questions. In addition, interviewees would discuss details specific to organizational subcultures into which the interviewing managers were not socialized. There were also the many interpersonal issues that go alongside assessing other people's work. The head of IT described the situation as follows:

> . . . we struggle to get feedback on how they can better improve their performance but at the same time we don't want to turn the interview into a process where it sounds like we are picking faults and looking for gaps. So we are trying to get an overall picture, but sometimes people are either not sure of what we expect from them, or reluctant to give brutally honest feedback, or they give recent feedback, and we try and say, "you know, what about the whole project?"...

For example, stakeholders would often assess the competence of a technologist with appraisal such as, 'Oh, James is pretty good' and the interviewer would have no context in which to assess the weight of this evaluation. Some stakeholders would say, 'James was adequate for my needs' and have no interest in further elaboration. Others, according to the head of the IT department, would 'sing the praises of everybody'.

The head of department noted that there was an essential indeterminancy in judgements of capacity[1] of this kind. The statement that 'James was good' might mean, 'James excelled in every capacity. I would never work on a project without him', or, 'He turned up on time, he gave me what I needed, he wasn't all that great, but I wouldn't have expected much'. Some stakeholders were hesitant to give negative feedback because they did not want a business analyst that they 'liked as a person' to be penalized. Thus, while the interviewers followed a loose outline of the general areas in which behaviour was to be assessed, the overall problem remained that there were a range of stakeholders with different levels of optimism and pessimism in their feedback and no effective system for calibrating different people's assessments.

In addition, the interviewing manager would often have very limited knowledge about the context of the business analysts and stakeholders. These managers were faced with the situation of reviewing the performance of a business analyst without knowing the specific behaviours that were expected by management or how to benchmark these behaviours. In addition, some stakeholders had a lot of experience with systems analysis, while for others, this was their first time working on an IT project. These inexperienced stakeholders would often give responses such as, 'Well, he seemed to do a good job, but I don't know'. In such cases it would not be logical to expect the stakeholder to assess the practice of technologist.

The head of IT also acknowledged that the business analysts had problems with self-assessment, that is, with describing their performance in terms that might be meaningful to the interviewing manager:

> . . . one of the challenges we have as managers is agreeing with our people on how they performed on a project . . . There's not a big discrepancy but obviously, when you work really hard, you think you have done a good job. Other people might think you've done a bad job or that you did an exceptional job but it's hard to rate yourself. And the other thing is sometimes we think the business analysts didn't do a good job because they upset the business, and so therefore they will almost necessarily get bad feedback and they might upset the business by saying, "look that's a bad idea we should do a different technology" or something like that and, hopefully, get people on board, but they may walk away thinking either, "that went well" and the stakeholder thinks "they let me down", or, "geez, I really struggled" and the stakeholder thinks they did a good job.

He noted that this was not merely a problem of inadequate verbal skill, but of the difficulty of putting certain practices into words:

> It's not a case like in some jobs where you can go, "sit down and here's how I'll tell you how to do a better job. Here is what I would do". It's often they know how to do it better, but they may struggle to explore that or express that. So, it would be valuable to us if we got some useful information on that.

It is this struggle to construe 'performance' in language that is the focus of the field study presented in this chapter.

Interviewers and interview protocols

Two independent classes of interviewers conducted the interviews: a grammar-targeted interviewer trained by the researcher, and managers from the host organization. The grammar-targeted interviewer was the same interviewer used in Field Study 2. The interviewers from the host organization were three managers within the IT department who had each been assigned the task of informally reviewing the performance of a business analyst working on a project under the jurisdiction of the IT department.

Three managers in the IT department of the host organization conducted the content-targeted interviews in accordance with the performance review processes native to the department. The individual managers determined the topics for these interviews. While the specific questions were not formally assigned by a departmental pro forma, managers generally covered the following areas set out in a performance review summary document:

- People and teamwork.
- Partners and customers.
- Delivering profitable IT outcomes.
- Projects and technical support.
- Development.

The complementary interviews undertaken by the grammar-targeted interviewer used the grammar-targeted protocol given in Appendix A. The interview topics for the grammar-targeted interviews were designed to match those of the content-targeted interviews so that the two kinds of interviews could be meaningfully compared. The interviewer was provided with the general content areas that the content-targeted interviews covered, but not with the exact questions that were asked by the content-targeted interviewers. The interview topics covered the following areas:

- The business analyst's role.
- The business analyst's perception of their own performance.
- The manager's perception of the business analyst's performance.

These areas included topics such as the business analyst's communication skills, teamwork skills and relationship with stakeholders.

Since the interview the interviewing managers in the host organization determined the topics to be covered in the performance reviews, the grammar-targeted interviews had to be scheduled to follow the content-targeted interviews. This limitation meant that alternating the interview styles was not possible. While this is a limitation of the study, and impacts upon the validity of the findings, it should be noted that the study is exploratory, and that the comparison between the grammar-targeted and content-targeted interviews is a quasi-experiment since a range of intervening variables cannot be controlled due to the nature of the field environment.

Transcription, sampling and linguistic analysis of corpus

The grammar-targeted and content-targeted interviews were transcribed. Phases of discourse were sampled from the latter on the basis that they exemplified the grammar-targeted interview method. In other words they contained instances where under-representation in a speaker's discourse was unpacked by a grammar-targeted question. Corresponding samples were taken from the content-targeted corpus where under-representation on the same topic remained intact.

The grammar-targeted interview responses formed a corpus of 3,279 clauses and the content-targeted interview responses formed a corpus of 2,114 clauses. The phases sampled from the grammar-targeted interview corpus were analysed in terms of the unpacking of under-representation. This instance-level approach complements the quantitative approach undertaken in Field Study 2. The instances of unpacked under-representation were compared with the content-targeted interview corpus. The aim was first to determine whether the original content was covered in the interviews, and if so, whether it was packed up in a grammatical form that meant it was not available for deconstruction by the interview participants.

Appraisal theory

Evaluative language is clearly central to performance reviews. Evaluation is a domain of interpersonal meaning where language is used to express attitudes and to adopt stances about other texts. Appraisal theory argues that the emotional reaction to the world through infant protolanguage develops as we are socialized into a culture and into institutions (Martin and White 2005). Feeling becomes institutionalized as ethics and morality, forming the JUDGEMENT system with which we construe rules and regulations regarding behaviour (e.g. 'He is doing the **wrong** thing'). Feeling is also institutionalized as aesthetics and value, forming the APPRECIATION system with which we generate assessments based on our reactions to phenomena (e.g. 'I think it is **beautiful**').

Appraisal systems are discourse semantic systems. While appraisal analysis did not form part of the lexicogrammatical probing in the interviews, this chapter will consider appraisal in exploring the post-interview transcribed texts to further illuminate under-representation in the area of evaluation. Figure 5.1 provides examples of each region of appraisal as a system network as theorized by Martin and White (2005). The network adopts the convention whereby capitalized labels above the arrows indicate different systems of meaning, and the lowercase labels at the end of each path mark features within systems. A square bracket represents a choice between two options in a system (an 'or' relation), while a brace represents simultaneous choices (an 'and' relation). For

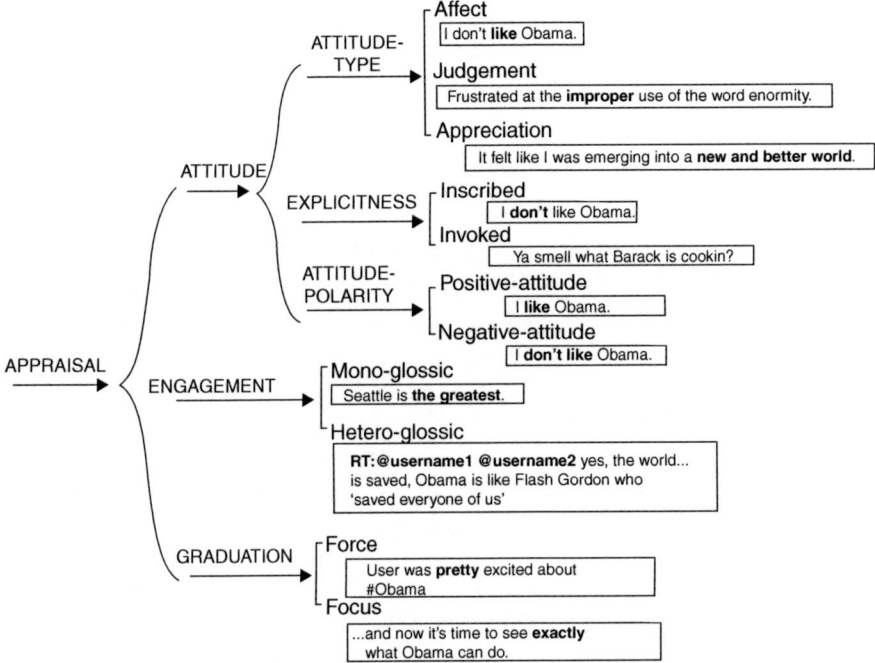

Figure 5.1 The appraisal system.

example, the ATTITUDE system involves three more delicate systems from which a choice can be made:

- AFFECT – expressing emotion
- JUDGEMENT – assessing behaviour
- APPRECIATION – estimating value

The examples in the boxes (taken from Zappavigna (2012)) illustrate each type of attitudinal appraisal. This network may be further specified to greater levels of delicacy depending on the kind of analysis in which it is being used.

Depending on the target and source of the evaluation, lexis such as 'good' can work with any of the ATTITUDE systems. Consider the difference between JUDGEMENT in the following:

Thank god it is the weekend, time off for **good** behaviour

and AFFECT:

I feel really **good** about this review.

or APPRECIATION:

It has been a hard week. I need to drink some **good** wine.

As we will see in this chapter, 'good' is a common appraisal item in the interviews, realizing under-representation in the form of generalization.

The JUDGEMENT *system*

Since judgement was a commonly used resource in the interviews often associated with under-representation via nominalization it will be explained here in more detail. Instead of making an aesthetic assessment, the JUDGEMENT system critiques human behaviour: what people say and believe. This can be further regionalized into two areas of meaning: 'social esteem' and 'social sanction':

> **Judgements** of **esteem** have to do with 'normality' (how unusual someone is), 'capacity' (how capable they are) and 'tenacity' (how resolute they are); **judgements** of **sanction** have to do with 'veracity' (how truthful someone is) and 'propriety' (how ethical someone is). (Martin and White 2005: 52)

Social esteem can be further delineated into NORMALITY, CAPACITY and TENACITY. NORMALITY considers behaviour in terms of deviation from the status quo, CAPACITY in terms of ability and TENACITY in terms of endurance. The capacity system was a frequent resource drawn upon in the performance reviews considered in the chapter, for example when one of the analysts says:

> if I'm not doing **well** in this project at this phase, then I'd be in trouble.

Social sanction delineates behaviour as truthfulness or decorum. For instance when Business Analyst 3 says the following she is making an assessment about PROPRIETY:

> I don't think it's appropriate for me to go in there and just shake that team when there's already like a team leader.

What is a 'performance review' in the technical discourse of IT professionals?

In the context of IT projects, the term 'performance review' is a nominalization that embeds ideas about what it means for someone 'to perform well' and what it means for someone 'to assess' this performance. It condenses processes central to forming judgements of CAPACITY. Descriptions of performance produced by employees and their managers can often be conflicting at the level of content.

This study will show how there may also sometimes be in discord at the tacit level of grammar.

The aim of performance reviewing is usually professed to be to gain an understanding of an employee's experience of their own work *as they perceive it* in relation to their manager co-construal of their performance. There were a range of nominalizations associated with 'good performance' in the interviews across a range of process types associated with different areas of work (Table 5.1). The collocation of generalizations such as 'good' or 'alright' with these types of nominalizations renders below-view processes central to both experiencing and critiquing 'performing well'. For example, embedded within the term 'good understanding' are assumptions about how people negotiate meaning and convey that they have understood each other. An example of unpacking this type of under-representation was seen in the elaboration of the term 'clarity' as used by the project manager in Field Study 2.

The sections in this chapter which follow discuss the tendency for under-representation about 'performance' to be unpacked in the grammar-targeted interviews while remaining part of 'taken as given' meaning in the content-targeted interviews. We explore cases of grammar extending, aligning and misaligning with content in a speaker's talk to investigate how the managers, stakeholders and business analysts in the study understand 'good performance'. In other words, we seek to investigate their tacit knowledge about 'performing well' in Organization Z.

Table 5.1 Nominalizations associated with 'good performance' in the interviews

Nominalization	Nominalized process	Process type	Work area
Expectation	To expect	Mental	Role definition
Feedback	To feed back	Verbal (metaphorical)	Project management
Understanding	To understand	Mental	Communication with stakeholders
Experience	To experience	Material	Role definition
Management	To manage	Material	Project management
Knowledge	To know	Mental	Knowledge management
Information	To inform	Verbal	knowledge management
Responsibility	To be responsible for	Relational	Role definition
Solution	To solve	Material	System development

Grammar extending content: What does 'good' mean?

One of the central problems in the department's performance review process was the tendency of participants to employ appraisal that was very general. This included instances of under-representation by generalization such as 'good', 'well' and 'alright'. Less of this type of generalized JUDGEMENT occurred in the grammar-targeted interviews compared with the content-targeted interviews. For example, there were less instances of 'good' used in this way in the grammar-targeted interviews (Figure 5.2). This means that there were proportionally more clauses in the content-targeted interviews where the manager, stakeholder or business analyst chose to use the generalization 'good' to describe some aspect of their experience of working with technology. While instances of 'good' are only a small part of the system by which appraisal is realized, the difference in quantity here points to a more complex shift in the level of under-representation occurring in the grammar. The implication for the performance review interviews is that more congruent, and thus less tacit, descriptions of performance can be collected with a grammar-targeted interview method.

In contrast, generalized appraisal was rarely deconstructed by the managers conducting the in-house performance review interviews. For example, Manager 2 construes assessment of CAPACITY ('good' and 'well') in relation to Business Analyst 2's ability to integrate into a team (Turn 2, Table 5.2). Such generalized evaluative lexis is highly indeterminate without considering co-text appraisal

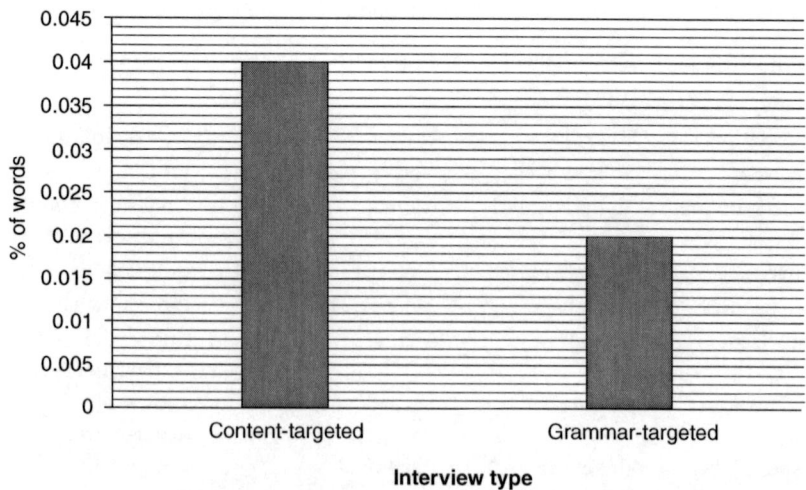

Figure 5.2 Comparing the use of 'good' as judgement of capacity in the two interview types.

Table 5.2 'Good', Manager 2, content-targeted interview (emphasis added)

Turn	Speaker	Talk
1	Interviewer	Organization Z has a bunch of core values and various things. Do you think he fits in with all of those?
2	Manager 2	Yeah, he does. He's one of those guys who **fits in well**. So he's **pretty good** there. There's no, there's no need to bring him, to talk to him at all about any of that stuff, to be honest with you.

patterning or by further probing the structure. The interviewer, however, does not seek further clarification from the interviewee. Does fitting in 'well' mean that Business Analyst 2 has a highly developed capacity to communicate with his team mates, or does it simply mean that he is not in direct conflict with the team? Glossing over how Manager 2 construes 'fitting in well' means that the opportunity to understand his tacit criteria for recognizing 'one of those guys that fits in well', and, in turn, his assumptions about the interpersonal stratum of project work, are missed.

When such instances of generalization occur in the grammar-targeted interviews they are typically unpacked by the interviewer. The business analysts and managers both used the term 'performance' to describe their activities on projects. However, each had a different tacit construal of 'performing well'. 'Fitting in well' is elaborated in the extract shown Table 5.3. By attempting to unpack 'good' as it is used by Manager 2, the grammar-targeted interviewer was able to elicit meaning that remained tacit in the exchange in the corresponding content-targeted interview (Table 5.2). Manager 2, as a project manager, construes 'good' as the capacity of the business analyst 'to fit in' in a way that causes minimal impact on the manager's schedule. This is in accord with other comments that the manager makes about Organization Z being a 'lean' organization where employees have little time to engage in activity that is not directly 'billable'. In this way, 'fitting in' is about conforming to the cultural norms dictated by the economic climate in the organization.

Manager 2 elaborates 'good' as a series of verbal projections about what Manager 2 can 'say' to his employee in the case where the employee fits the criteria of being 'good' (Table 5.3). If we compare the two extracts (Tables 5.2 and 5.3) a difference in construal is apparent, with the content-targeted example manifesting more evaluative generalization and the grammar-targeted example more instances of congruent explanation. The content-targeted interviews manifest and evaluative patterning that generalized assessment of not just of procedural work, but interpersonal meaning relating to such work. An example

Table 5.3 'Good', Manager 2, grammar-targeted interview (emphasis added)

Turn	Speaker	Talk
2	Interviewer	So, what does '**good**' mean?
3	Manager 2	For me, as a project manager, it means someone that you can say, 'Here's a piece of work. This is why we are trying to do it. A little bit of an understanding of what the objective is that we are trying to get out of it. In terms of what we usually do, here's a number of people that you are going to need to talk to get some information from whether it's underlying data from one of our systems or, you know, knowledge on what the rules are to for example underwrite business or something like that, some set of business rules we want to get, you know, an answer out of that information. Is there an opportunity in there that we can realize to make more money or increase something or other?'. So for me '**good**' means he is effective at taking that piece of work, understanding what needs to be done, going away and pretty much self-managing, checking in once a day or as required. If he's got an issue, he'll say, 'Can I have 5 minutes?' and we'll sit down and work it through and we can either reinforce that he's on the right track and he can keep going. Veering off track, pull him back on or if the information isn't there as required, we'll work out an option to move forward.

of unpacking this interpersonal component is the verbal projection in Turn 3 from Table 5.3:

> . . . it means someone that you can say "Here's a piece of work. . .

In this example, the clause about the manager 'saying' projects the clause that was said ("Here's a piece of work . . ."). The statements in the projected clauses are contestable in a way that the nominalization 'good performance' is not. As Halliday and Martin (1993: 39) point out 'you can argue with a clause but you can't argue with a nominal group'. Put simply, I can argue with the propositions that someone makes at the level of content but it is much more difficult to contest assumptions embedded in their grammatical choices. This is the reason why, for example, it is so difficult to argue with a person who has a good knowledge of the linguistic art of rhetoric.

'Good' was a frequented instance of evaluative lexis used to appraise a range of propositions that are important to how the speakers construe their work and their relationships with their peers (64 instances) in the content-targeted

Table 5.4 Words that collocate with 'good' in the content-targeted interview corpus

Words collocating with good
Understanding
Decision
Coverage
Value
Analytical skills
Summary
Relationship
Balance

interview sample. Common collocates of good are shown in Table 5.4. When such collocations occur in the content-targeted interviewers, the terms are taken 'as given', as if a 'good decision' or a 'good balance' are transparent terms. In some cases, the speakers themselves will offer an elaboration, but in the majority of instances, these terms remain unchallenged. They are part of what is assumed to be a common ground or shared habitus that the interviewer and subject do not deconstruct.

An example where unpacking 'good' misaligns with the content

The extract shown below is an exchange between the Business Analyst 1 and the content-targeted interviewer asking a general question about his performance. While the interviewer chooses a question about the process of performing rather than the artefact 'performance', and in this sense avoids some of the pitfalls of under-representation, the generalization 'pretty' remains unprobed in the text. At the level of discourse semantics 'pretty' is an example of tempering of ATTITUDE via the GRADUATION system (e.g. 'pretty reasonably', 'pretty happy' and 'pretty confident') that softens the focus of what is said. It raises the question 'pretty X in comparison to what other evaluative assessment'?

Table 5.6 is an extract taken from the grammar-targeted interview with the same business analyst. In this extract the grammar-targeted interviewer directly probes the analyst's construal of 'good performance'. The analyst responds by construing performing well as a process of internal accountability that can be tangibly measured (manifest as verbal processes where he asks himself a series of pass/fail style questions). These questions are yes/no interrogatives rather than WH interrogatives (Turn 2) and constrains what counts as a valid appraisal

Table 5.5 'Performance', Business Analyst 1, content-targeted interview

Turn	Speaker	Talk
1	Interviewer	On a more general approach, if you like, how do you think you've performed?
2	Business Analyst 1	Well, I think **pretty reasonably**, I mean, something like fee for service is probably an area that I am most comfortable in, and the beginning of the project is the part that I enjoy, so if, you know, if I'm not doing **well** in this project at this phase, then I'd be in trouble, so I'm **pretty** happy with the way things are going, but –
3	Interviewer	It's still challenging though, by the sounds of things, 200 business requirements across seven systems.
4	Business Analyst 1	Yes. Yeah, I mean, it's really, it's all new things that I haven't done before in terms of the scale, the complexity –
5	Interviewer	But the general functionality you're **pretty** confident with, yeah?
6	Business Analyst 1	I mean, that type of system and business model and so on is what I'm used to or my background is sort of in that area.
7	Interviewer	But, still, the particulars of this scenario are challenging you.
8	Business Analyst 1	Yep.

metric. As the interview continues the analyst construes 'good' performance as the number of 'boxes' that he can 'tick off':

> ... if I could tick off all those things, I think I'd be doing a pretty good job.

This extract renders visible assumptions about performing 'pretty reasonably'. On the one hand in the content-targeted interview the analyst employs evaluative lexis suggesting a qualitative approach to assessing performance ('comfortable', 'enjoy', 'trouble' and 'happy'), on the other hand when his grammar is probed about what he means by 'performance' more quantitative processes of 'ticking things off' are construed. There seems a misalignment in the semantic construal in the content interviews with the meaning revealed in the grammar-targeted interview. This is an example of the kind of misalignment between content and grammar identified in Chapter 2. The incongruity suggests that this is an instance of tacit knowledge about appraisal metrics and that the subject is not necessarily aware that he applies a quantitative appraisal metric while talking about performance as an instrinsically qualitative process.

Table 5.6 'Performance', Business Analyst 1, grammar-targeted interview

Turn	Speaker	Talk
1	Interviewer	So what's performance and particularly your performance mean for you?
2	Business Analyst 1	Well, I suppose the way this process is defined, I'd sort of think in terms of that, because what this is **saying** is, you know, that we have a number of measures here, and that's what I've said that I'll do this year. So good performance for me is really ticking those boxes off or **saying**, 'Yep, I did get 92 per cent billable hours' or 'I did produce three documents of this type' or 'I did do this'.
3	Interviewer	Ok, so it's about quantitative things?
4	Business Analyst 1	Well, again it's a mix, because in terms of whatever's in that measures column. That's what I'm trying to focus on, **saying**, my performance will be judged by however many of those measures I can think of sort of thing or satisfy, and I suppose at the beginning of the year, because I get to help define what those measures are, then I'll try to make them relevant to what I think is good performance, or would be, that is, I suppose I try and think if I could tick off all those things, I think I'd be doing a pretty good job.
5	Interviewer	Right, right.
6	Business Analyst 1	So therefore when I think of my performance, it's how many of those things I can tick off and **say**, 'Yes, I've done those' or –
7	Interviewer	So good performance, what would constitute good performance?
8	Business Analyst 1	I suppose, good performance would be satisfying a high percentage of those measures, so 75 per cent plus, I suppose.

An example where the content and grammar appear aligned

The in-house interviews with the business analysts focused on self-appraisal by the analyst. Table 5.7 is an extract from such an interview with Business Analyst 2 where he is asked to appraise his 'performance'. If we focus just on the under-representation via generalization in this extract, it is apparent that 'good' occurs at two crucial points in the business analyst's talk (see bold text in extract). These are the points at which the following assumptions are effaced:

- How do I know when I am doing a 'good' job?
- How do I know when I possess 'good written communication, oral communication, network skills and analytical skills'?

Table 5.7 'Performance', Business Analyst 2, content-targeted interview

Turn	Speaker	Talk
1	Interviewer	If you had to sum up your own **performance**, how do you think you have gone in the last 12 months?
2	Business Analyst 2	Well, I'm definitely moving up because 6 months ago I was on level 9, now I'm on level 10.
3	Interviewer	Well, that's **good**.
4	Business Analyst 2	But, I was on level 14 last year.
5	Interviewer	Do you think you'll ever get to 25?
6	Business Analyst 2	No, I don't. Look, I think there's always room for improvement because, especially being a contractor, you don't want to become too complacent. I like to challenge myself which is why I have set these goals outside of work. It's kind of personal training goals, but, yeah, look, I think I'd like to think I'm doing a **good** job, both from a technical perspective and also a business perspective. I think as a BA, you have to have a number of skills, not just, it's not like, I guess, a programmer where they can literally sit in a room in front of a computer and just cut code. With a BA, you've got to have **good** written communication, oral communication, network skills, and analytical skills, and all of that.

The interviewer, however, does not take up these issues but instead moves on to a question about the speaker's perceived weaknesses. The talk in Turn 6 seems to be more about the speaker's opinion about the 'BA', as an idealized subject position, more than it is about the speaker's experience of his day-to-day work environment.

Table 5.8 is the same business analyst's response to a question about his performance over the last year in the grammar-targeted interview. The interviewer attempts to unpack 'a good job' in Turn 3. However, little below-view meaning about how the subject construes 'good performance' is revealed. Instead of a more congruent agnate realization, the business analyst introduces additional under-representation into the discourse: the nominalization, 'expectation' (which in this particular example, the grammar-targeted interviewer fails to probe).

A possible explanation for the failure of the grammar-targeted interview to uncover tacit knowledge is that grammar and content appear aligned in this example. In both the content-targeted and grammar-targeted extracts, Business Analyst 2 talks about 'challenging himself' and uses a grammar where he is the dominant agent. Thus content about locating himself as the entity who is

Table 5.8 'Unpacking 'a good job', Business Analyst 2, grammar-targeted interview

Turn	Subject	Talk
2	Business Analyst 2	I'm wonderful. Nah, nah! [laughs] I mean, I think I've done alright. Look, I think I've done **a good job**. I mean, I've done what I've been employed to do. I've challenged myself. I used to work in more of a technology planner area and I've since moved to this new area where I focused not on the planners, but more on the products which is the superannuation products and the retail products, the risk products. So, yeah, look, I think I've done a reasonable or a **good** job. There's always room for improvement.
3	Interviewer	So what's **'a good job'** mean?
4	Business Analyst 2	Given – Met expectations of the teams I've been working with, of my managers. Outside of work, I've pushed myself to do additional training, and, yeah, look, I like to exceed expectations as well. So –

responsible for 'good performance' aligns with a grammatical construal of himself as the participant who causes 'good performance' to happen.

What are the practical implications of generalization such as 'good'?

If generalization such as 'good' and other vague appraisal items remain packed-up in performance reviews, the tacit assumptions that inform the appraisal will not be addressed. This means that they will instead be taken as given. However, glossing over such phenomena and assuming that the interviewer and interviewee share the same meanings about working with technology is problematic. The risk is that the performance reviewer (where not adequately socialized into the interviewees' technical discourses) will reconstrue the interviewee's meanings without adequate understanding of the context.

The probing of 'performance' was designed to more fully construe what the agnate process of 'performing well' meant in the interviewee's own terms. The grammar-targeted method is useful, in this way, not only for overcoming differences in how interviewers and interviewees view 'performance' but in addressing differences between the speakers' construals. For example, in the following section we see an example where understanding the different and particular construals of experience made by a manager and a business analyst was crucial to explaining conflict over the validity of a manager's assessment of that analyst.

An example of misalignment of content and grammar: Unpacking 'role'

This section investigates a particular instance where there was an incongruity between the content and grammar used by two individuals, Business Analyst 3 and Manager 3. The incongruity resulted in conflict about role definition, the origins of which were explicitly described by the participants as unclear. The term 'role' was used throughout the interviews to refer to the scope of a person's work activity to which some higher ranking member of the organization expects they will perform. The conflict centred upon the problem that the business analyst felt that she was expected to perform activities that were not specified by her manager. For example, Business Analyst 3, when asked about the feedback that was given to her in the content-targeted interview about Manager 3's behaviour stated:

> It is sort of expected from me that I should try and provide more than is expected.

The business analyst and Manager 3 'pointed the finger' at each other grammatically over who was responsible for defining the business analyst's role on the project. This was despite the content-level consensus being that it is the manager's responsibility to define the business analyst's role, seen in statements such as the following by the manager:

> So, I therefore would answer you that it was ultimately my responsibility for the role that she was performing.

However, despite this description of accountability regarding the role residing with the manager, his grammar shifts the locus of this responsibility to the business analyst. Contrastively the grammatical construal of the business analyst locates the manager as the participant responsible for the 'role' (Table 5.9). The sections that follow consider the nature and implications of this difference in how the two speakers allocate responsibility through how they distribute agency in their grammar.

Table 5.9 Difference in the construal of responsibility for 'role' in the talk of Manager 3 and Business Analyst 3

	Manager 3	Business Analyst 3
Content	Manager is responsible	Manager is responsible
Grammar	Business analyst is responsible	Manager is responsible

The manager's perspective

While the manager locates Business Analyst 3's work role as within his domain of responsibility, at the tacit level he shifts this responsibility to the business analyst. His grammar tended to cast the business analyst as an agent in material processes about not only enacting, but more importantly, defining or 'carving out' her role (Table 5.10). These material processes construe the employee as causing the role to happen: not an illogical grammatical choice since she is the person carrying out the tasks. However, she is also the agent in clauses defining the role. This is an instance of misalignment between the explicit and tacit construal, or in alternative terms, the content and the grammar.

The tendency identified in these instances is echoed when we approach the manager's talk as a corpus. The business analyst is the dominant agent in Manager 3's discourse when he is talking about the concept of 'role' in 178 effective (as opposed to middle) clauses (Figure 5.3). The semantic domains of the agent are explained in Table 5.11.

The manager locates himself as agent in 12 per cent of cases, while he positions the business analyst as agent in 36 per cent of cases (Figure 5.3). In this way, his grammar shifts responsibility from himself to the business analyst when he talks about the role. This pattern is echoed across the entire sample of discourse from this interviewee. In a similar way, the relatively high incidence of 'Impersonal' clauses appears to be another tacit strategy used by the manager to distribute agency elsewhere or to be vague about the locus of responsibility.

The manager concedes at an explicit level, as I mentioned earlier, that responsibility for the role lies with him when he says 'it was ultimately my responsibility for the role that she was performing'. However, he goes on to make a number of grammatical moves that undermine this concession. These

Table 5.10 Examples of Business Analyst 3 as an agent in material processes about the 'role' as described by Manager 3

Process	Process type	context
To carve	Material	She's got a responsibility there as well to carve her role and fit into the environment as well.
To carve out	Material	To some extent she carved out the role that she ultimately ended up with.
To deliver	Material	She did well within the bounds of what she was able to deliver in the role.
To take into	Material	What she ended up doing was a function of what she was able or comfortable to take into her role.

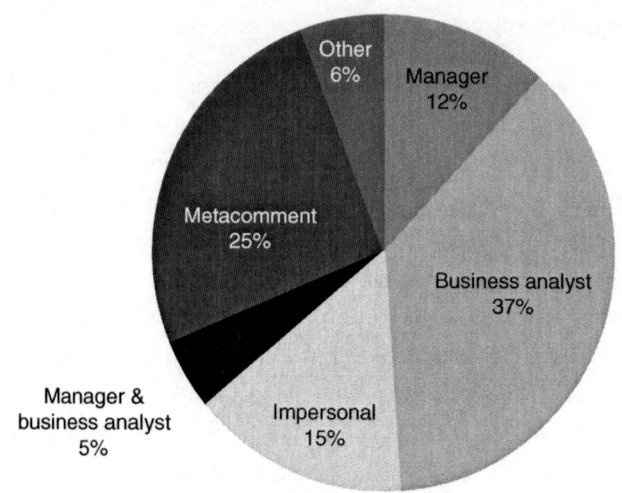

Figure 5.3 Distribution of agency in clauses about 'role', Manager 3, grammar-targeted interview.

Table 5.11 Type of agent

Agent categories	Explanation
Manager	Manager 3, the interviewee
Business analyst	Business Analyst 3, the manager's employee on a project
Metacomment[2]	Clauses which project such as 'I think', 'I suppose', etc.
Manager and business analyst	Manager 3 and business analyst as joint agent, e.g. 'we'
Impersonal	Non-specific 'you' or 'we'
Other	All other agents, e.g. clients, stakeholders, developers, etc.

grammatical moves begin with a hypotactic 'if' clause (Turn 2 of Table 5.12). The manager shifts responsibility to the irrealis by the adverbs 'ultimately' and 'officially'. In this way, he reduces the contestibility of his 'responsibility' as it becomes something that cannot be contested in the realis domain. These grammatical moves culminate with the manager stating, at the end of Turn 2, 'she's got a responsibility there as well to carve her role and fit into the environment as well', assigning, if in part, explicit responsibility to Business Analyst 3, while obscuring the extent of the delegation via the nominalization.

Returning to the content-targeted interviews, we see similar covert patterns that remain unpacked. Table 5.13 is the phase in the content-targeted interview where the manager talks about 'responsibility':

I never really felt she took additional ownership . . .

Table 5.12 'Responsibility', Manager 3, grammar-targeted interview (emphasis added)

Turn	Speaker	Talk
1	Interviewer	So, who took responsibility for the management of the relationship between you? She did or you did?
2	Manager 3	I asked her to come in and do a role, so I therefore would answer you that it was ultimately **my responsibility** for the role that she was performing. You asked me before whether I had a formal feedback discussion with her regarding this. No, I didn't. Would I say it was my responsibility to do that? I'd say, 'Yes, it was' **if** I felt the situation necessitated it, which I didn't, so I didn't, but, yeah, **ultimately** I see that's my responsibility. I also believe that any individual is responsible you know for their own being in a workplace environment, and they are accountable for what they do in that environment, so although I say, **officially**, I'm responsible for her work and her position in the team, she's got a responsibility there as well to carve her role and fit into the environment as well.

Table 5.13 'Responsibility', Manager 3, content-targeted interview

Turn	Speaker	Talk
1	Manager 3	So, she was able to track the status of things, chair the meetings, etc., catalogue the status, produce the daily reports on the staff, but **I never really felt she took additional ownership** of trying to understand that real need of trying to manage all the parties, so she tended to be a little bit **passive** in the role versus, you know, **actively** managing it.
2	Interviewer	So actively managing the Organization Z stakeholders?
3	Manager 3	I think just making, to me it was purely a case of making something of the role and she was, like, if I would go to her and say, 'You know, Business Analyst 2, please do this report, or, Business Analyst 2, let's get this report right', she would do that, and she'd produce the stuff as required, but I never felt like **her brain engaged the extra step** in terms of, 'well hang on, why's he asking me to do this stuff?' and **owning** the role and **owning** the function and delivering that.
4	Interviewer	So you felt that she could have, I guess, have made the role a bit more than what it was?
5	Manager 3	Yeah.
6	Interviewer	Especially, I guess, as a project manager coming in at that level.

This clause complex is characteristic of how Manager 3 distributes agency. Business Analyst 3 is the agent in the projected clause. She is the entity 'taking ownership', while the manager is cast as the senser making the evaluation.

The business analyst is the target of the following appraisal by the manager (Table 5.14):

> ... she performed to a level that was acceptable and we worked with.

The embedded clause, 'that was acceptable' reduces the contestibility of Manager 3's description of the business analyst's performance because the agent saying 'that something is acceptable' is omitted and hence the acceptability criteria cannot be probed. Similarly, his use of a generalized 'we' under-specifies the actor. The interviewer responds to the grammatical construal by asking a question designed to elaborate the 'we', as seen in Turn 3 of Table 5.14. The manager's response distributes the 'we' across a variety of participants, diluting his own responsibility. The implications of this move are seen in the following section dealing with the business analyst's perspective.

Table 5.14 'Alright', Manager 3, grammar-targeted interview

Turn	Subject	Talk
1	Interviewer	So, when you say she was 'alright', what does 'alright' mean?
2	Manager 3	It means she performed to a level that was acceptable and we worked with. I think that within the bounds of the original role that we scoped and that I wanted her to perform to with respect to what I originally was looking for, she didn't really fulfil that full function but it didn't matter, because we had other people like me to fulfil the bits she was missing out on. So it never really became a big issue, but I think, if I am purely trying to appraise Business Analyst 3's performance, give her constructive feedback, there's clearly a role there that we wanted her to step into that she didn't. She did parts of that, but not as strong as she may have been able to.
3	Interviewer	When you say 'we wanted her to step into', who's the 'we'?
4	Manager 3	'We' is – I talk on respect of the, the project team upstairs. That's effectively me, because I've got carriage of the problem, right, but I represent, I guess, the, all the production stakeholders of the system, so our people who we – When I say 'we', I say that because there are developers up there fixing problems. There are business analysts up there analysing issues that are happening. They're all a team, so even though it's ultimately my responsibility, it's more than just me who needs that function performed.

The business analyst's perspective

The previous section demonstrated how Manager 3's grammar shifted responsibility for the defining and managing the role of Business Analyst 3. This section shows how Business Analyst 3 shifts this responsibility back to the manager. The business analyst's grammar construes that manager as the dominant agent when she talks about the role she performed (Figure 5.4). The majority of the agency is ascribed to her manager (35%). The following is an example of a clause casting the manager as agent:

In order for him to be able to resolve all these production support issues.

The below-view nature of this grammatical finger-pointing about the business analyst's work means that it is difficult for a performance reviewer who deals solely with content to understand the nature of the problem. For example, understanding how the manager and business analyst are tacitly construing each other as agents responsible for defining what is required within the business analyst's role means that assumptions underlying statements such as the following can be made visible:

. . . and she'd produce the stuff as required, but I never felt like her brain engaged the extra step in terms of "well hang on, why's he asking me to do this stuff?" and owning the role, and owning the function, and delivering that . . .

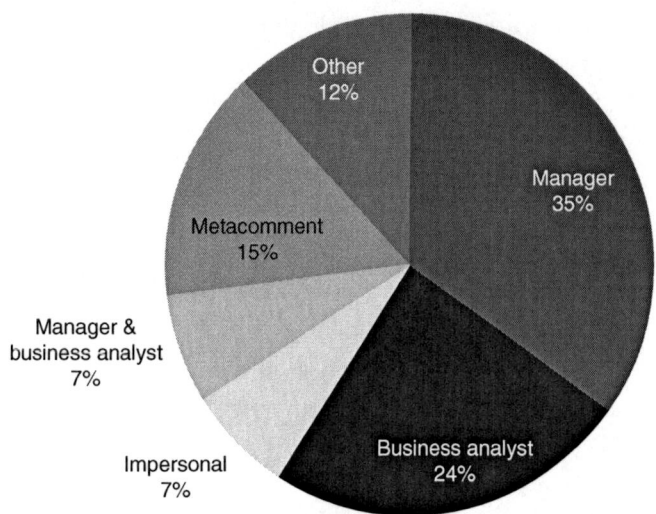

Figure 5.4 Distribution of agency in talk about 'role', Business Analyst 3, grammar-targeted interview.

This is an instance from the content-targeted interview with the manager where he appears unaware of how notions of 'requiring', 'owning' and 'delivering' are competing in his discourse. The 'extra step' that he implies is part of effectively performing the role that seems to be about enacting the unexpressed. The following section investigates how such ideas about 'expecting someone to do something' were packed up in nominalizations.

Unpacking the nominalization 'expectation'

The results presented so far have focused upon under-representation by generalization about 'performing well'. Alongside this type of under-representation was the packing up of interpersonal meaning about 'why a person works well with another person' via nominalization. Various types of interpersonal phenomena were under-represented such as personality traits, opinions and behaviours (Table 5.15).

The nominalization 'expectation' was unpacked in the grammar-targeted interviews with Business Analyst 3 and Manager 3. The aim was to understand the tacit assumptions they made about what it means 'to expect something from someone else'. Nominalizations associated with the idea of 'someone expecting something from someone' in the speakers' talk were both about meeting project goals and about communication between people (Table 5.16). Each of these nominalizations embeds a series of processes, participants and circumstances about these types of activities.

Appraisal collocated with the nominalization 'expectation' (Table 5.17) added another layer of complexity to the problem of understanding the assumptions about performing well that the speakers made because the nominalization meant that the specific processes and participants being appraised, typically

Table 5.15 Examples of nominalization that were the target of questions in the grammar-targeted interviews

Nominalization	Nominalized process
Expectation	To expect
Productivity	To produce
Approachable	To approach
Diligent worker	To work (and to be diligent)
Leader	To lead
Feedback	To feed back
Knowledge sharing	To know, to share
Predictability	To predict

Table 5.16 Nominalizations associated with 'expectation' in the interviews

Nominalization	Nominalized process
Improvement	To improve
Solution	To solve
Management	To manage
Feedback	To feed back
Agreement	To agree

Table 5.17 Appraisal collocating with 'expectation'

Appraisal	Type
Appropriate	JUDGEMENT: SOCIAL SANCTION: PROPRIETY
Fairly solid	JUDGEMENT: SOCIAL ESTEEM: CAPACITY
Fairly high	JUDGEMENT: SOCIAL ESTEEM: CAPACITY
Strange	JUDGEMENT: SOCIAL ESTEEM: NORMALITY

by the JUDGEMENT system, were obscured, being embedded in the nominal groups. Thus the criteria establishing propriety, capacity and normality in the text remained tacit.

For example, in the content-targeted interview with Manager 3, the manager says:

> . . . the project management bit I always recognised we needed to be strong in, because there are a lot areas we needed to align. That was a fairly solid expectation from my side as well, but I felt over time that the actual the role she tended to get more into was . . . a bit more reactive perhaps than proactive around what it needed to be.

In this extract, 'fairly solid expectation' seems an innocuous term that might be paraphrased as being about the case where 'someone expects someone to do something with a reasonable degree of certainty'. However, the nominalization naturalizes both the concept that 'expecting the something' is reasonable and that the 'someone can perform the thing that is expected of them'. A more congruent such as 'I expect X from X' would allow these concepts to be deconstructed in a way that the nominalized form does not: in this instance, the manager expects that the business analyst will perform her project management functions well. However, elsewhere in the interview the manager concedes that he did not tell Business Analyst 3 that she was not fulfilling particular functions that he expected her to perform (Table 5.18). While the content-targeted interviewer has picked

Table 5.18 Unvoiced expectation, Manager 3, content-targeted interview

Turn	Speaker	Talk
1	Manager 3	… when the dust settled, what she (Business Analyst 3) was doing was a lot less than what the original intention was for that role.
2	Interviewer	Ok, alright, and did you actually, I guess, spell that out for Business Analyst 3 or was it an expectation that at her level she would realize that needed to be done?
3	Manager 3	No, not really. I mean, it was a case of we filled the gaps through other means. It probably meant through other people doing those pieces of work that weren't being done.

up on the important point that the 'expectation' is unvoiced by the manager, the interviewer does not further probe the response and the topic is dropped.

By way of contrast, the grammar-targeted interviewer probes the nominalization 'the right expectation' in the interview with Business Analyst 3. As the subject talks about what it means for the manager to expect her to perform certain activities she reveals that while she 'thought it was very clear as to what [she] was expected to do', her manager has been disappointed that she has not performed tasks that she feels he has not explicitly defined. The interviewer attempts to unpack this analyst's construal of what it means to express an 'expectation'.

However, continued probing reveals that the situation is more complex when the business analyst is confronted with aspects of the 'role' that require her to make decisions that she deems involve an interpersonal component about what is 'appropriate' in a particular situation. Parallel to the idea of 'someone expecting something to be done' is the notion of 'who decides whether something is appropriate'. The former is more about material action, while the latter foregrounds the interpersonal aspect of such action. 'Appropriate' is judgement: propriety: positive in the appraisal system. While Business Analyst 3 assigns agency to her manager when talking about 'role', she covertly locates herself as the entity who decides when a course of action is 'appropriate'. Positioning herself and her managers in this way causes a misalignment that she was unable to resolve. An example is the business analyst's 'failure' in the eyes of Manager 3 to perform certain tasks. For example, Manager 3 was displeased that Business Analyst 3 did not contribute in meetings with the client in the way that Manager 3 envisaged (Table 5.19).

Table 5.19 Contribution in meetings, Manager 3, content-targeted interview

Turn	Speaker	Talk
1	Manager 3	Business Analyst 3 never really contributed to those sessions.
2	Interviewer	Oh, didn't she?
3	Manager 3	She came along to her credit, and she brought the numbers, and she'd always have the spreadsheets for me or whoever to speak to. It's probably not fair to be critical of her for not doing that better, but she didn't really, I don't know, I think there's probably a question in there of developmentally for Business Analyst 3. She's in that room, it's an opportunity.

Business Analyst 3 provided the following explanation in the grammar-targeted interview for her behaviour regarding the project meetings:

> Well first of all, as I said before, I don't think it's appropriate for me to go in there and just shake that team when there's already like a team leader. I don't want to undermine the team leader.

Following this explanation from the business analyst, the grammar-targeted interview unpacks the agent(s) who decide if something is 'appropriate' (i.e. the elided participants defining the judgement of PROPRIETY) (Table 5.20). This unpacking reveals that Business Analyst 3 positions herself as the agent in mental processes of deciding whether something is 'appropriate' (Turn 6). Thus, we see a further incongruity in the business analyst's language. While, as previously noted, she construes the manager as responsible for her role, here the business analyst herself is the agent who decides when it is 'appropriate' to do something. The further incongruity explains the inaction of the business analyst, for example, her failure to attend various key meetings. Simple misalignment between the tacit construals of responsibility identified in previous sections (manager as agent/business analyst as agent) explain the conflict over role definition, but the further internal misalignment in the business analyst's discourse, that is, the way she attributes responsibility about the role to the manager while also attributing decisions about the 'appropriateness' of some kinds of actions (conforming to her construal of PROPRIETY).

Table 5.20 Unpacking 'appropriate', Business Analyst 3, grammar-targeted interview

Turn	Speaker	Talk
1	Interviewer	So **who** determines what's appropriate?
2	Business Analyst 3	It's me.
3	Interviewer	Ok.
4	Business Analyst 3	But sometimes what you think is appropriate or inappropriate others might not see that. Do you know what I mean? It's very subjective, I suppose.
5	Interviewer	So, was there a space in there somewhere which left a gap between you and Manager 3 which you both could have made some contribution to close?
6	Business Analyst 3	Probably. We probably could have worked together because the feeling that I got was that, well, from the feedback, he expected me to do all this by myself. Like to just go in there and as I said, 'I don't have the technical knowledge'. And if I had the technical knowledge, I would maybe feel more comfortable in doing that, but I don't. And that's why I thought it was **inappropriate** for me to do that. And specifically if I'm providing a service because person x's team, they're seen as internal consultants and they're providing a service for other teams and I don't think it's appropriate that I go in there and shake-up an existing, established team. Does that make sense?

What are the implication of misalignment between content and grammar?

The below-view nature of the misalignment in content and grammar about role definition that we have seen in the discourse of Business Analyst 3 and Manager 3 mean that it is difficult for these individuals to determine why they are in conflict. Consequently, a performance reviewer is at a double disadvantage, as they may be confused by the apparent transparency of the speakers' explicit construal. The situation is not merely a case where two people disagree on something. Instead this is the case where two people have different kinds of tacit knowledge about their practice. The individuals cannot get to the point of constructively disagreeing because they do not have a common construal of the problem itself. Thus, the major implication of identifying this kind of misalignment is the opportunity it allows for people to resolve their differences: it gives them the opportunity to be grammatically 'on the same page', to appropriate a popular management metaphor. When grammar and content are out of alignment it is less likely that people are doing what they say they are doing. This means that without specific strategies for identifying misalignment of this kind, the performance reviewer cannot be certain whether they are dealing with an accurate representation of the state of affairs in question.

This field study has investigated what can be thought of as the below-view stratum of performance reviewing, that is, the tacit assumptions made by interviewers and interviewee's when they talk about 'good performance'. It has described how grammatical analysis of under-representation can uncover instances of incongruity or, alternatively, alignment between content and grammar, and instances where the grammar extends the content. The ability to probe grammar and identify these instances offers the performance reviewer a more nuanced instrument for interpreting the meanings made by interviewees as they talk about their work.

Notes

1   Judgement forms part of the Attitude system within Martin and White's (2005) model of appraisal.
2   The category 'Metacomment' is distinguished from the general 'Manager' category since these clauses 'function not as a direct representation of (non-linguistic) experience but as a representation of a (linguistic) representation' (Halliday and Matthiessen 2004).

6

Conclusion

Introduction

This book has explored an unconscious dimension of language. We have been concerned with the grammatical patterns that people use to construe experience as a way of understanding their tacit knowledge. This type of perspective on communication is not commonly used outside linguistics since many disciplines adopt an ideationally focused standpoint on meaning, that is, a perspective that focuses on content. These disciplines tend to construe content as 'words':

> Certain aspects of language are closer to conscious awareness than others; these are the more exposed parts of language, which are also the parts that tend to get studied first. In Western thinking about language, the most exposed aspect of language has been the "word": to talk is to "put things into words". (Halliday and Matthiessen 1999: 568)

It is thus unsurprising that most approaches to tacit knowledge have not considered the possibility that it may be carried in the grammatical patterns of language, and researchers have looked outside language to understand knowledge.

This turn away from language has arisen alongside the long-held tradition that argues that language obscures our lens on reality. Instead theoretical gazes thought to be more rigorous than linguistics (e.g. the scientific method) have been privileged:

> This belief in the distorting effect of language was propounded by the early European humanists, who held that mediæval scholars had focussed too strongly on language, whereas the real task of the scientist was to see through

the verbal disguise and penetrate the reality underneath . . . (Halliday and Matthiessen 1999: 444–5)

The field studies presented in this book have attempted to counter this kind of anti-linguistic stance found in work on tacit knowledge. By adopting a rich, functional model of language, using SFL, I have shown how linguistic analysis can be used to explicate tacit knowledge.

This book has introduced an interview method, the grammar-targeted interview method, that employs a questioning style aimed at probing grammatical patterns. I have introduced a model of 'under-representation' in spoken discourse. This model was used to define a manageable set of features that might be probed in real time by an interviewer. The field studies using this method have reported on tacit knowledge in two ways: in terms of grammatical patterning assessed quantitatively across a corpus, and in terms of more qualitative grammatical analysis of instances of specific language examples.

What type of tacit knowledge was unpacked via grammar-targeted questions?

The tacit knowledge uncovered in the three field studies involved abstract meanings about technology and technical processes in organizations as well as about managing people and relationships. It was thus 'practical' knowledge in the semiotic rather somatic sense, where the latter is the commonly cited example of tacit knowledge: riding a bike. In other words, what has been exposed in the interviewee's talk is the implicit assumptions carried in their grammar about their work.

Important tacit knowledge that the technologists held was about the system and its operation. This included implicit meanings about technical systems and their scope, and particular ways of thinking about delivering services to users. It typically involved under-representation via generalization (e.g. the term 'system' itself) and nominalization (e.g. 'requirement'). Field Study 1 foregrounded the potential of technical terminology to camouflage non-optimal ways of approaching requirements analysis (e.g. approaching requirements as 'system requirements' and failing to engage with the user community).

Another important kind of implicit patterning significant in the field studies was how the speakers allocated responsibility to participants in their talk. Tacit knowledge in this area was about power relations within the organization. How agency was distributed revealed how the speakers viewed different types of work relationships (e.g. the relationship between the technical team and the uses, and the relationship between managers and business analysts). The field studies demonstrated how responsibility could be unconsciously tempered by individuals (e.g. the CIO in Field Study 1 dissipating responsibility about cultural change, and the 'grammatical finger-pointing' between Manager 3 and Business Analyst 3 over accountability about a role in Field Study 3).

While most examples of tacit knowledge that are cited in the literature involve practical skills such as the fashioning of a physical object by an artisan (e.g. Nonaka and Takeuchi's (1995) example of bread-baking), this is largely tacit knowledge at one order of experience – it is somatic tacit knowledge. To ignore more abstract forms of tacit knowledge such as those explored in the field studies presented in this book, is to negate the role of tacit knowledge in the complex meanings negotiated in modern organizations. Indeed Polanyi figures both kinds of knowledge as interwoven.

Technology allows us to operate at an order of experience higher than that of concrete objects. Alongside technological advance is the evolution of language as a 'semiotic refraction of our own existence in the physical, biological, social and semiotic modes' (Halliday and Matthiessen 1999: 602). The abstraction afforded by language allows us to move beyond the purely physical to work with complex artefacts such as technical systems and organizational processes. When working at this order of experience multifaceted arrays of meaning are packed up in language. It is fortunate that we have the capacity to pack up such meaning since the semantic and grammatical burden of constantly detailing all assumed concepts would otherwise be overwhelming.

The IT implications of the tacit knowledge uncovered

The IT consequences of the four main types of tacit knowledge uncovered in the field studies are summarized in Table 6.1. This is intended to give the reader a sense of the very practical impact of implicit meaning on people working in organizations. For example, the manager in Field Study 1 talking about the kinds of cultural changes he wants to make in an organization is unlikely to be successful when deploying a grammar that dissipates his responsibility at getting the process going.

However, even when meanings remain below-view, there is always the possibility of change: by changing our language we change our practices. Halliday has suggested that people developing technology might begin to alter the kind of language that they use so that it is less remote from the experience of those ultimately using the technology:

> Perhaps our technical discourse, while it must have its nominalisations in order to create systematic taxonomies, could nevertheless be nudged away from its obsession with pseudo-things, towards more democratic forms which lessen the semiotic distance – both the experiential distance, which makes the language of technical knowledge so remote from the experiences of everyday life, and the interpersonal distance, which separates those who have the knowledge from those who are left outside. (Halliday 1993: 78)

The less under-represented discourse produced in the grammar-targeted interviews, with its reduced preference for nominalization, might be though of as a step towards lessening the semiotic distance to which Halliday here refers.

Table 6.1 The IT implications of the types of tacit knowledge identified in the field studies

	Tacit knowledge	IT consequences
1	The construal of technical terminology and construction of technical artefacts:	
	– Requirements analysis is undertaken as a technocratic activity. For example, systems are construed as technical artefacts rather than complexes involving people processes and technology (Field Study 2).	– User resistance of a system that does not meet their needs.
2	The allocation of responsibility:	
	– Accountability for cultural change required for successful knowledge management is effaced (Field Study 1). – Confusion over conflict about responsibility for roles (Field Study 3).	– Failure of the culture to change due to inadequate ownership of the problem of management. – Unresolved conflict about role definition.
3	The construal of performance:	
	– Difficulty interpreting context-specific generalization (Field Study 3).	– Inaccurate performance reviews.
4	The construal of shared knowledge:	
	– Understanding between individuals assumed to be a tangible commodity (Field Study 2).	– True consensus is not achieved.

In these field studies I have explored whether under-representation in spoken discourse about IT can be unpacked through a grammar-targeted interview method. However, I have not considered the complementary question of whether the material unpacked in the interviews can improve the work practices of the interviewees when it is presented to them. Such inquiry would require a controlled experiment measuring improved performance by subjects on specific tasks. Such an experiment might test whether subjects who have undergone the grammar-targeted interview method change the way in which they work with IT. The general question would be whether making a person aware of tacit knowledge embedded in their grammar has an impact on the way they work. No doubt controlling all the possible variables for this type of study would be very difficult.

A more complex issue is how tacit knowledge explicated through the grammar-targeted technique might assist the practice of people other than the original speaker. While I have piloted the grammar-targeted interview method in different kinds of corporate organizations, I have not made claims about how to involve the method in larger organizational processes of training and development. This is because the issue of communicating unpacked tacit knowledge to other individuals involves a large range of intervening variables relating to education and learning.

A language-oriented approach to eliciting tacit knowledge, of the kind pursued in this book, may appear radical given the dominance of Polanyi's concept of 'knowing more than we can tell'. However, if we acknowledge the role of tacit processes in spoken discourse, analysing and probing language patterns appears a viable way of eliciting tacit knowledge. We tell more than we realize we know.

Appendix A: The Grammar-Targeted Interview Protocol

1. The interviewer asks a general question of the form 'Tell me about your particular area of expertise' (or if the task/domain is sufficiently specified 'Tell me about task X').
2. The interviewee responds.
3. The interviewer interrupts the interviewee when he/she has identified a grammatical feature of under-representation about the particular content-area of interest and asks a question aimed at unpacking the grammatical feature.
5. The interviewee responds to the question.
6. The interviewer repeats steps 3 and 4 until he/she has constructed a coherent argument for a particular reading of the interviewee's tacit knowledge about some topic. The argument is coherent in the sense that it is supported by multiple patterns of grammatical features.
7. When the interviewer has achieved an understanding of the concept/skill that is the topic of the interview he may present his 'reading' to the interviewee, asking a question of the form 'Now I think I have understood what you mean about X. How do you feel about this reading?'.
9. The interviewer and interviewee may engage in unstructured discourse relating to what has occurred in the interview.
10. The interviewer will conclude the interview at an interpersonally appropriate juncture.

Appendix B: Interview Topics, Field Study 2

Round 1

The aim of this is interview is to elicit the following:

- What the subject believes is the aim of the project and their definition of a content management system.
- The subject's expertise in the project.
- How the subject transfers knowledge within the project.
- What the subject believes are the challenges they face in the project.

Round 2

This interview aims to elicit the subject's knowledge transfer processes as they relate to their work in the last week. This includes the following:

- barriers to knowledge transfer
- the content of the knowledge transfer
- the mode of knowledge transfer
- how knowledge transfer relates to the critical success factors of the project
- the individual's current work (in the last week):

  - what are they working on?
  - how are they working on it?
  - with whom are they working?
  - what difficulties are they experiencing?

Round 3

This interview should cover the following:

- What is the current status of the project?
- Is the project meeting it goals?

- How does the subject understand how the project is progressing?
- What kind of communication processes are involved in ensuring that the team knows the project status?

In addition, the current work of the participants is an ongoing topic:

- What are they currently working on? (i.e. since the last interview)
- How are they currently working on it?
- With whom are they currently working?
- What difficulties are they experiencing in their current work?

Round 4

This interview deals with the following:

- What have you achieved in the project and where is the project currently in terms of status?
- Summarize what you did in the project personally. What kind of approach did you take?
- What are the weaknesses in what you have done in the project? What are the weakness in the project overall?
- What are the strengths in what you have done in the project?
- What are the strengths in the project overall?
- How will the project continue? What still needs to be done?

Appendix C: Statistical Analysis of Interview Corpora

Table C.1 Amount of nominalization for each subject and interview type $N = 3$; $N = 12$ for the totals shown in the bottom row

Interviewee	Content-targeted interview nominalization (%)		Grammar-targeted interview nominalization (%)	
	Mean	Standard deviation	Mean	Standard deviation
1	25.7	6.68	13.3	5.03
2	19.1	5.38	14.0	0.67
3	18.0	7.47	8.89	3.36
4	21.1	1.47	12.7	3.50
Total	21.0	5.76	12.2	3.64

Table C.2 Difference in the distribution of agency in the content-targeted and grammar-targeted interviews

	Value	df	Asymptotic significance (two-sided)
Pearson chi-square	29.05332076	3	2.18239E-06
Likelihood ratio	29.29509122	3	1.94142E-06
Linear-by-linear association	14.26060475	1	0.000159161
Number of valid cases	2,640		

Table C.3 Amount of clauses containing a generalization for each subject and interview type

Interview round	Content-targeted interview generalization (%)		Grammar-targeted interview generalization (%)	
	Mean	Standard deviation	Mean	Standard deviation
1	47.33277539	1.732557209	20.44444444	3.355481971
2	32.72901905	3.347272257	14.44444444	4.337604732
3	39.38888889	5.478070761	16.44444444	4.073400618
4	41.14227134	5.922917236	18.40048559	5.7030579

Table C.4 Amount of modalized clauses for each subject and interview type

Interview round	Content-targeted interview modalized clauses (%)		Grammar-targeted interview modalized clauses (%)	
	Mean	Standard deviation	Mean	Standard deviation
1	15.83820195	8.523729583	18.22222222	5.17830231
2	23.99244214	3.705780875	20.88888889	4.018475849
3	17.5	2.204792759	13.11111111	3.421067626
4	31.19382396	10.70591855	19.66462207	6.164223266

Appendix D: Transitivity of Clauses Containing 'Requirements'

Table D.1 Transitivity in clauses containing requirement

Subject	Process	Process type	Participant type
Project manager	To be	Existential	Medium
	To relate to	Relational	Medium
	To be defined as	Relational	Medium
	To fit into	Relational	Medium
	To provide	Material	Medium
	To use	Material	Medium
	To state	Verbal	Medium
	To make	Material	Medium
	To have	Relational	Medium
	To be	Relational	Agent
	To steer clear of	Material	Medium
	To pass as	Relational	Medium
	To document	Mental	Medium
Information architect	To be	Relational	Medium
	To have	Relational	Medium
	To bunch	Relational	Medium
	To cover	Relational	Agent
	To isolate	Relational	Medium
	To be	Existential	Medium
	To call	Relational	Medium
	To feed into	Relational	Medium
	To develop	Material	Medium
	To gather	Material	Medium
	To filter	Material	Medium
	To be derived	Relational	Medium
	To be elaborated	Relational	Medium
	To derive	Relational	Medium
	To try to get perfect	Relational	Medium

Continues

Table D.1 Cont'd.

Subject	Process	Process type	Participant type
Technologist 1	To capture	Material	Medium
	To make a difference in	Material	Medium
	To put into	Material	Medium
	To be	Relational	Medium
	To be needed	Mental	Medium
	To need	Mental	Medium
	To be part of	Relational	Medium
	To define	Relational	Medium
Technologist 2	To need	Mental	Agent
	To be	Relational	Agent

Appendix E: Extracts in which 'Requirements' are Construed as Aspects of the System

Table E.1 Unpacking 'requirement', Technologist 1, Grammar-targeted Interview 3

Turn	Speaker	Talk
1	Interviewer	To, to move onto requirements which is a lot of what this is about? What's your understanding of the differences between a requirement and a feature?
2	Technologist 1	A requirement is a capability of the system. A feature I think is, is more what the system must do in order to fulfil a need. So requirement can be a feature, it can be a need, it can be – let's see what else could it be – a problem. That kind of thing as well so a requirement to me is an overall desire I guess pretty much.
3		So it's any type of description about what you want the system to do?
4		Yes.

Table E.2 Unpacking 'requirement', project manager, Grammar-targeted Interview 4

Turn	Speaker	Talk
1	Interviewer	Is it different to a user requirement?
2	Project manager	I don't think we've used the term user requirement but I would say that a user requirement was a subset of the full set of requirements or maybe a different term. I think people would use it in different, can be maybe a bit ambiguous which is perhaps why we have steered clear of it but if you were to say who is the user in that circumstance. If you were saying. I can understand that people could have a set of user requirements and that if you satisfied all of those you'd probably have a system that met all of their objectives. So it might, it might pass as the requirements.

Table E.3 Unpacking 'requirement', project manager, Grammar-targeted Interview 4

Turn	Speaker	Talk
1	Interviewer	So what now is a requirement? What's your idea of what constitutes a requirement?
2	Project manager	What now is a requirement?
3	Interviewer	Yeah, what's your idea of what constitutes a requirement?
4	Project manager	A requirement is a, a functional or non-functional aspect of the system, aspect that must be performed by the system.

Appendix F: Response to a Question about Knowledge Transfer, Project Manager, Content-Targeted Interview 2

Table F.1 Understanding knowledge transfer, project manager, Content-targeted Interview 2

Turn	Speaker	Talk
1	Interviewer	That's wonderful, I have covered one lot of questions. Another section deals with basically knowledge management, knowledge transfer but knowledge as in general term right now, and the questions deal with the content of knowledge transfer, mode of knowledge transfer, manner, barriers to knowledge transfer and its impact on the success of the project. So I will repeat them again for you. How is, sorry, what is being transferred among team members and how it is being transferred? Lets handle those two.
2	Project manager	Are we just talking about team members or stakeholders and so on?
3	Interviewer	No, every person involved in the project.
4	Project manager	Every person involved in the project.
5	Interviewer	Yes.
6	Project manager	Users.
7	Interviewer	And users as well.
8	Project manager	The whole lot. Well I think first I should say that I think it could be a whole lot better. It's, it's one of the areas that with trying, that we haven't focused on as much as I'd like to because we have just had so many other issues to solve within the team. So I think we have been very introspective and we have probably got a lot of knowledge transfer happening in the team. So, maybe I should address that separately. But knowledge transfer among stakeholders and wider users has been limited to the meetings that we had initially to talk about the project and to get their input into what they thought was important. And we did that on a fairly ad hoc basis.

Continues

Table F.1 Cont'd.

Turn	Speaker	Talk
		We just identified a bunch of naturally forming groups that we could get people together and discuss the project and elicit their requirements and those were like New South Wales team meetings, producers' meetings or maybe getting people together in a particular area like news or science and I would give a short presentation about the project and the objectives and then we would discuss what their problems were with the existing system and what they would like to see fixed.
12	Interviewer	So would you then agree that in terms of barriers to this knowledge dissipation one of the barriers is really a motivational barrier or lack of motivation or sociological factor saying you know you mentioned that there are people who for whom this particular project is not their life, they have other jobs to do and this just comes along, tags along to their daily routine. So then it doesn't really matter how many more meetings you have, emails you send, intranet updates you publish. They are still going to lag behind because there is not motivation.
13	Project manager	That could be correct, yes. They're not switched on to the, to the information that's being presented to them and they even delete the email when it comes into their inbox.
14	Interviewer	Yeah it's like it's not effecting them directly right now. That is true of the people around the stakeholders but not true of the stakeholders.
15	Project manager	No, they're probably quite interested.
16	Interviewer	The stakeholders realize the value that this project has to their own careers and things like that.

Appendix G: Participants and Processes in Clauses about 'Tracing'

Table G.1 Participants in clauses in which the process 'tracing' or a process describing 'tracing' occurs in the grammar-targeted interviews

Speaker	Process	Process type	Agent	Medium
Project manager	To trace	Material	Requirement	Scope
	To cover off	Material	Requirement artefact	Scope
	To cover	Material	Requirement artefact	Scope
	To trace from	Material	Thing	–
	To trace to	Material	Thing	–
	To flow from	Material	–	Original request
	To help uncover	Material	Tracing	Areas where you missed out requirements
	To trace to	Material	Feature	Stakeholder request
Information architect	To feed into	Material	Requirement	Requirement
	To trickle into	Material	Requirements	Features
	To trickle into	Material	Features	Use cases and test cases
	To be derived	Relational	Requirement	Another requirement
	To Derive From	Relational	Requirement	Requirement
	To trace back to	Material	–	The source
	To distill	Material	We	Stakeholder requirements
	To expand into	Material	We	Use cases
	To track	Material	–	Where the origin of the requirement is located
	To meet	Material	Requirement	A need
Technologist 1	To take	Material	I	Someone's thoughts and concepts
	To translate	Verbal	–	Someone's thoughts and concepts

Appendix H: Interview Topics, Field Study 3

Topics for interview with Business Analyst 1

- The subject's feedback to the stakeholder.
- The subject's sharing of skills and knowledge with other team members.
- Whether the subject had a proactive stance on projects.
- How the subject handled the balance between the sponsor and the project manager.
- The subject's management of risk and control.
- The subject's performance on billable targets.
- The peer review panel.
- The subject's performance on meeting deliverables.
- The subject's performance on reporting requirements.
- The subject's opinion on his performance.
- The subject's opinion on whether there were any areas where he could improve?
- The development plan for the subject.

Topics for interview with Stakeholder 1

- The business analyst's role on the project.
- The business analyst's knowledge about the host organization's systems.
- How the stakeholder finds working with the business analyst.
- Examples of the business analyst being helpful.
- The business analyst's demeanour and interaction with his team.
- The business analyst's interaction with the subject.
- The business analyst's presentation skills.
- Reports or feedback from the team or others about the business analyst.
- Any conflict between the business analyst's work on the project and other commitments such as development courses.
- The business analyst's meeting technique.

- Frequency of the subject's meetings with the business analyst.
- What the business analyst does if he doesn't know something.
- Examples of the business analyst sharing knowledge or mentoring others.
- The business analyst's input into risk management.
- The business analyst's specific skills.
- The subject's rating of the business analyst against other employees in general.
- The subject's inclination to work with the business analyst again.
- Areas where the business analyst could improve his performance.
- Whether the business analyst offered counsel or guidance to others.
- General points on the business analyst's performance not covered in the above.

Topics for interview with Business Analyst 2

- The subject's rapport with his team mates.
- The subject's conflict resolution with his team mates.
- The subject's response to difficult questions.
- The subject's ability to make managers aware of risks.
- How the subject dealt with a manager not listening to him.
- Whether the subject raised compliance breeches.
- The subject's relationship with the business managers.
- Instances where the business wanted something the subject didn't agree with.
- Summary of the subject's performance over the last 12 months.
- The subject's strengths.
- The subject's weaknesses.
- The subject's follow-up/feedback skills.

Topics for interview with Manager 2

- Whether the business analyst was a team player.
- Whether the business analyst offered help when he possessed skills that others do not.
- The business analyst's fit with the host organization's core values.
- Risk identification and risk notification by the business analyst.

- The business analyst's relationship with the business users.
- The quality of the business analyst's deliverables.
- The relevance of the business analyst's solutions.
- The business analyst's response to criticism.
- Whether the business analyst is worth a salary increase.
- The business analyst's overall performance.
- The business analyst's capacity to be a team leader.
- Whether the host organization is getting value from the business analyst.

Topics for interview with Business Analyst 3

- Summary of the project and expectations that the stakeholder had of the subject.
- The stakeholder's opinion that the subject could have done more managing of her relationship with the client.The stakeholder's opinion that the subject lost opportunities to raise her profile.
- The subject's feeling that the stakeholder did not explain his expectations of her.
- The subject's feelings about her behaviour.
- The expectations that the stakeholder did not articulate.
- Who owns the role of managing the relationship with clients.
- The subject's thoughts on the stakeholder's feedback.
- Conflict between the stakeholder and other managers over resources.
- The stakeholder's style of management.
- How a person's role is defined in the host organization.

Topics for interview with Manager 3

- Expectations of the subject for the business analyst's tasks.
- The business analyst's performance on her tasks.
- The performance outcomes for the business analyst.
- The subject's feedback to the business analyst on her performance.
- Examples of the business analyst's performance.
- Strengths of the business analyst.
- The business analyst's management of her relationship with the client.
- What the subject most valued about the business analyst.

- The subject's suggestions about improvements to consolidate the business analyst's performance.
- The extent to which the business analyst met the subject's expectations on her tasks.
- The extent to which the current role challenged the business analyst.
- Future roles to develop the business analyst.
- The business analyst's relationship with her team members and clients.
- The business analyst's interaction with developers.

Appendix I: Transitivity of Clauses Containing 'Role'

Table I.1 Processes, process type and agent for processes where 'role' is a participant. Manager 3, grammar-targeted interview

Process	Process type	Agent
[elided]	Existential	–
To be	Existential	–
To be scoped	Material	–
To do	Material	–
To carve	Material	Business Analyst 3
To carve out	Material	Business Analyst 3
To deliver	Material	Business Analyst 3
To do	Material	Business Analyst 3
To do	Material	Business Analyst 3
To do	Material	Business Analyst 3
To fill	Material	Business Analyst 3
To get	Material	Business Analyst 3
To look for	Material	Business Analyst 3
To look for	Material	Business Analyst 3
To perform	Material	Business Analyst 3
To take into	Material	Business Analyst 3
To come in and do	Material	Business Analyst 3
To scope	Material	Predefined functions for the role
To evolve	Material	Role
To do	Material	Somebody
To put around	Material	Us
To carve out	Material	Us
To scope	Material	We
To step into	Material	We
To want from	Mental	Business Analyst 3
To want out of	Mental	Business Analyst 3
To want	Mental	I
To be	Relational	–
To be	Relational	–
To be	Relational	–

Continues

Table I.1 Cont'd.

Process	Process type	Agent
To be	Relational	–
To be	Relational	–
To be	Relational	–
To be	Relational	–
To be in	Relational	–
To be sufficient for	Relational	–
To dictate	Verbal	PM roles

Table I.2 Processes, process type and agent for processes where 'role' is a participant. Manager 3, content-targeted interview

Process	Type	Agent
To be in	Existential	–
To be	Existential	–
To be	Existential	–
To do	Material	Business Analyst 3
To step into	Material	Business Analyst 3
To go into	Material	Business Analyst 3
To be able to do	Material	Business Analyst 3
To own	Material	Passive
To own	Material	Passive
To make something out of	Material	Passive
To come into	Material	Someone who was new
To be engaged	Mental	Someone
To want	Mental	We
To be passive	Relational	Business Analyst 3
To have	Relational	We
To be	Relational	–
To be	Relational	–
To be	Relational	–
To be	Relational	–
To have	Relational	–
To be	Relational	–
To be	Relational	–
To be	Relational	–
To give direction	Verbal	I
To do		The Role

Table I.3 Processes, process type and agent for processes where 'role' is a participant. Business Analyst 3, grammar-targeted interview

Process	Type	Agent
To be	Existential	
To ask to do	Material	A manager
To do	Material	An outsider
To take on	Material	Manager 3
To be appropriate to do	Material	–
To perform	Material	–
To expect	Mental	Manager 3
To assume	Mental	We
To be	Relational	–
To be	Relational	–
To be	Relational	–
To Be	Relational	–
To be	Relational	–
To speak with	Verbal	Business Analyst 3
To talk about	Verbal	

Table I.4 Processes, process type and agent for processes where 'role' is a participant. Business Analyst 3, content-targeted interview

Process	Process type	Agent
To do	Material	Somebody else

Bibliography

Ambrosini, V. (2001). Tacit knowledge: some suggestions for operationalization. *Journal of Management Studies* 38(6): 811–29.

Anderson, J. R. (1976). *Language, Memory and Thought.* New York: Hillsdale.

Applen, J. D. (2002). Tacit knowledge, knowledge management, and active user participation in website navigation. *IEEE Transactions on Professional Communication* 45(4): 302–6.

Aristotle (1998). *The Nicomachean Ethics.* Oxford, UK: Oxford University Press.

Ashmore, M. (1989). *The Reflexive Thesis: Wrighting Sociology of Scientific Knowledge.* Chicago, IL: University of Chicago Press.

Bachelard, G. (1984). *The New Scientific Spirit*, tr. Arthur Goldhammer. Boston: Beacon Press.

Bargh, J. A. (1999). The unbearable automaticity of being. *American Psychologist* 54(7): 462–79.

Bateson, G. (1972). *Steps to an Ecology of Mind.* San Francisco, CA: Chandler Publishing Company.

Baumard, P. (1999). *Tacit Knowledge in Organizations.* London: Sage.

Bernstein, B. B. (1971). *Class, Codes and Control.* London: Routledge & Kegan Paul.

Boiral, O. (2002). Tacit knowledge and environmental management. *Long Range Planning* 35(3): 291–317.

Boland, R. J. and R. V. Tenkasi (1995). Perspective making and perspective taking in communities of knowing. *Organization Science* 4(4): 350–72.

Bordum, A. (2002). From tacit knowing to tacit knowledge – emancipation or ideology? *Critical Quarterly* 44(3): 50–4.

Bourdieu, P. (1977). *Outline of a Theory of Practice.* Cambridge; New York: Cambridge University Press.

— (1990). *In Other Words: Essays Towards a Reflexive Sociology.* Stanford, CA: Stanford University Press.

Bourdieu, P. and T. Eagleton (1994). Doxa and common life: an interview. In S. Žižek (ed.), *Mapping Ideology* (pp. 265–77). London: Verso.

Busch, P. (2008). *Tacit Knowledge in Organizational Learning.* Hershey, PA: IGI.

Busch, P. and D. Richards (2000). Triangulated measurement of articulable tacit knowledge using formal concept analysis. *Proceeding of the 11th Australasian Conference on Information Systems*, December 6–8, Brisbane.

Busch, P. A. et al. (2001). Visual mapping of articulable tacit knowledge. *Australian Symposium on Information Visualisation*, Sydney, Australian Computer Society.

Butt, D. (1985). *Talking and Thinking: The Patterns of Behaviour.* Victoria: Deakin University Press.

— (1996). Theories, maps and descriptions. In R. Hasan, D. Butt and C. Cloran (eds), *Functional Descriptions: Theory in Practice* (pp. xv–xxxv). Amsterdam; Philadelphia: John Benjamins Pub.

Butt, D., R. Fahey, S. Feez, S. Spinks and C. Yallop (2000). *Using Functional Grammar: An Explorer's Guide.* Sydney, Australia: National Centre for English Language Teaching and research, Macquarie University.

Byrd, T. A. et al. (1992). A synthesis of research on requirements analysis and knowledge acquisition. *Management Information Systems Quarterly* 16(1): 117–38.

Callon, M. (1994). Is science a public good? *Science, Technology and Human Values* 19(4): 395–424.

Castillo, J. (2002). A note on the concept of tacit knowledge. *Journal of Management Inquiry* 11(1): 46–57.

Chalmers, A. F. (1982). *What Is This Thing Called Science?* Queensland: Queensland University Press.

Chomsky, N. (1965). *Aspects of the Theory of Syntax.* Cambridge, MA: MIT Press.

— (1986). *Knowledge of Language: Its Nature, Origin, and Use.* New York: Praeger.

Christie, F. and J. R. Martin (eds) (2008). *Language, Knowledge and Pedagogy: Functional Linguistic and Sociological Perspectives.* London; New York: Continuum.

Coffin, C. (2006). *Historical Discourse: The Language of Time, Cause and Evaluation.* London: Continuum.

Collins, H. M. (2001a). Tacit knowledge, trust and the Q of Sapphire. *Social Studies of Science* 31(1): 71–85.

— (2001b). What is tacit knowledge? In T. R. Schatzki, K. Knorr-Cetina and E. V. Savigny (eds), *The Practice Turn in Contemporary Theory* (pp. 107–19). London; New York: Routledge.

— (2010). *Tacit and Explicit Knowledge.* Chicago, IL: University of Chicago Press.

Cook, S. D. N. and J. S. Brown (1999). Bridging epistemologies: the generative dance between organizational knowledge and organizational knowing. *Organization Science* 10(4): 381–400.

Day, R. (2005). Clearing up 'implicit knowledge': implications for knowledge management, information science, psychology, and social epistemology. *Journal of the American Society for Information Science and Technology* 56(6): 630–5.

Deely, J. N. et al. (1986). *Frontiers in Semiotics.* Bloomington, IN: Indiana University Press.

Douglas, M. (1975). *Implicit Meanings: Essays in Anthropology.* London; Boston: Routledge & Keagn Paul.

Eggins, S. (1994). *An Introduction to Systemic Functional Linguistics.* London: Pinter Publishers.

Eraut, M. (2000). Non-formal learning and tacit knowledge in professional work. *British Journal of Educational Psychology* 70: 113–36.

Evans, G. (1981). Reply: semantic theory and tacit knowledge. In S. H. Holtzman and
C. M. Leich (eds), *Wittgenstein, to Follow a Rule* (pp. 118–37). London; Boston:
Routledge & Kegan Paul.

Ferrara, K. (1988). Variation in narration: retellings in therapeutic discourse. In
K. Ferrara, B. Brown, K. Walters and J. Baugh (eds), *Linguistic Change and Contact*.
Austin, TX: University of Texas.

Feyerabend, P. K. (1975). *Against Method: Outline of an Anarchistic Theory of
Knowledge*. London: Humanities Press.

Firth, J. R. (1957). *Papers in Linguistics 1934–1951*. London: Oxford University Press.

Foucault, M. (1973). *The Birth of the Clinic: An Archaeology of Medical Perception*.
London: Tavistock.

— (2002). *Archaeology of Knowledge*. London: Routledge.

Freud, S. (1994). A note on the unconscious in psycho-analysis. In B. A. Farrell (ed.),
Philosophy and Psychoanalysis (pp. 3–8) New York: Macmillan College Publishing
Company.

Freud, S. and J. Strachey (1970). *An Outline of Psycho-Analysis*. New York: W.W. Norton.

Gopnik, A. and A. N. Meltzoff (1997). *Words, Thoughts, and Theories*. Cambridge, MA:
MIT Press.

Grene, M. (1977). Tacit knowing: grounds for a revolution in philosophy. *Journal of the
British Society for Phenomenology* 8(3): 164–71.

Gulick, W. B. (1992–3). Polanyi's theory of meaning: exposition, elaboration, and
reconstruction. *Polanyiana* 2(4) and 3(1): 7–42.

Hall, Nigel (1994). The emergence of literacy. In Barry Stierer and Janet Maybin (eds),
Language, Literacy and Learning in Educational Practice: A Reader (pp. 15–29).
Clevedon, Avon, England; Philadelphia: Multilingual Matters in association with the
Open University.

Halliday, M. A. K. (1961). Categories of the theory of grammar. *Word* 17(3): 241–92.

— (1973). *Language in a Social Perspective. Explorations in the Functions of Language*.
London: Edward Arnold.

— (1978). *Language as Social Semiotic: The Social Interpretation of Language and
Meaning*. Baltimore, MD: University Park Press.

— (1989). *Spoken and Written Language*. Oxford: Oxford University Press.

— (1993). *Language in a Changing World. Occasional Paper Number 13*. Sydney:
Applied Linguistics Association of Australia.

— (1994). *An Introduction to Functional Grammar* (2nd edn). London: E. Arnold.

— (1998). Things and relations: regrammaticising experience as technical knowledge. In
J. R. Martin and R. Veel (eds), *Reading Science: Critical and Functional Perspectives on
Discourses of Science* (pp. 185–235). London; New York: Routledge.

— (2000). Grammar and daily life. In M. Lamb, D. G. Lockwood, J. E. Copeland and
P. H. Fries (eds), *Functional Approaches to Language, Culture, and Cognition: Papers
in Honor of Sydney Amsterdam* (pp. 221–37). Philadelphia: John Benjamins.

— (2004). *The Language of Science*. London: Continuum.

Halliday, M. A. K. and J. R. Martin (1993). *Writing Science: Literacy and Discursive Power.* London: Falmer Press.

Halliday, M. A. K. and C. M. I. M. Matthiessen (1999). *Construing Experience Through Meaning: A Language-Based Approach to Cognition.* London: Cassell.

— (2004). *An Introduction to Functional Grammar* (3rd edn). London: Arnold.

Halliday, M. A. K. and J. Webster (2002). *On Grammar.* London: Continuum.

Harper, D. (ed.) (2001). *Online Etymological Dictionary,* available at: www.etymonline. com/ (last accessed 15/10/04).

Hasan, R., G. Williams, D. Butt and C. Cloran (1996). *Ways of Saying, Ways of Meaning: Selected Papers of Ruqaiya Hasan.* London; New York: Cassell.

Hershel, R. T. et al. (2001). Tacit to explicit knowledge conversion: knowledge exchange protocols. *Journal of Knowledge Management* 5(1): 107–16.

Hutchins, E. (1995). *Cognition in the Wild.* Cambridge, MA: MIT Press.

Huysman, M. (2004). Communities of practice: facilitating social learning while frustrating organizational learning. In H. Tsoukas and N. Mylonopoulos (eds), *Organizations as Knowledge Systems: Knowledge, Learning, and Dynamic Capabilities* (pp. 67–85). New York: Palgrave Macmillan.

Iedema, R. (1995). *Literacy of Administration (Write it Right Literacy in Industry Research Project – Stage 3).* Sydney: Metropolitan East Disadvantaged Schools Program.

— (1997). The language of administration: organizing human activity in formal institutions. In J. R. Martin and F. Christie (eds), *Genre and Institutions: Social Processes in the Workplace and School* (pp. 73–100). London; Washington: Cassell.

— (2003). *Discourses of Post-Bureaucratic Organization.* Philadelphia, PA: John Benjamins Pub.

Jacobs, S. (2007). Michael Polanyi and Thomas Kuhn: priority and credit. *Tradition and Discovery* 33(2): 25–36.

Johnson, B. and B. Lundvall (2001). Why all this fuss about codified and tacit knowledge? *Industrial and Corporate Change* 11(2): 245–62.

Jung, C. G. and R. F. C. Hull (1959). *The Archetypes and the Collective Unconscious.* London: Routledge & Kegan Paul.

Kant, I. (2001). *Lectures on Metaphysics.* Cambridge, UK: Cambridge University Press.

Kipfer, B. A. (ed.) (2003). *Roget's Interactive Thesaurus* (1st edn) (v 1.0.0). CA: Lexico Publishing Group, LLC.

Klein, W. (1986). *Second Language Acquisition.* Cambridge, UK: Cambridge University Press.

Korner, H., D. McInnes and D. Rose (1992). *Scientific Literacy (Write it Right Literacy in Industry Research Project – Stage 1).* Sydney: Metropolitan East Disadvantaged Schools Program [reprinted by New South Wales Adult Migrant Education Service, Sydney, 2007].

Kubota, H. and T. Nishida (2000). Exchanging tacit community knowledge by talking-virtualized-egos. *Proceedings of the Fourth International Conference on Autonomous Agents.* Barcelona: ACM press.

Kuhn, T. S. (1962). *The Structure of Scientific Revolutions.* Chicago; London: University of Chicago Press.

— (1993). Metaphor in science. In A. Ortony (ed.), *Metaphor and Thought* (pp. 409–19). Cambridge; New York, NY: Cambridge University Press.

Lakoff, G. and M. Johnson (1980). *Metaphors We Live By.* Chicago, IL: University of Chicago Press.

— (1999). *Philosophy in the Flesh: The Embodied Mind and its Challenge to Western Thought.* New York: Basic Books.

Latour, B. (2004). A dialog on actor-network-theory with a (somewhat) Socratic professor. In C. Avgerou, C. Ciborra and F. F. Land (eds), *The Social Study of Information and Communication Study* (pp. 62–76). Oxford: Oxford University Press.

Latour, B. and S. Woolgar (1979). *Laboratory Life: The Social Construction of Scientific Facts.* Beverly Hills, CA: Sage Publications.

Lecourt, D. (1975). *Marxism and Epistemology: Bachelard, Canguilhem and Foucault.* London: Nlb.

Lemke, J. L. (1984). *Semiotics and Education, Toronto Semiotic Circle Monographs Series.* Toronto: Victoria University.

— (1995). *Textual Politics: Discourse and Social Dynamics.* London: Taylor and Francis.

Lynch, M. (2001). Ethnomethodology and the logic of practice. In T. R. Schatzki, K. Knorr-Cetina and E. V. Savigny (eds), *The Practice Turn in Contemporary Theory* (pp. 30–148). London; New York: Routledge.

Malinowski, B. (1935). *Coral Gardens and their Magic.* London: Allen and Unwin.

Mann, P. (2001). Tacit knowledge in an age of reform. *International Journal of Human Resource Management* 12(1): 76–90.

Martin, J. R. (1987). The meaning of features in systemic linguistics. In R. Fawcett and M. A. K. Halliday (eds), *New Developments in Systemic Linguistics Vol. 1. Theory and Description.* (pp. 14–40). London: Pinter [reprinted in *SFL Theory* 2010, 44–98].

— (1993). 'Technology, bureaucracy and schooling: Discursive resources and control', *Cultural Dynamics* 6: 84–130.

— (2008a). Incongruent and proud: de-vilifying 'nominalization'. *Discourse and Society* 19(6): 801–10.

— (2008b). Tenderness: realisation and instantiation in a Botswanan town. In N. Nørgaard (ed.), *Odense Working Papers in Language and Communication Special Issue of Papers from 34th International Systemic Functional Congress* (pp. 30–62). Odense: University of Southern Denmark, Institute of Language and Communication [reprinted in *SFL Theory* 2010, pp. 484–513].

Martin, J. R. and R. Veel (1998). *Reading Science: Critical and Functional Perspectives on Discourses of Science.* London; New York: Routledge.

Martin, J. R. and P. R. R. White (2005). *The Language of Evaluation: Appraisal in English.* New York: Palgrave Macmillan.

Martin, J. R. and R. Wodak (eds) (2003). *Re/Reading the Past: Critical and Functional Perspectives on Discourses of History.* Amsterdam: John Benjamins.

Matthiessen, C. M. I. M. (1995). *Lexicogrammatical Cartography: English Systems.* Tokyo: International Language Sciences.

— (1997). *Glossary of Systemic Functional Terms,* available at: http://minerva.ling. mq.edu.au/ (last accessed 18/5/04).

— (2010). *Key Terms in Systemic Functional Linguistics.* London: Continuum.

McKenna, B. and P. Graham (2000). Technocratic discourse: a primer. *Journal of Technical Writing and Communication* 30(3): 219–47.

Moss, E. (1995). *The Grammar of Consciousness: An Exploration of Tacit Knowing.* New York: St. Martin's Press.

Mukarovský, J. (1964). Standard language and poetic language. In P. Garvin (ed.), *A Prague School Reader on Esthetics, Literary Structure and Style* (pp. 17–30). Washington, DC: Georgetown University Press.

Nonaka, I. and H. Takeuchi (1995). *The Knowledge-Creating Company: How Japanese Companies Create the Dynamics of Innovation.* New York: Oxford University Press.

O'Donnell, M. (2002). *Systemic Coder (Version 4.5).* Madrid: Wagsoft Systems.

O'Halloran, K. (2006). *Mathematical Discourse: Language, Symbolism and Visual Images.* London: Continuum.

Peirce, C. S. et al. (1931). *Collected Papers of Charles Sanders Peirce.* Cambridge: Harvard University Press.

Pinch, T. et al. (1996). Inside knowledge: second order measures of skill. *Sociological Review* 44(2): 163–87.

Polanyi, M. (1958). *Personal Knowledge: Towards a Post-Critical Philosophy.* Chicago, IL: Chicago University Press.

— (1966a). The logic of tacit inference. *Philosophy* 41(1): 1–18.

— (1966b). *The Tacit Dimension.* London: Routledge & Kegan Paul.

— (1967). Sense-giving and sense-reading. *Philosophy* 42(162): 301–25.

— (1969). *Knowing and Being; Essays.* Chicago, IL: University of Chicago Press.

Polanyi, M. and H. Prosch (1977). *Meaning.* Chicago, IL: University of Chicago Press.

Ravetz, J. R. (1971). *Scientific Knowledge and its Social Problems.* Oxford: Clarendon Press.

Reber, A. S. (1967) Implicit learning of artificial grammars. *Journal of Verbal Learning and Verbal Behaviour* 5: 855–63.

— (1993). *Implicit Learning and Tacit Knowledge: An Essay on the Cognitive Unconscious.* New York; Oxford: Oxford University Press; Clarendon Press.

Reddy, M. (1979). The conduit metaphor. In A. Ortony (ed.), Metaphor and Thought (pp. 284–324). Cambridge: Cambridge University Press.

Reuber, A. R. (1990). Using a tacit knowledge methodology to define expertise. *Proceedings of the 1990 ACM SIGBDP Conference on Trends and Directions in Expert Systems.* Orlando, FL: ACM Press.

Richards, D. and P. A. Busch (2000). Measuring, formalising and modelling tacit knowledge. *International Congress on Intelligent Systems and Applications,* Wollongong, Australia.

Richards, I. A. (1936). *The Philosophy of Rhetoric.* Oxford: Oxford University Press.

Roget's II: The New Thesaurus (1995). Xreferplus, available at: www.xreferplus.com/
    entry/751220.

Roget's New Millennium Thesaurus (2006). 1st edn (v 1.0.5), edited by Barbara Ann
    Kipfer.

Rose, D. (1998). Science discourse and industrial hierarchy. In J. R. Martin and R. Veel
    (eds), *Reading Science: Critical and Functional Perspectives on Discourses of Science*
    (pp. 236–65). London; New York: Routledge.

— (2012). Genre in the Sydney school. In J. Gee and M. Handford (eds), *The Routledge
    Handbook of Discourse Analysis* (pp. 209–25). London: Routledge.

Ryle, G. (1949). *The Concept of Mind.* London: Hutchinson's University Library.

Sanders, A. F. (1988). *Michael Polanyi's Post-Critical Epistemology: A Reconstruction of
    Some Aspects of "Tacit Knowing".* Amsterdam: Rodopi.

Sapir, E. (1949). *The Pyschological Reality of Phonemes. Language, Culture and
    Personality.* Berkeley, CA: University of California Press.

Schulz, M. and L. A. Jobe (2001). Codification and tacitness as knowledge management
    strategies: an empirical exploration. *The Journal of High Technology Management
    Research* 12(1): 139–65.

Schuster, J. (1984). Methodologies as mythic structures: a preface to future
    historiography of method. *Metascience: Annual Review of the Australasian
    Association for the History, Philosophy and Social Studies of Science* 1(2): 17.

Simon-Vandenbergen, A. M., M. Taverniers and L. Ravelli (2003). *Grammatical
    Metaphor: Views from Systemic Functional Linguistics.* Amsterdam; Philadelphia:
    John Benjamins Pub.

Spearman, C. E. (1927). *The Abilities of Man.* London: Macmillan.

Spender, J. C. (1993). Competitive advantage from tacit knowledge? Unpacking
    the concept and its strategic implications. *Academy of Management Proceedings,*
    37–41.

Starbuck, W. H. (1992). Learning by knowledge-intensive firms. *Journal of Management
    Studies* 29(6): 713–41.

Starke, F. A. et al. (2003). Coping with the sudden loss of an indispensable employee.
    The Journal of Applied Behavioral Science 39(2): 208–28.

Stenmark, D. (2001). Leveraging tacit organizational knowledge. *Journal of Management
    Information Systems* 17(3): 9–24.

Sternberg, R. J. (1985). *Beyond IQ: A Triarchic Theory of Human Intelligence.*
    Cambridge; New York: Cambridge University Press.

Sternberg, R. J. and E. Grigorenko (2001). Practical intelligence and the principal.
    Spotlight on Student Success, 603.

Sternberg, R. J. and J. A Horvath (eds) (1999). *Tacit Knowledge in Professional Practice:
    Researcher and Practitioner Perspectives: Researcher and practitioner perspectives.*
    Mahwah, NJ: Lawrence Erlbaum and Associates.

Suchman, L. A. (1987). *Plans and Situated Actions: The Problem of Human–Machine
    Communication.* Cambridge; New York: Cambridge University Press.

Swan, J. et al. (1999). Knowledge management and innovation: networks and networking. *Journal of Knowledge Management* 3(4): 262–75.

Swarts, J. (2000). Document collaboration and tacit knowledge. *Proceedings of IEEE Professional Communication Society International Communication Conference*, Cambridge, MA, IEE Educational Activities Department.

Thompson, G. (2000). *Introducing Functional Grammar*. London: Hodder Headline Group.

Tóth, Z. N. (2008). The transparency of words: a Polanyian explanation for the process of translation. *Polanyiana* 1–2(17): 38–42.

Tsoukas, H. (2003). Do we really understand tacit knowledge? In M. Easterby-Smith and M. A. Lyles (eds), *The Blackwell Handbook of Organizational Learning and Knowledge Management* (pp. 411–27). Cambridge, MA: Blackwell Publishing

Turner, S. P. (1994). *The Social Theory of Practices: Tradition, Tacit Knowledge and Presuppositions*. Cambridge: Polity Press.

— (2001). Throwing out the tacit rule book: learning and practices. In T. R. Schatzki, K. Knorr-Cetina and E. V. Savigny (eds), *The Practice Turn in Contemporary Theory* (pp. 120–30). London; New York: Routledge.

Wagner, R. K. (1987). Tacit knowledge in everyday intelligent behaviour. *Journal of Personality and Social Psychology* 52: 1236–47.

Wagner, R. K. and J. Sternberg (1991). *Tacit Knowledge Inventory for Managers: User Manual*. San Antonio, TX: The Psychological Corporation.

— (2000). Tacit knowledge and management in the everyday world. In R. J. Sternberg (ed.), *Practical Intelligence in Everyday Life* (pp. xiv, 288). Cambridge, UK; New York: Cambridge University Press.

Wenger, E. (1998). *Communities of Practice: Learning, Meaning, and Identity*. Cambridge, UK; New York: Cambridge University Press.

Whorf, B. L. and J. B. Carroll (1956). *Language, Thought and Reality: Selected Writings of Benjamin Lee Whorf*. Cambridge, MA: MIT Press.

Wignell, P. (1998). Technicality and abstraction in social science. In J. R. Martin and Robert Veel (eds), *Reading Science: Critical and Functional Perspectives on Discourses of Science* (pp. 297–326). London: Routledge.

— (2007). *On the Discourse of Social Science*. Darwin, Australia: Charles Darwin University Press .

Wittgenstein, L. (1953/2001). *Tractatus Logico-Philosophicus*. London: Routledge.

Zappavigna, M. (2012). *The Discourse of Twitter and Social Media*. London: Continuum.

Zappavigna-Lee, M. (2005). Explicating tacit knowledge embedded in nominalisation. *Australian Conference on Information Systems*, Sydney.

Zappavigna-Lee, M. and J. Patrick (2004a). Eliciting tacit knowledge from spoken discourse about requirements analysis. *Australian Conference for Knowledge Management & Intelligent Decision Support*, Melbourne.

— (2004b). Literacy, tacit knowledge and organisational learning. *16th Euro-International Systemic Functional Linguistics Workshop*, Madrid.

— (2005a). Tacit knowledge and discourse analysis. *Encyclopedia of Information Science and Technology.* Idea Group Reference.

— (2005b). Tacit knowledge in communities of practice. *Encyclopedia of Communities of Practice in Information and Knowledge Management.* Idea Group Reference.

— (2010). Eliciting tacit knowledge about requirement analysis with a Grammar-targeted Interview Method (GIM). *European Journal of Information Systems* 19: 49–59.

Zappavigna-Lee, M., M. O'Donnell and C. Whitelaw (2004). Inter-coder reliability and process type. *16th Euro-International Systemic Functional Linguistics Workshop,* Madrid.

Zappavigna-Lee, M., J. Patrick and A. Stern (2002). Knowledge management as social semiotic: discourse analysis as a measure of quality. In F. Burstein and H. K. Linger (eds), *The Role of Quality in Knowledge Management* (pp. 55–72). Melbourne: Australian Scholarly Publications.

Zappavigna-Lee, M. et al. (2003). Assessing knowledge management services through discourse analysis. *Seventh Pacific Asia Conference on Information Systems,* Adelaide.

Zeira, A. (2000). Unravelling 'tacit knowledge': what social workers do and why they do it. *Social Service Review* 74: 105–23.

Zollo, M. and G. Winter (2002). Deliberate learning and the evolution of dynamic capabilities. *Organization Science* 13(3): 339–53.

Index